American Cocktail

American Cocktail

— *A "Colored Girl" in the World* —

Anita Reynolds
with Howard M. Miller

EDITED AND WITH INTRODUCTION AND NOTES BY
George Hutchinson

FOREWORD BY
Patricia Williams

Harvard University Press

Cambridge, Massachusetts
London, England
2014

Library of Congress Cataloging-in-Publication Data
Reynolds, Anita Thompson Dickinson, 1901–1980.
American cocktail : a "colored girl" in the world / Anita Reynolds with
    Howard M. Miller ; edited and with introduction and notes by George
    Hutchinson ; foreword by Patricia Williams.
        pages   cm
Includes bibliographical references and index.
ISBN 978-0-674-07305-0 (hardcover : alk. paper)
    1. Reynolds, Anita Thompson Dickinson, 1901–1980.   2. African
American women—Biography.   3. Motion picture actresses—United
States—Biography.   4. African American women entertainers—Biography.
5. African American psychologists—Biography.   I. Hutchinson, George,
1953– editor.   II. Miller, Howard M.   III. Title.

    E185.97.R49A3   2014
    791.4302'8092—dc23
    [B]   2013032113

Contents

Illustrations

Foreword

by Patricia Williams

Oceans of ink have been spilled about those complicated souls supposedly caught in the racial "middle" of America's eternal identity wars. Well before the anodyne—and misleading—term "biracial" came into being, there was the long-suffering figure of the tragic mulatto. When I was growing up, we of the Civil Rights era were called "grey babies." Somewhere between the times of Puddn'head Wilson and Barack Obama, there were also octoroons, quadroons, mestizos, maroons, sepia sisters, meriney men, high-toned folk, yellow women, rooster reds, tea-honeys with milk, cinnamon sugars, and sallow gals. Each wave of immigration to this country has brought its happy mixtures of indigenous peoples: African slaves, Italian laborers, German and Irish indentured servants, Chinese railroad workers, South Asian refugees, Japanese and Korean war brides, Spanish conquistadores, and Russian Jews. Yet somehow each of those waves has been erased from memory as the children of those unions have been—sadly, even forcibly for the most part—assimilated as either "black" or "white."

This particular bit of American history tends to get lost, over and over again, as each generation eliminates the ubiquitous truth—since colonial times—of multiracial, multicultural, multiethnic relationships, by burying such border-crossings as unusual, dangerous, and against God's law. Indeed, given the violent history of masters "breeding" their own exploitable stocks of sex slaves, to say nothing of the realities of Jim Crow anti-miscegenation laws, the children of such unions have borne peculiarly Dickensian burdens as the best-worst proof of such vexed entanglements. The dominant plot line for pretty mulattas has always been a tale of unrequited love, lost reputation, rape, and ruination topped off by a Dickensian leap—or shove—off a very high bridge. To break the curse of such destiny, such a one must always keep her knees locked, her hair under a hat, her back straight, her mind on alarm and alert. If she prays hard enough, she will make a good teacher, a Florence Nightingale of a nurse, a solemn preacher's wife. . . . Langston Hughes even wrote a poem about it, called Cross: "My old man died in a fine big house / My ma died in a shack / I wonder where I'm going to die / Being neither white nor black?"

Enter Anita Thompson Dickinson Reynolds. Interestingly enough, she was Langston Hughes's cousin, and if the narrative of the tragic mulatta is a mite overwritten, then her life both reinforced and defied that plotted destiny in intriguing ways. Just to start with, she was named after Giuseppe Garibaldi's first wife, Anita, an ardent feminist whom her grandmother had befriended in Boston. Born in 1901, Reynolds was someone who might well have met a sad end had she passed her entire life in the United States. Indeed, the mailman to whom she proudly announced her fifteenth birthday replied darkly: "I'm sorry to hear that. With those bedroom eyes you're in for one hell of a life." The foreboding in that encounter underscores the degree to which the purported tragedy tucked into the status of being mulatta is a presumption of irresistible sexual invitation, coupled with exceptional vulnerability to violent exploitation.

For all that, Reynolds grew up in an extraordinarily privileged environment, not extremely wealthy by white standards, but carefree and protected enough to have been marked by close to a noblewoman's taste for languid amusement. Perhaps because of that, she was unusually comfortable with her own sexuality, again particularly given the times. Her unapologetic sense of entitlement to the enjoyment of her own body runs through this book like a meandering river of life's many satisfactions. Nor was her libidinal energy only or even mostly about sex. From the time she was a very young girl, she delighted in all things sensual: dance and textures and food and smell and color and music. Her moral life was marked by little in the way of easily identifiable ideology, and more by aesthetic sensibility. She gorged on whatever was joyful and beautiful; she dismissed light-heartedly the normal rituals of middle-class modesty and racial propriety.

By her early twenties, Reynolds had taken accurate stock of her own impatient disposition and moved to Paris. She absconded with the tuition money her father sent for her enrollment at Wellesley College, and booked passage on the next ocean liner to Europe. She describes one of the encounters with the rigidly proper black bourgeoisie that ultimately motivated her departure: when she attempted to bring H. L. Mencken to a party, the hostess sniffed: "Why, we don't have white men at our parties. We don't have white people at all. But if we did, they would certainly have to be our social equals, and no journalist would ever fit in our parties.

Unless you know white people in the diplomatic corps, don't ask to invite them." Even today there are high echelons of black society that might enforce those lines with unnerving vigilance, but for the most part, such an exchange would strike the contemporary ear as somewhat absurd. Again, it helps to consider the times: the light-skinned black middle and upper classes were—and are—largely descended from the illegitimate children of slave masters; and American culture of the day treated the rape of black women by white men with impunity. "Respectable" women were heavily charged with signaling their unavailability in no uncertain terms. The behavior codes that grew up in reaction to that reality were strict, ultraconservative, littered with lines that could not be crossed.

Reynolds hated those strictures. She was, to great extent, a party girl, "liberated" yet status-conscious, ethereal yet earthy, terribly well-educated if often dismally class-bound in her own right. Her prize-winning review essay of an anthology of F. Scott Fitzgerald's short stories, published in 1922, presages the arc of her own life, as a "modern cocktail in which ex-soldiers, Socialists, college failures, flappers, and alcohol are shaken together and mixed like oil and water" (Appendix 1).

And so Reynolds was a smart, upper-class, sexually unrepentant black woman at a time when there was precious little model for that. (Indeed, is there yet such a thing on the American scene?) She was playful about the cultural confusion her ambiguous phenotype inspired in others, but also burdened, self-protective. She was a strong woman—though not in the muscular sense toward which that term so often points. Rather she was manipulative, arch, calculating and rather uncomfortably reminiscent of Scarlett O'Hara in full curtains-into-evening-gown mode. She was driven by a restless searching quality, which kept her on the move, flitting from place to place, language to language (Spanish, French, Arabic), profession to profession (dancer, clinical psychologist, art historian, teacher, model, actress, author), and relationship to relationship.

Reynolds grew up in Los Angeles, in a family whose members embodied all the complexities of American identity. There seemed not to be the usual tension among family members who passed for white and those who didn't. While she recalls something "secret and hidden" in the stories of those who passed, she describes a generally accepting humor about it that was "ironic beyond anything I could hope to understand or appreciate." Of course most of them were light-skinned enough to be racially ambiguous, all were very well-educated and fairly well-to-do; so the consequence of identifying as "colored" was not as divisive as it might have been where color distinctions were oppressive and unrelenting.

Her large and far-flung family also didn't live in the South, but in all the most liberal, artily integrated places in the United States: Boston, Chicago, Hollywood, Baltimore—places where the color line was not quite as closely patrolled. Moreover, as she grew up and pursued her astonishingly varied career, she chose to live in geographies where attitudes were progressive and racial integration possible: Harlem, Greenwich Village, London, Morocco, and Paris. These were places of great cultural foment in literature, the arts, theatre, fashion, and politics. The list of her friends and mentors reads like one long list of dropped names: Her first dance teacher was Ruth St. Denis. Bill "Bojangles" Robinson taught her to tap. A. Philip Randolph and Booker T. Washington frequently stayed at her parents' home. She knew Douglas Fairbanks, e.e. cummings, A'Lelia Walker, Walter White, and reputedly had an affair with W. E. B. Du Bois. She mentions sending her mother "a little sketch of me made by Matisse as we sat in the Deux Magots." She modeled for Coco Chanel ("I often wore her own dresses, discarded after she had worn them just once."). Man Ray was among her best friends. She partied with André Gide, Claude McKay, Ernest Hemingway, Kristians Tonny, Paul Bowles, Antonin Artaud, Djuna Barnes, Ford Madox Ford, William Carlos Williams, Ralph Bunche, Jean Patou, Baron von Munchausen, James Weldon Johnson, Carl Van Vechten, and "my old friend Fernand Léger." She mingled with Gertrude Stein, James Joyce, and Kay Boyle (one of whose daughters was named Apple well before Gwyneth Paltrow's). Over the course of her life, she ambled casually through a dizzying array of literary friendships, as when "I was walking home with W. H. Auden . . ."; or when she decided not to call upon Ezra Pound because "I didn't care much for his admiration and support of the fascists"; or when she identified Antoine de Saint-Exupéry as "the most beautiful ugly man I had ever seen." *American Cocktail* is one long testament to Reynolds's having met everyone there was to know of importance in the twentieth century. Plus, she could even claim to have been engaged or "nearly engaged" to rather a few of them.

Thus, Reynolds walked through otherwise awful racial times within a relatively secure bubble of privilege, enjoying the benefits of beauty, nearly white skin, schooling at Columbia Teacher's College and the Sorbonne, and very quick wits. If blondes have stereotypically had more fun in the dominant culture, it must be said that beautiful light-skinned black women like Reynolds enjoyed something of a similar "pass." "Most of my contemporaries, both black and white, have had chiefly tales of woe to tell," she

writes. "I feel a little guilty saying how much fun I have had being a colored girl in the twentieth century."

Reynolds was a woman who milked her "exoticism" for everything it was worth—which was quite a lot by any measure. She
seemed endlessly conflicted about her racial identity and, while
never really denying who she was, played with the shades of her
being in a way chameleons would envy. She flitted among pre-
senting herself as "jazz baby," high-toned, mulatta, "American
Indian," "East Indian," "high yaller easy lay," half-breed, "wild
baby," island child, exotic, mixed breed, Creole, "part Cherokee,"
half-caste, "brown-skinned baby," "yellow peril," metisse, "sugar
cane," "noble savage," and the eponymous "American cocktail."
She becomes a peculiarly passive opportunist: she allowed a Maryland marriage clerk to believe she was white in order to marry
Dwight Dickinson, in Maryland in 1941, when anti-miscegenation
laws would have otherwise prohibited that; and she engages in a
lengthy affair with the very wealthy Guy de Châteaubriant, who
was "my idea of a gentleman." What did he see in her? As she
describes it, a "civilized" woman yet with "all the charm of the
jungle."

Ah yes, it is hard to disagree when she sighs, "I was a bird in
dizzy flight, going from flower to flower, with never a full meal,
but enjoying every sip."

And quite honestly, she really would be a lot less interesting if
she weren't black and American and rather like a fly on the wall
during interesting times. You sort of wish you could get her to
focus less on the crystal chandeliers, Aubusson carpets, and the
call of the clubs—you just want her to scan the headlines.

Alas no: "I leave it to the historians to record the exterior events
of the time. We were busy attending the vernissages of the Berman

brothers and Dalí, Miró, Max Ernst, Bracque, Man Ray, Giacometti, Tchelitchew, Tzara, Brancusi, Léger, Derain and Picasso. . . . Oh there were so many things to do and read and attend to each month, each more amusing and delightful than the other."

For all her worldly connections, therefore, this autobiography is strangely and tantalizingly spare in meaty historical detail. Reynolds sets the reader up in a catbird seat to exciting encounters among major figures of the Civil Rights movement, the Harlem Renaissance, the Surrealist art movement, the Paris fashion scene, and the rise of fascism in Europe. But if they're all there, moving from stage right to stage left in the theater of her life, they are given astonishingly few lines. We see her conversing with Picasso on the eve of the Spanish Civil War; we learn that Alice B. Toklas glared at her from across a room while her then-lover painted a portrait of the more affable Gertrude Stein; we know that she breakfasted with the dour wife of Marshal Pétain on the morning the Vichy regime is installed. But we strain in vain for audio. Instead one must piece the substantive background together from Reynolds's breathless descriptions of the color of the wallpaper or the smell of fresh linens or the make of her roadster or some delicacy served at luncheon.

It's all quite interesting as a study in manners, but her persistent ellipses seem more than mere oversight, and rather the product of a consciously formulated snobbery related to a self-involved guardedness around the question of race. "They were the most civilized people I had ever known," she writes of a motley cohort of wealthy international dilettantes, "quite possibly because no one ever mentioned politics or policies, ideologies, nationalities, religions or any other subject that might be considered in the least controversial." Of course no one in that merry company held a job or had to: they swam every morning, had lunch, enjoyed a siesta, returned to the beach, visited, then "just loaf[ed] around before getting dressed for dinner."

This love for a world so free from want, so free from the need to theorize about distributive justice, inflects the entire memoir. "I fell into the superficial social life like falling into a feather bed that I had always looked for. . . . Certainly I never felt hurt by the so-called 'easy arrogance of wealth.' The arrogance never touched me, perhaps because my own matched it. I was certainly more at home with inherited wealth than in the presence of the uneasy arrogance of persons struck with their racial superiority or of the newly rich."

Hence, this is a book where it helps to read between the lines for cultural details of the times she describes. Reynolds is frequently so inattentive to context that the excellently juicy footnotes become indispensable reading, and surely lend her text some of its most interesting historical heft. For example, she describes having had an abortion and leaving a lover because he was murkily implicated in a fight in which "one musician shot at another in the streets." It's all very engagingly torrid, but it's only in a footnote that we learn this was an infamous and very well-publicized gunfight with none other than jazz great Sidney Bechet.

Similarly, she begins some of her stories with great substantive promise: "[M]ost of the religious, financial, big business, military and even the political greats of the time were willing to collaborate with the Nazis. They were so afraid that Léon Blum and the socialists would bring Russia into Paris, they were perfectly willing to sell the country, turn over the keys to the factories, turn the government over to the Nazis." But characteristically enough, she quickly veers off course, because "Leftists, rightists, bourgeoisie, nobility—I went shining through it all with an inner light, for I had a deep secret love."

Yes, it's time for another affair.

It is possible to enjoy this book simply for the indulgently entertaining life she leads. She had an adventurous life, particularly for someone raised by a mother who is consistently described as a well-bred Boston Brahmin. Her company included pedophiles, opium smokers, and alcoholics—even if many of them were also world-class intellects. For example, William Seabrook, as she states in one toss-away sentence, had "just written a sensational thing about black magic in Haiti and wanted to continue his research in Africa." She is invited to come along, but passes on the trip with him and his wife because "I wasn't interested." But she never details exactly why Seabrook's work was so sensational: lost to contemporary audiences is the fact that his books on Satanism, death rites, and the occult introduced the word "zombie" to Western audiences. If he is remembered at all today, it is for his experimentation with cannibalism and his deliciously detailed description of what human flesh tastes like (veal, not chicken).

An apolitical, nonideological critic, Reynolds is nevertheless an engaging storyteller, a gifted writer. But she deflects away from her own best potential. Early in her career, she published a story about a girl who was "supposed to have been raped" by a man who was lynched. Without further clues as to the ambiguities suggested, she says simply that the story was accepted by a London literary magazine that asked her to write more, and wished to make it into a series. But "I had no more to say." Living in France, she says, "I was not reminded of the horrors of American lynchings every day, nor did I care to be. One must feel deeply to want to write about these things, but at the time, I wanted to be living a light, gay way, not feeling deeply about much of anything."

And so she didn't. Still, she is not without a sense of analogy and the profound links among all forms of prejudice: in 1930 she felt accepted in France even as she was aware of "intergroup tensions," as "when someone was referred to as a Jew or a sacré Jesuit or a Puritan Protestant. . . . Fear and animosity towards the Germans was also widespread. . . . Fascism was starting to show itself, communism was well-established by then and the 'master race' was feeling the pinch in Asia and Africa." Yet even as she observes this reality, she presents it only as the filler in a conversation ("I was personally convinced that they could all get together and stop this nonsense") with a rich man who offered her a thousand dollars to "spend the afternoon with me."

She makes clear what she did not believe in: communism, fascism, nationalism, religion, sexism, and so on. But in not taking any position on so many of the issues about which she wrote and events in which she was directly involved—such as that elegant breakfast with Marshal Pétain's wife on the eve of France's capitulation to the Nazis—it's necessarily tempting to read into the gaps in her story. The startling absence of self-reflection at certain points leaves the reader to ponder other of her unseemly priorities and blind spots. She turned down an invitation to meet F. Scott Fitzgerald, for instance, with a cuttingly dismissive parenthetical: "My friends were upper class Negroes and the Greenwich Village crowd which included Eugene O'Neill and Edna St. Vincent Millay. The newly rich Irish arriving in the mid-20s did not attract me at all; rather dull and unintelligent, I'd heard."

Similarly, Reynolds sneers when, at a card party, Paul Robeson's wife complained that the British shared the same color prejudice as Americans: "She surely would never have been invited to an American bridge party with women of that class, yet she was completely accepted by the English." This, only two pages after Reynolds's "Anglo-Saxon" mother-in-law worried that "you mustn't get sunburned" because "people who live in hot countries have thickened skulls and can't think too well." Reynolds found that bit of phrenological poppycock "greatly amusing" and seemed not to connect it at all to the racialized thinking about which Mrs. Robeson so fretted.

It is a blindness that grows more glaring as World War II neared. In 1933, "with Hitler raving on the radio like a mad, hysterical bitch," she lists herself as "not among the fighting adherents of any political philosophy. I might have taken a pot shot at Hitler had I either been Jewish or seriously enough involved in the German situation to risk my life." But she was neither, and instead took off for "a pleasure trip" to Spain "in a light-hearted mood," where she dined and danced even as the Spanish Civil War broke out all around her. She stayed there until food became so scarce "it seemed as though there would soon be nothing left to eat but anchovies and honey." Returning to France, she was mildly distressed by the rise of a wealthy right wing: "All the have-gots were saying they would rather have Hitler in the Élysée than Léon Blum [the French leader, a communist.] Still, I danced as usual in the afternoon at Le Boeuf."

As conditions grew more desperate, she joined the Red Cross: "But even with my officer's rank, lieutenant, which, by the way, netted me about five cents a day, I couldn't dissuade the 'authorities' from taking a Jewish neighbor, Charlotte, to put her in 'protective custodial camp' (concentration camp) when they came to the building to get her." And that's that. The very next paragraph moves briskly on to describe in lengthier and loving detail all the drawings, prints, and Chanel dresses she packed as she prepared to decamp from Paris to the south of France.

It is there, as she sat on the border of Spain where Jews were fleeing ahead of the Nazis, that Mme. Pétain asked her why she was helping "the rats who were deserting the sinking ship." Reynolds writes, "That slight contact with what seemed to me to be anti-Semitism on her part inspired me to go to any length to try to help the refugees." Perhaps it is a stylistic tic for lady-like understatement typical of her time, but even as Reynolds positions herself as a resister, she comes across as an oddly casual and generally thoughtless one. Indeed, one of the most interesting takeaways from this memoir is the degree Reynolds's intuitive sense of justice remains tone-deaf to the malleability and hybridity of cultural prejudices. In the spaces of her story, one can glean important object lessons about how class, education, color, and celebrity might—even today—constantly play against each other in complicated, ever-vibrant, and divisive ways.

But this book is not merely about one woman's brilliantly multitalented career, or her wildly successful if sometimes solipsistic ability to go clubbing with every known celebrity of the time. It is also testament to the concentrated geography of talent that had pooled in Los Angeles as capital of the emerging film industry, and in New York and Paris as centers of art and literature. Reynolds possessed front-row seats to the exceptional human energy unleashed in the Roaring Twenties and Thirties. She was surrounded by people who used their libidos as well as their logic to challenge and remake culture. It was the era of Dadaism, surrealism, fauvism, cubism, automatism, Fabianism, and modernism. It was the Jazz Age, when transgression was a dominant theme in politics, psychology, and economics; when returning to a state of innocence, or starting over, was touted as positive social experiment. Her disinhibitions were those of the time. Too easily dismissed as frivolity or wildness, that spirited foment also broke down many theretofore-intractable social conventions about wealth, race, class, and place. Those open doors, those crossed thresholds, ultimately led, in successive decades, to social movements based on racial integration, social welfare, women's rights, sexual freedom, and anticolonialism. Through the lens of this memoir, one can appreciate the unprecedented crucible of opposites bubbling then: of global and local, arm's length and intimate, classical and experimental, canonical and interdisciplinary, east and west, north and south, black, white, and intermezzo. Anita Thompson Dickinson Reynolds embodied the indomitable human cocktail whose ingredients inspired an Old World to dance its way into an entirely new age.

Introduction

by George Hutchinson

In the novel *Quicksand,* Nella Larsen introduces a character named Audrey Denney as a probe into the psychology of the bourgeois but politically progressive "race woman" of the 1920s in the United States. Audrey Denney lives downtown, on 22nd Street, near Greenwich Village, and moves freely between blacks and whites. Anne Grey, Helga Crane's well-heeled friend in Harlem, detests her for this:

> It's a wonder she hasn't some white man hanging about. The disgusting creature! . . . She ought to be ostracized."
>
> "Why?" asked Helga curiously, noting at the same time that three of the men in their own party had deserted and were now congregated about the offending Miss Denney.
>
> "Because she goes about with white people," came Anne's indignant answer, "and they know she's colored."
>
> "I'm afraid I don't quite see, Anne. Would it be all right if they didn't know she was colored?"
>
> . . . . .

> "Why, she gives parties for white and colored people to-
> gether. And she goes to white people's parties. It's worse than
> disgusting, it's positively obscene."
>
> "Oh, come, Anne, you haven't been to any of the parties, I
> know, so how can you be so positive about the matter!"[1]

Not knowing that Helga herself was born to an interracial couple, Anne goes on to reveal the depth of her contempt for Denney's "treacherous" behavior, which is shared by Anne's circle of
friends. Helga gives up on the discussion, feeling "that it would
be useless to tell them what she felt for the beautiful, calm, cool
girl who had the assurance, the courage, so placidly to ignore racial barriers and give her attention to people, was not contempt,
but envious admiration. So she remained silent, watching the girl.[2]
One of Larsen's most evocative characters, Audrey Denney serves
Helga Crane as the ideal of an alternative way of being in the
world, "raced" and yet not restricted by race, desired and desiring
yet self-possessed, a model of feminine agency irrespective of racial boundaries.

While doing research on Nella Larsen at Howard University
several years ago, I was waiting for some material relating to Larsen
when I came across the shelf list for the papers of someone named
Anita Thompson Dickinson Reynolds. As her span of life closely
overlapped with Larsen's and she had spent some years in New
York, I wondered if they might have known each other. I asked
to see some of her correspondence and then turned to several
manuscripts of an autobiography. Expecting nothing of interest
to my project, yet hopeful, I was quickly drawn into a life story
the likes of which I had never encountered. It turned out that
Anita was close to a number of Larsen's closest friends in this pe-

riod, including particularly Dorothy Peterson of Brooklyn (Larsen's best friend), black Greenwich Villagers Dorothy and Jim Harris, Grace Nail and James Weldon Johnson, and Walter and Gladys White. This was the crowd with which Larsen regularly socialized. It seemed impossible that Larsen and Anita Thompson were not acquainted. Anita reflected on the prudishness of the Harlem black professional class, their suspicion of the white bohemians, and her own greater comfort in the Village, where she ultimately settled for a while—which, she said, raised some eyebrows. She hosted "mixed parties" and mingled freely with white men, although her boyfriends in New York were black. She disliked the segregated nature of black high society, and she loved to dance. In fact, she danced professionally in her teens and twenties. This connection stuck with me. In the Dorothy Peterson Papers I later found a letter Dorothy had written to Carl Van Vechten referring to "Anita Thompson," with whom Dorothy was browsing the shops at Christmastime in 1941. (Thompson married Dwight Dickinson in the 1940s and, after divorcing Dickinson, Guy Reynolds in the 1960s; hence the name Anita Thompson Dickinson Reynolds.) Nella Larsen had cut off her friends and dropped out of sight four years earlier. But suddenly Dorothy and Anita came upon her in a shop on 10th Street, and Larsen spoke with them. Anita was shocked at Larsen's appearance. It was also clear from this letter that Anita Thompson and Nella Larsen had known each other in years past. I reflected back on the autobiography I had come upon at Howard University and, knowing that Larsen often created her characters as composites of people she knew, wondered if the character Audrey Denney was modeled on Anita Thompson, who had all of the characteristics ascribed to the fictional character.

I acquired a copy of the final version of Reynolds's memoir in order to read it more closely and in doing so became entranced by the story not for its relation to Nella Larsen, but in its own right. Anita Reynolds turned out to be considerably more remarkable than Audrey Denney, and I found her manuscript, as coauthored with Howard Miller, impossible to put down. Here, it turned out, was the story of an African American intellectual, dancer, silent film actress, model, inspiration of poems and fictional characters, part-time journalist, protégé of famed surrealists, vamp, and all-around bohemian, told in a style I had never known before. In it a person who inspired so much—and such diverse—fantasy comes out of the novel, the poem, the chorus line, the film still, the Man Ray portrait, the Chanel advertisement to tell her own tale, one in which her voice and attitude are as vividly unique and engaging as her life story.

Covering the years from Reynolds's birth to her flight from the German conquest of France, the memoir gives a revealing glimpse into the variations on blackness in one woman's life, a life that even Nella Larsen would have had difficulty imagining. It allows a view of international modernism, and of racial passing, from a unique angle. It provides, as well, a marked contrast to the autobiographies of Anita's cousin Langston Hughes and her friend Claude McKay, whose forms of intellectual vagabondage have been at the center of many constructions of black transnational experience.

Anita Thompson was politically aware, a left-wing liberal, quite familiar with Marxism but never a communist, never much of a "joiner" in any sense. She was an epicurean individualist striving for independence against long odds. Of the Communist Party, she writes: "It reminded me of a furniture company which advertised: 'We stand behind every bed we sell.' I didn't want them standing behind my bed." Released from the stranglehold of U.S. racial politics and their implications for black women of her class, and possessed of a hedonistic life philosophy, she traversed racial boundaries in pursuit of knowledge, excitement, pleasure, freedom, and, at times, security. This is not to say that she was free of race; her choices and their effects were also conditioned by racial divisions not only as they were drawn in the United States but as they functioned in France, England, Spain, and North Africa. Hers is a fascinating story of one woman's life that provokes reflection on the modernist cultures of the interwar period from a peculiar angle, in which the intersections of female sexuality, class, race, and place achieve an almost surreal and fantastic historical density.

At the time Anita Reynolds wrote, or rather recorded, her autobiography, she was a psychologist and part-time university instructor at the College of the Virgin Islands. She was married to a white American hotel owner and real estate entrepreneur, with whom she found pleasant companionship and freedom to do as she wished. It was the mid-1970s, and the feminist movement was in full swing. Women were demanding equality in the workplace and orgasms in the bedroom, and Thompson pointedly writes her story with these demands in mind, detailing her sexual experiences, including her first orgasm—with another woman—and speaking proudly of her mother's professional achievements (being the first female CPA in the United States) and of her feminism. She speaks in no uncertain terms of male chauvinism and selfishness in sex while nonetheless prizing traditional "gentlemanly" behavior.

The sexual frankness in Reynolds's autobiography is striking next to the reticence of Hughes's *The Big Sea* or McKay's *A Long*

Way from Home—or even next to the autobiographies of performers such as Josephine Baker and Ada "Bricktop" Smith. The difference can be attributed in part to the fact that Reynolds was working on her book mainly in the 1970s, when such frankness was widespread, but it also seems to have to do with her personality, her psychological training, and a lack of concern for her "reputation" precisely because she was *not* a public figure or a well-known artist. It may also have to do with her bohemian unconcern, dating to the late 1920s, about racial and sexual norms.

The 1970s reverberated still with the militancy of the black power movement and calls for black autonomy, and Reynolds writes with these movements also in mind, referring at one point to the first American "Black Muslim" she met—in Tunisia. Throughout her story, she speaks frankly and with anger, and often with sarcasm, about anti-black racism, but she does so as an avid integrationist who believes the world has had enough of racial division. The peoples of the world need to "get together" and form "one big family," she argues at several points in her story. The sentiment undoubtedly derives from her own experiences of national and racial division in the twentieth century and the memory of fascism's rise in Europe; but she also locates its origins in her own family heritage, which was "red, white, and black," in her own telling. "At home, and in conversation with Grandma," she noted in the first draft of her memoir, "we learned that we belonged on neither side of the tracks but in the middle—dodging trains headed in opposite directions."[3]

Many of Anita's relatives passed as white; but her immediate family did not find this entirely tragic. They regarded it as a defensible choice in the face of American racism and found the ironies of the color line thus opened up to them sources of endless, if

this," she continued, "is the hope that mankind, that all people on the globe, may understand the advantages of integration, amalgamation, the taking of the best out of each culture, and of all people living as one, intermarrying, intermingling, and making one human race."[6] It is a sentiment that resonates with Josephine Baker's feelings in her later life. Reynolds had seen enough in her long life of the "unintelligent futility of killing so many people in the name of nationalism, communism, fascism, racism, Zionism, Protestantism, Catholicism, or any 'ism.'"[7] She believed that in the next century "everyone is going to have a good time mixing with everybody else." And in the first draft of her memoir (transcribed directly from tapes), she dedicated it "to all those who have seen in me a person and not a race."[8] She then crossed out "race" and replaced it with "problem." Take it as you will.

Anita Reynolds was born Anita Thompson in Provident Hospital of Chicago—the first black-owned and black-directed hospital in the United States—on March 28, 1901, attended by Daniel Hale Williams, the African American doctor famed for first performing successful open-heart surgery. She was named after Anita Garibaldi, the feminist wife of the Italian liberator Giuseppe Garibaldi, whom her beloved maternal grandmother had allegedly known (although this seems unlikely). This grandmother, according to the first draft of the memoir and notes Anita wrote for photographs to accompany the memoir, was born in 1850 near Richmond of a planter father and an "Indian-Negro?" mother who had escaped slavery with the aid of a German sea captain who took her as a cabin girl to Boston about 1862, when she was twelve. (The memoir speaks of the "Indian-Negro?" great-grandmother as "a Cherokee Indian," which would make the grandmother half-white and half-Cherokee.) She lived with the captain's family—who also educated her—continued to make runs back and forth to Norfolk as cabin girl, and became a "very active member of the abolitionist group in Boston."[9] In fact, she worked directly with Charles Sumner, "who was her hero and . . . teacher, she said."[10] Shortly after the Civil War, she married Bertrand Thompson, "one of Jerome Bonaparte's bastards," a "mulatto" veteran of the Union Navy whom she met at the Essex Club in Boston, an organization of "freed and escaped slaves and persons of mixed blood" that helped escaped slaves settle in the North. He had been taught the jeweler's trade by Jesuits but was a Freemason and "a Voltaire skeptic," as Anita's mother proudly told her.[11]

Anita's mother, Beatrice Sumner Thompson, had been born and partly raised in Cambridge, Massachusetts, and was a "bluestocking" feminist with a Boston Brahmin accent and golden hair. The family eventually moved to Denver, where Anita's uncle Clarence was born in 1888. Beatrice could easily pass as white but chose to identify as Negro. She had been saved from marriage to her fiancée of eight years, a handsome Pennsylvania Dutchman, by concern about his drinking and the fortunate intervention of a Creole beau brummel from Louisiana, a man of elegant manners, striped pants and cutaways, and a good eye for fine jewelry. He was at the time a traveling salesman for a Chicago jeweler and met Beatrice on a trip to Denver. His first wife, named Lottie, had divorced him in 1898 to marry the celebrated black entertainer Bert Williams. After marriage Beatrice and Samuel set up their household in Chicago, at 5120 Indiana Avenue, where they lived when Anita was born in 1901.[12] Two years later Beatrice gave birth to a son, Sumner Mattelle Thompson, who would be nicknamed "Tada" and became protective Anita's bosom buddy until he passed into the white world while she was in Europe in the 1930s.

Anita's extended family was huge, and well-connected to the New Negro elite of the early twentieth century. When Anita's grandfather died, her grandmother moved to Los Angeles, at 22nd and Los Angeles Streets, where a number of relatives (including, eventually, Anita's mother with children) joined her. Many relatives on the father's side remained on the eastern seaboard in prominent positions. As a result Reynolds is able to give unique glimpses of black "high society" in Los Angeles, Chicago, New York, and Washington. Her father's brother, Noah Thompson (who lived in a "double" with Anita's family in Chicago when she was young), served for some years as secretary to Booker T. Washington, and later as publicist for Marcus Garvey, the charismatic head of the United Negro Improvement Association and "self-styled Provisional President of Africa." In 1922, however, the redoubtable Noah Thompson went on the floor of the UNIA convention to battle what he considered Garvey's quixotic business schemes and demagogic tactics, then returned to Los Angeles to persuade most of its Garvey followers to leave the UNIA.[13] Noah's wife's family owned the Baltimore *Afro-American,* one of the three or four most influential black newspapers of the early twentieth century, and one closely associated with the colored aristocracy of Washington, D.C. When well-heeled and even famous African Americans like James Weldon Johnson and W. E. B. Du Bois visited Los Angeles, they stayed with Anita's family since the "nice" hotels would not receive them. One of these stays culminated in her first sexual experience with a man, apparently none other than W. E. B. Du Bois, who was more than thirty years her senior. She termed the experience her introduction to "the real thing" at age twenty-two, and "far less agreeable" than her first sexual experience, with her high school friend Dorothea Childs. "It served me right," Anita tells us, "because I allowed an 'intellectual giant' to persuade me that 'virtue is its own and only reward,' and that 'flirting and spooning if you don't mean business is beneath the dignity of a liberated woman.' Of course, being a liberated flapper of the lost generation (no wonder it was lost!), I fell for this ludicrous line."[14]

Anita's family had influential friends in the white world as well. Charles Schwab of Bethlehem Steel, a childhood friend of her father's, helped him beat a murder rap in Los Angeles. During her high school years, Anita and her friend Dorothea (whose boyfriend was a cameraman) attended Charles Chaplin's "anarchist bull sessions" in Hollywood, and she knew Douglas Fairbanks personally. Her uncle Clarence Bertrand Thompson (the one who "passed") was a Harvard alumnus and successful businessman. He had been an associate of the famous business reformer, Frederick W. Taylor, whose Taylor Scientific Management system revolutionized modern industry. He would go on to a distinguished and multifaceted career in business management and eventually the sciences. Clarence enjoyed joking and telling stories with his sister and mother (Anita's mother and grandmother) about "passing" members of the family. In Anita's youth he was married to a white woman, a cousin of the governor of Ohio. The white aunt knew Anita's family and was perfectly aware of their racial designation. She got along particularly well with her mother-in-law (Anita's grandmother), but when together they never advertised Anita's mother's "colored marriage." Years later Clarence divorced, moved to France just after World War I to help reorganize national industries there (for which he was awarded knighthood in the Légion d'Honneur), and married a German woman who never knew he was other than white until Anita informed her, to her chagrin, years after his death. He returned to the United States just before the fascist occupation, having helped to build the French munitions industry in the lead-up to World War II.

Anita Thompson Reynolds's life thus traversed numerous spheres considered iconic, and usually separate, in transatlantic modernism—the nationwide colored aristocracy, Douglas Fairbanks and Charlie Chaplin's Hollywood and early black cinema, the Greenwich Village bohemia of the early 1920s, high Harlem and the Broadway revues of the late 1920s, surrealist Paris, the world of French high fashion in the early 1930s, Spanish Morocco, Barcelona at the start of the Spanish Civil War, English aristocracy, France in the tense years of Léon Blum's socialist administration and then in the chaotic weeks of the Nazi invasion, and refugee New York in the early 1940s.

She gives priceless glimpses of each space she inhabits and the people she meets, from a unique point of view, and her observations about Langston Hughes, Du Bois, Claude McKay, Man Ray, Antonin Artaud, André Derain, Robert Desnos, Kristians Tonny, among others—will be of interest to biographers, historians, and literary as well as art history scholars. Here's A'Lelia Walker, heiress of Madame C. J. Walker's hair-straightening and cosmetics empire, while living with the Thompsons in Los Angeles and marketing her mother's products to the beauty parlors there: "After breakfast . . . she got busy turning the kitchen into her workshop, boiling petroleum jelly, adding some perfume then ladling the concoction into little cans labeled *Madam Walker's Hair Straightener.* Each time she tipped the ladle, she would amuse us by saying, 'one dollar, one dollar.' I thought that was certainly an easy way to get rich."

The memoir directs modest attention to Anita's film career— much too modest, given the later interest in early black film and black performance history. She was regarded as the most promising black actress of "the race" in the early 1920s, mainly by reason of her starring role opposite Clarence Brooks in *By Right of Birth* (1921). This was a historic film in black cinema history, a six-reeler, the most substantial and successful of those produced by the first black film company, Lincoln Motion Pictures, although it has attracted little scholarly attention, since it exists today only in fragments totaling twenty-three minutes, at the Library of Congress. Reviewers of the film for both black and white newspapers noted Anita Thompson's fitness for the role and the quality of her acting, and for several years into the mid-1920s black newspapers would refer to her as a "Movie Picture Queen," "New York's doll baby," and "the lovely screen-stage beauty." A columnist for the *Pittsburgh Courier,* asked about the race's greatest actress, said he couldn't decide between Evelyn Preer (who starred in Oscar Micheaux films), Anita Thompson, and Edna Morton.[15] But her role in the Hollywood blockbuster *The Thief of Bagdad,* starring Douglas Fairbanks, was also more prominent than she lets on in the memoir. She appears throughout the film as a waiting maid for the princess who stars opposite Fairbanks's thief (and of course marries him in the end). But there was no future in the early 1920s for a "colored" actress, and Anita Thompson was surely aware of this, as was her mother, who considered acting in Hollywood films "the next thing to appearing in a circus."

As Anita grows into adulthood and settles in New York, then Paris, we see things from the perspective of a bright young woman making her way, often somewhat recklessly, by wit, grace, and sex appeal. In New York, at first among the haute bourgeoisie, she is surprised by the conservatism: "There was nothing simple about what respectable colored people thought were their moral standards. The women, especially, were so prudish, at least so it seemed to me, I got the impression they were afraid to be mistaken for an 'easy lay' even by their husbands. / Everything in colored society was formal. I remember, that some women were called Mrs. Doctor Smith or Mrs. Lawyer Serotee, basking in whatever profession her husband was active in. I found this all very different from my life in Los Angeles, where we talked freely about birth control, the Lucy Stone League, and the advisability of women keeping their maiden names after being married." Her Hollywood background significantly accounts for the fact that this daughter of the haute bourgeoisie would turn out to provide the most notable case of footloose expatriate hedonism in African American women's autobiography.

In Greenwich Village, Anita tells us, she felt more at home than in Harlem. Her acquaintances included a heroine of sexual liberation she had long admired who, in person, seemed not to live up to the hype. "I found it hard to believe that Miss [Edna St. Vincent] Millay was someone who 'burned her candle at both ends'; she seemed to be such a nicely brought-up young woman, I imagined she went to bed at eight o'clock with a volume of Tennyson. [Eugene] O'Neill struck me as a typical journalist, a slender man and pleasant to chat with."

Readers will notice a remarkable independence of spirit in Reynolds's life from early on, a spirit that is unmistakable in the style of the memoir itself, its uniquely brash yet self-deprecating voice. When her father refuses to fund her education at Columbia

Teachers College, hoping to force her to return to Los Angeles, she raises tuition money by finding a job as a dancer. About the same time she was getting to know the white bohemians of "the Village," Anita was living on "Strivers' Row" in Harlem—the famous collection of brownstones on 138th and 139th Streets—with the Austins, one of the most well-known families of high Harlem's social set. This gave her the opportunity to meet their neighbor, the showman Flournoy Miller, who gave her a spot on the chorus line of the revue *Runnin' Wild,* one of the most successful black Broadway revues of the 1920s, now famous for having set off the worldwide Charleston craze. It ran for twenty-seven weeks and 213 performances in the fall and winter of 1923–1924, while Anita was also attending Columbia Teachers College to become an art educator. The nickname her grandmother gave her, "Jazz Baby," had proven prophetic. It came from a popular song, the smash hit of 1919:

> *I'm a jazz baby,*
> *I wanna be jazzin' all the time!*
> *There's something in the tone of a saxophone*
> *That makes me do a little wiggle all my own.*
> *'Cause I'm a jazz baby!*
> *Full of jazzbo harmony!*
> *The Walk the Dog and Ball the Jack that cause all the talk,*
> *Is just a copy of the way I naturally walk*
> *'Cause I'm a jazz baby.*[16]

True to her sobriquet, Anita attended class by day and danced by night. The "stage-door johnnies" who took her out to the Cotton Club found her exotic as a Columbia co-ed, while the

Columbia students she dated found her chorus-girl persona equally intoxicating. Growing restive under the condescension and concern of her famous boyfriend, Charlie West (All-American football star and an M.D.), she allowed her marriage prospects in the black fraternity and sorority crowd to fade away, being uncomfortable with their "Puritanism."

When her father finally broke down and sent her money to enroll in the highly respectable Wellesley College so she could stay on the East Coast under close supervision, and away from bohemian New York, Anita used the money to buy passage to Paris and begin art school at the Louvre, leaving on September 28, 1928.[17] Her parents only learned of her arrival there from her Uncle Clarence, then passing as white and helping to rebuild French industry. He wrote the Thompsons, disapprovingly, that she had shown up at his door looking "like an actress"—which, in a sense, she was. She imagined herself looking like Gloria Swanson.

Reynolds's descriptions of her life in Paris, which dominate the memoir, often throw doubt on well-known scholarly accounts of black Paris, which emphasize the development of a mostly male African American community, or a diasporic black community, largely separated from the white American expatriate writers and artists, with whom black Americans interacted only superficially.[18] Although this may well have been true for some black expatriates, it does not fit Anita Thompson's case—nor, significantly enough, the experiences of Nella Larsen, Dorothy Peterson (a director of various Harlem theater groups), Nora Holt (nightclub performer), Claude McKay, Walter White (novelist and NAACP officer), and others whom Thompson knew from New York. Indeed, Anita may have met McKay through Louise Bryant, the left-wing journalist to whom he dedicated his novel *Banjo,* and she rarely saw him with other black people in Paris—although, her correspondence shows, she introduced McKay and Countee Cullen to each other for the first time at the American Express office there: "Can you imagine," she wrote her brother, "they've been near each other dozens of times—anxious to know each other—and never met before? I like them both and it's really only the poets and other no gooders that keep drawing me back to their group. Tho' with Claude—black as he is—one never meets spades but the most charming people. This week we've been the guests of Louise Bryant to whom his 'Home to Harlem' is dedicated."[19] A year and a half later, she wrote her mother that she might go visit McKay in Morocco: "Don't think that is scandalous; he is a fairy. And he aint got no time for nothing my color no how . . . even if I were a boy. HA!"[20] She believed he was in Morocco, like André Gide and others, mainly because of an interest in Arab boys.

Much of the historical interest of the memoir in its second half derives from the perspective on surrealist circles it provides. Under the wings of Louise Bryant and Man Ray, Anita had entered a niche more than ready to receive her. Dada had just given way to surrealism—in both of which Man Ray was a major protagonist—and *La Revue Nègre* of 1926, which made Josephine Baker's reputation, had seemed to point the way toward the renewal of European art, by some accounts. Simultaneously "modern" and "primitive," "sophisticated" and "naïve," it exemplified just what the Parisian avant-garde and its liberal observers were looking for. As Anita's friend Jacques Baron later recalled, "the music hall, in all its joy, provided in a substantial measure a place for marvels. All the art of the black Americans was a revelation to old Europe. It wasn't only the pain of humanity. It was a conjuration of heaven against earth. Perhaps there was a god in heaven who was not simply an entrepreneur of vulgar spectacles."[21] African sculpture had already inspired a major break in European visual arts, but the African American musical revue of the 1920s was something new and different. And Anita Thompson had danced in such a revue, on Broadway. Moreover, Charlie Chaplin, an artistic hero of the surrealists, is someone Anita could talk about as an acquaintance. The surrealists were also fascinated by "westerns" of the silent film era, and she had starred in one. She had acted on sets with Douglas Fairbanks as an Arab waiting maid in *The Thief of Bagdad*. Jacques Baron described the Paris surrealists' fascination with American cinema and music: "The Far West traversed our walls, in a passionate ride with Douglas Fairbanks under the sign of Zorro. As for Charlot of the early period, he wasn't merely Charlie Chaplin but the eternal emigrant whom we all are. There was also jazz."[22]

Interest in the exotic—realms and beings outside space and time—related to the exoticizing of women, particularly non-white women. Describing the way Paris functioned as an exotic realm for the surrealists, Baron compares the city to a woman of the tropics, "Like a woman one loves and calls 'my bird of the islands' or 'my orchid of Brazil' in order to situate her outside space and time, or in some unvisited hot corner of the world."[23] Baron, as Anita Reynolds tells us, wrote a poem about her in which her feet "never touched the ground." She also partly inspired Eric de Haulleville's surrealist novel, *Le Voyage aux Iles Galapagos* (Marseilles: Les Cahiers du Sud, 1934), in which a shipwrecked sailor falls in love with an exotic South Pacific island girl who reminds him, uncannily, of his wife "Anita."

White men entranced by the young American could fantasize about her in multiple locations, and surrealism, if nothing else encouraged fantasy. Her first long-time lover and potential husband, Kristians Tonny (who illustrated de Haulleville's novel *Genre épique*), was a Dutch fan of James Fenimore Cooper novels since boyhood; he liked to imagine her an American Indian. Her first husband, a veteran of the British colonial army in India, fantasized about her as an "East Indian" maiden. And her later French lover, Guy de Chateaubriant, who loved sailing in the Antilles, thought of her as "his dream of the island child come true, the creole, the exotic girl of the islands." These were fantasies, according to Reynolds, that she did not mind indulging, even while laughing at them: "I might have been La Dame aux Camélias [in her relationship with Chateaubriant], except that I was a healthy American and not likely to die of TB or love or anything else if I could help it. I was an American edition of Back Street Love who could laugh at herself and the whole situation." Yet Anita Thompson was something of a surrealist herself, valuing the interpenetration of the unconscious and conscious worlds. "Like a psychotic, a schizophrenic, I lived a life of waking and dreaming. When I was with Guy [de Chateaubriant] I was in the dream world, and when I was with Charles or Cecile [Schramm] or Jacques [Baron], my dream world lay just beneath the surface, coming to me any morning or evening."

In a sense, her roles in Paris were extensions of earlier ones in Los Angeles and Hollywood. Anita's dancing career began when the famous choreographer Ruth St. Denis picked her out to be a South Asian "nautch" dancer. Her mother promptly snatched her away, deciding that, if dance she must, she should learn the "Greek" style of dancing made famous by Isadora Duncan. But since Norma

Gould's high-toned dance school did not accept black or Jewish girls, Gould passed Anita off as Mexican. On the Hollywood set of *The Thief of Bagdad,* she played an Arab, and in *By Right of Birth* (1920), a black-directed film, she starred as a girl adopted by a white couple who thought she was Native American and discovered at about college age that she was a Negro: "I had to pull on my face most dramatically and utter with astonishment: 'My God, I'm a Negro!' It was difficult to stifle the giggles." In Greenwich Village, the set designer Cleon Throckmorton of the Provincetown Players once put on an "Antony and Cleopatra" party in which Anita was Cleopatra of the Nile.

Young and exotic in appearance to Europeans, racially ambiguous, Anita was also well-educated and a student of art. As a teenager, she had been a reader of *The Smart Set* (to which her parents subscribed) and later its successor *American Mercury*—one of the defining literary magazines of the era. (The sophisticated wit of the journal is detectable in Thompson's style, full of ironic deflation of patriotism, chauvinism, and moral self-righteousness.) She was very much au courant with the changing mores of the time, and while still in high school had even reviewed Fitzgerald's *Tales of the Jazz Age* for *The Messenger,* a New York–based black socialist magazine at the time edited by A. Philip Randolph and Chandler Owen, friends of her family. At the age of fifteen she had been introduced to the Hollywood avant-garde surrounding Chaplin; she knew all about Freud, Adler, and Jung, "and we talked freely about the current political issues." By the time she reached Paris, no one could take her for genuinely "primitive," but they imagined her so. Her life had already passed through cultural dimensions and juxtapositions that were, in a loose sense, "surreal." And they would become more so.

Reynolds's own racial identifications shifted as well. Growing up in Los Angeles, the African Americans she knew were all light-skinned and often thought of themselves as "mulatto" or "half-breeds." She distinguishes her own family ethnically from such "African-type" black Americans as A'Lelia Walker. Anita was always incensed by American anti-black racism, and her mother was a leader of the NAACP in Los Angeles. During the Chicago riots of 1919, she was proud of her cousins who transported guns for blacks' defense against the rioting whites. And yet, during at least her young adulthood, Thompson thought of herself as a "mixed-blood," and distinguished this identity from that of "Negro." In a letter of 1930 to her brother, she wrote, "My honest conclusion is that the only hope of salvation lays with the half-castes. In a hundred years America will be all half-caste. I'm sure there's no stopping it . . . [T]he world's getting smaller and smaller, all people are being mixed up—whether they want to be or not—and we half-breeds have everything in our favor. Despite the inferiority complex which holds them in subjection to-day, the 'gens de couleur' are stronger morally and physically than the 'sangs purs' . . . we're just shining examples of superiority."[24]

While Thompson for the most part disdained white Americans for their racism and identified with the black freedom struggle, she was hardly heroic in her own racial politics. She admits repeatedly that she was too caught up in pleasure and excitement to get too serious about anything. In fact, this unflattering characteristic helps account for the very range of her connections and experiences. In an undated letter to her mother, she wrote that she had just received a letter from her former boyfriend, Charles West, in which "He gave me all the news social political and athletic—a jig lynched t'other day, too. God be praised—how can all you sane people rest there? I could kill all the vile white people in the world. But I have other things to do now." And again, to her mother in 1929 Anita wrote, "This Nordic and Latin myth that binds the globe has about everyone (but the Chinese, perhaps) bamfussiled, and the only thing to be done about it is to make the most of it, that is Imperialism and rest, individually. Causes are senseless!"[25]

The memoir itself reveals that its author thought, despite what W. E. B. Du Bois once referred to as her "Bolshevik" sympathies, imperialism had its good points, and that she had no use for racial or ethnic nationalisms, even in service of anti-colonial movements. The national resentments of various European groups were palpable in Paris, as were those between the Africans in Paris and the French. She felt people needed to bridge their differences "and stop this nonsense. They all needed each other, particularly the undeveloped nations that seemed so anxious to throw off their colonial status and thus throw away the opportunity to build up their nation."

In Morocco, she stayed with Claude McKay a few weeks. They disagreed in their attitudes toward blackness. McKay "felt most strongly that anyone who had black blood should be Africanized. In Paris, for instance, anytime we went anywhere, he asked me to mat up my hair, which was about the only way I could have looked African. . . . I argued in Morocco as I had in Paris that there were already too many different races and nationalities, and it was far past time we all got together to be one family." Yet her impression was that, as much as McKay wanted her to "Africanize" herself, he spent all his time with white people.

After meeting the white American journalist Donald Duff, a friend of Claude McKay and Countee Cullen who was well-known in Harlem and was always ready to fight with other whites over the "race problem," Anita wrote: "Still he is most sensible, says he agrees that there is no hope of the jigs ever doing more than grabbing monkey-fashion all that the others are leaving to them. He says I should pass all together and not be identified with any unpopular minority unless I can be entirely independent."[26] It does not appear that Anita ever "passed altogether"; she did not "hide" her blackness. Usually, when asked, she termed herself "an 'American cocktail,' for among the French that included Indians, Negroes and everything else that made up a different kind of American. . . . The 'cocktails' were often welcome in many places where white Americans were not." Biographers and students of Kristians Tonny, who refer to her as Anita Matelle—the name she adopted in Paris, borrowing her brother's middle name—never mention that she was African American or "black" (although one uses the term "creool" in Dutch), which suggests that Tonny himself did not think of her as such, although he surely knew of her racial background.

It is not surprising that she took to the surrealists, and they to her, for they prized unexpected conjunctions, chance encounters, unhinged desire, the merging of the unconscious with the conscious mind, dream and "reality." And yet Anita remains hard-nosed and realistic, ever the outsider, watching and wondering at the scenes in which she plays a part. She had to have her wits about her, for even with her mother's periodic infusions of cash—her father having washed his hands of her—she needed money of her own to get by, as well as the companionship of men willing to buy her a meal or offer a place to live, sometimes as a long-term lover. The memoir mentions Arthur Wheeler's support for her as she worked on a book concerned with her family history, and his offer to give her an extra thousand dollars if she'd spend an afternoon in bed with him—an offer she refused. But he took her refusal in good humor and even told his wife about it, who laughed and said, "I wouldn't sleep with you for a thousand dollars myself." "They give me 3,000 francs a month," she wrote her mother, "until the book is finished without any strings. . . . This is the first time I ever got something for nothing and if you'd like to write someone in Paris, their address is 14 rue des Saints-Pêres, Paris 7e. . . . Just don't be too sweet, because they must be held to think that brains is rarer than cash. . . . What bull!"[27]

Not all white modernists in Paris were so taken with Anita "Matelle." She speaks of how Carl Van Vechten disapproved of and attempted to block her liaison with Kristians Tonny when it first began at a party in his Paris apartment. (Van Vechten eventually became "reconciled" to her friendship with Tonny, and she saw much of him in Toulon later.)[28] Van Vechten probably already knew—and certainly knew *of*—Anita Thompson through his friends in Harlem, black Brooklyn, and Greenwich Village, for he was good friends with her friend Dorothy Peterson. Van Vechten's disapproval may have had something to do with Gertrude Stein's, to which Reynolds does not allude even when mentioning Stein. (In correspondence at the end of her life, she observed that, "Although I considered Gertrude Stein quite mad, in fact <u>monstrous</u> in many ways, some of her observations are worth remembering.")[29] In an earlier draft of the memoir, she writes that Stein invited her to her salon only because Tonny would not go without her. Stein, she felt was "exploiting" him; she "was devious and bossy, and very few people liked her personally, but mutual exploitation was necessary during the depression."[30] Stein considered Kristians Tonny an artistic genius—he had painted a portrait of her and her dog that she liked—and paid for a lovely apartment for him to work in, in a new Art Deco building west of Montparnasse. He is one of the artists of whom she wrote a literary portrait (accompanied by his graphic self-portrait) in the book *Dix portraits*. However, she felt that Anita was distracting him from his work and connived with William Aspenwall Bradley and, apparently, the Wheelers, to send her off to Morocco.[31] According to the composer and later novelist Paul Bowles (an inspiration to the Beats), who knew them all, when Tonny figured out "the true reason for Anita's disappearance from the Paris scene," he took off for Morocco after her.[32] Anita, of course, knew little of the machinations that had led to her Moroccan sojourn. Bowles, who knew Anita in Morocco, did not have a much better opinion of Anita than Stein. In his autobiography, he wrote that "Tonny was so infatuated with Anita that he seemed not to be aware of her continuous flirtation with the younger male population in Tangier." According to Bowles, they "swarmed around her like bees over a honeysuckle vine."[33] In her memoir, Anita talks about the boutique she opened to sell trinkets to tourists. Bowles remembered the boutique in distinctly unflattering terms: "it was in a little street in the medina, near the Hotel Continental. It had a big mat on the ground, a painted étagère for displaying 'portefeuilles, et rien d'autres.' When she closed herself into the boutique with her Moroccan friends, the rumor circulated that she was running a bordello more than a gift shop."[34] Tonny grew so jealous of Anita's male Moroccan friends, and suspicious of her friendship with Claude McKay, that she felt she had to leave the house, and went to live with McKay for over a week. All of this earned Anita a reputation among Bowles's crowd as "une jolie putain," as one of his Arab friends put it.[35]

I had given Artaud an old walking stick from my days in California. It was made of Manzanita wood with twists and turns, and it had Mexican Indian carving and a metal tip. Artaud said it was a magic wand and used to go about Paris throwing this thing in the air and pointing it at people and telling them what he thought of them.

When he walked along the pavement, he would hit the cement with the metal tip so that sparks flew. He tried to persuade everyone that it certainly proved it was a magic stick.

Anita had carried the walking stick off and on for years and only gave it to Artaud because "he begged so for it," as she said in the first version of the memoir.[37] This is only one example of many in which the memoir fills in historical accounts of iconic persons and moments in the history of modernism.

Artaud's fiancée Cecile Schramm has always been a mysterious figure in his biography. She was Anita's best friend before, during, and after the time Artaud was seeing her. Anita—whom Artaud scholars have never been able to identify heretofore—is therefore able to give a more precise sense than ever before of the relationship and how it ended during a pivotal juncture of Artaud's tragic career. Moments such as these in "American Cocktail" give the work a documentary interest at every point of the author's remarkable narrative.

In its later stages, the story grows dark as Anita's first, English husband sinks into alcoholism, depression, and a respiratory illness, possibly tuberculosis; she abandons him in a sanatorium, convinced that their "marriage" had been fake, and then returns to a changed Paris. With the Nazis growing in power and French fascist sympathizers (including much of the upper class) growing increasingly fearful of Léon Blum's socialist government, a tone of dread gradually overcomes the narrator's light-hearted ironic wit, particularly when she goes to Spain as a journalist and witnesses the start of the Spanish Civil War in Barcelona. From this point on, fascism's shadow reappears with ever-increasing frequency, often close at hand—as when, working as a French Red Cross nurse in Brittany, Anita recounts the sympathy many of her colleagues showed for the Nazis and her upper-class lover's own fascist tendencies. Guy de Chateaubriant's father was in fact an admirer of Hitler, supported the Vichy regime, and was eventually sentenced to death as a "collaborator."[38] Many, indeed, were the aristocrats who believed Hitler would save France from the communists.

After the Germans obliterated Rotterdam from the air, Anita was advised, if she remained in France, to join the American Red Cross in Bordeaux. Before leaving Paris, she had a last talk with Man Ray on the phone: "He told me that he was an artist and not a politician, and that the war didn't interest him; he was going to stay in Paris."[39] One of the most unforgettable scenes comes at the moment of France's fall:

> The day and hour of the capitulation, I was in an excellent hotel in Biarritz, having lunch. The dining room was crowded. The windows looked out to sea. At a table near mine, Moysés and his nephew and an elderly gentleman sat. The filet of sole had just been put on the table, the second course, when the Marseillaise was played on the radio, and we, of course, all stood up. Pétain announced the capitulation and the fall of France. As we listened to his speech, tears filled everyone's

eyes. I glanced at Moysés, who had been our so lighthearted host at the Boeuf sur Le Toit for so many years, and his was the saddest face I could see. . . .

Real tragedies were being enacted all along the coast as refugees ran toward the sea and even into the sea. Many of them drowned before the crowds that came after them could pull them out. Their desperation was far beyond ours. We stood looking at them through the windows, and after the Marseillaise was played the second time, we sat down to finish our lunch.

In the following pages the tension builds as Anita, protected by her American passport, scrambles from one mobbed consulate to the next in Bordeaux, attempting to help refugees gain visas as the Panzer divisions closed in. As she finally flees France and crosses the Spanish border at Hendaye, she finds herself staying in the same high-class hotel as Madame Pétain, who invites Anita to join her for breakfast only to ask why she is helping the "rats" escape. And then she joins the mad dash for Lisbon to catch the last ship out of Europe, the *S.S. Manhattan,* sent specially from New York to rescue Americans. As it would turn out, one man she got to know on that train ride and ocean voyage was the white American Dwight Dickinson, a volunteer ambulance driver, who would be her next husband.[40] (When they married, in Maryland, she was forced to "pass" as white to get a license.)[41]

The memoir closes with a terse testament to the American way of categorizing and stigmatizing African Americans. When she had seen the American flag painted on the side of the ship in Lisbon just before boarding, she had wept with relief and joy, glad to be an American:

We followed a brightly lighted white wall that we were advised was the side of our ship. Then suddenly into the light came the American flag, painted on the ship, a huge American flag, lighted in the dark night.

When I saw it, I and some others I noticed had tears in [our] eyes. We were glad to be Americans. There were three Navy cruisers in the harbour.

It took many years for the stars in my eyes to dry from bright on blue to dark on black. They are still dark on a red, white, and black flag.

A boatload of reporters boarded the MANHATTAN before we landed. Many took photos of me as of someone of importance: Egyptian? Arab? East Indian? No one spoke to me in English or in French. I just looked so well-dressed in my Chanel Suit, and carrying my latest affectation—an ivory-topped walking stick.

But the next morning the NEW YORK TIMES headed an article on the arrival of "the last ship to return with escapees of the Panzer Division's closing the Spanish frontier from France" with a large photo of a stout American woman emerging from her cabin weighted with many cameras—the gear of a newspaper photographer. There was no mention of the center of so many reporters' attention on me.

They had learned, no doubt, that I was just an Afro-American expatriate of no importance, a common or garden variety coloured woman forced "home."

Many years later, visiting Baltimore, I learned from my cousins, the Murphys, owners of the *Afro-American* newspaper there, that my *"Manhattan"* photo had been posted to them.

Returned to the racial regime of the United States of America, Anita Thompson was once again black. She never truly readjusted to the racial customs of the United States. In the first version of the memoir she said, "I had found it very strange to feel like a 'race' in the presence of Negroes instead of like a person, as I had for so long in France. When I arrived in the U.S. in 1940 it seemed that everything had a racial tone." She could not understand the "Negro problem" as her old intellectual mentors A. Philip Randolph and W. E. B. Du Bois "saw it and tried to explain it to me."[42] She did not believe Negroes could be "led"; they would have to "explode from the inside."[43] She even speaks of her "rejection of Americans, black and white—that is, almost all of them."[44]

Anita Reynolds's deflated view of American identity coincides, ironically, with her identification as an American of "red, white and black" descent, an Americanism that remains, at the moment of her writing, unrepresentable. An absolutely unique record of black experience between the world wars, and a vivid, fast-paced narrative full of wit and sharply etched scenes, Reynolds's autobiography brings a new perspective to the various spheres of transatlantic modernism up to World War II. It is an unforgettable read, among the most amazing memoirs of the interwar period, and unlike any other.

A Note on the Text

by George Hutchinson

Following the events recounted in *American Cocktail,* Thompson stayed in New York and before long married Dwight Dickinson. Soon thereafter she joined the American Women's Voluntary Services agency of the Navy Department, for which she worked mainly at Sampson Naval Base near Geneva, New York, from 1941–1944. In spring of 1944, her marriage apparently over, she enrolled in the New School for Social Research and then got a degree in psychology from the William Alanson White Institute in New York. She worked as a psychologist at the New York Consultation Center and apparently at the historic Lafargue Clinic in Harlem in 1947–1948.[1] This was a pioneering interracial institution staffed by volunteers, created to bring mental health care to underserved African Americans and exploring anti-racist approaches to doing so. Richard Wright termed it, "the extension of the very concept of psychiatry into a new realm, the application of psychiatry to the masses, the turning of Freud upside down."[2] Ralph Ellison called it "an underground extension of democracy."[3] Moving to California upon the death of her father, Thompson became a psychologist at Child House, a psychoanalytically oriented nursery school in Los Angeles, for a year before moving back to New York and taking a job as a student advisor in Elizabeth Irwin High School, a progressive private school. She also taught a summer course on Ethnology at New York University in 1949 and served on the Commission on Intergroup Relations of the United Nations in the late 1940s, probably through the influence of Ralph Bunche. She became disaffected with her job at the high school, where she "couldn't stand the pressure of the Communists," who assumed that any intelligent Negro should be a member of the Communist Party.[4] In late 1950, during a trip to the Caribbean in search of greener pastures, she fell in love with the Virgin Islands. She returned in the summer of 1951 with a group of NYU School of Education teachers and students for a workshop on St. Thomas, and decided to settle in the Virgin Islands, soon thereafter getting a job as a psychologist with the Health Department on St. Croix. On St. Croix in the mid- to late 1950s, she met her last husband, Guy Reynolds, a retired naval officer who owned and managed a hotel and rental properties. She managed the Virgin Islands Employment Service from 1960–1964 and then taught psychology at the College of the Virgin Islands until she turned sixty-five. On St. Croix, as in New York and Paris, she passed between the different communities—white and black, islanders and mainlanders—trying to "get people together" and help them to overcome their distrust of one another.

In the 1960s, Reynolds reflected increasingly on her former life and occasionally wrote old friends like Ralph Bunche and Man Ray, inviting them to come stay in one of her and her husband's properties for free. Langston Hughes took her up on such offers a few times.[5] Friends on St. Croix admired her looks, her wit, her stylishness, and her stories. Following a trip to Europe in 1972, for which Man Ray and his wife Juliet Man Ray had booked her a room near their own residence in Paris for a month,[6] she returned to St. Croix,

> determined to take Man Ray's advice, to do again what he told me to do: "TALK your autobiography."
>
> With a tape recorder open I went about my daily chores—caring for house plants, cooking, listening to my FM, answering the telephone's friendly and business calls, yelling at the two over-protective police dogs, paging, dressing, often chatting with my husband just home from golf, or from his hotel lunch—or just sitting talking to myself and the Recorder.[7]

These reminiscences were aided by Reynolds's diaries and correspondence, which she reviewed before recording.[8] Jean Loesch, a close friend who worked in a local real estate office, encouraged her and transcribed the fifty tapes that resulted, correcting "many errors in English composition and syntax," according to Reynolds. The first tape begins,

> Jean dear—thank you for another good lunch in your pink marble villa above the sea. The food, wine, Empire décor—and you—take me from this bright Caribbean back to the dramatic Mediterranean of an earlier day.
>
> You made me especially happy today when you suggested that I should review for a larger audience my speckled career of about three-quarters of a century of enjoying being an American Negro. Most of my contemporaries, both black

and white, have had chiefly tales of woe to tell. I feel a little guilty saying how much fun I have had being a colored girl in the twentieth century.

Perhaps I should call my memoirs "The False Spring Violet." I feel that in the next century everyone is going to have a good time.

Reynolds went over the transcription typed by Loesch to correct errors and misspellings due to the fact that Loesch occasionally could only type out unfamiliar names and words or French phrases phonetically as she listened to the tapes. Reynolds also added, by hand, some details and reflections throughout the draft, and crossed out others. This first version of the memoir ended in the early 1950s, with some brief reflections on Reynolds's life later in the Virgin Islands. She attempted to interest publishers, but, "Even in this amateur style," Reynolds later wrote, "no publisher could handle such a mess . . . no editor nor agent (like William Aspenwall Bradley or Klaus Mann) who had encouraged me to 'say it any way' is here today to gather the pieces."[9] She turned to Howard Miller, a young teacher at the time for whom she and her husband were also landlords, for help in shaping and rewriting the original typescript. She found Miller's initial revisions of the original "excellent. I like it, and I trust that, when completed, the MS will be published." She added, "I have no experience writing. I am a talker. I love to lecture. I love conversation. But literature is beyond my wildest dreams."[10] The revisions by Miller had chiefly to do with reshaping and reducing, breaking the manuscript into chapters, ending the memoir with Thompson's return to New York on the *Manhattan*, and reorganizing for chronological consistency. The opening scene in the

Foreword, for example, originally came much later in the recorded reminiscence, and generally speaking the memoir had a number of organizational problems in its early transcript version. Yet the voice of the narrative did not change. Miller preserved the phrasing and the pacing of the sketches and stories out of which the memoir is built, for the most part adhering to what one finds in the tapes and in Jean Loesch's transcript of Anita Reynolds's tape recordings. The most dramatic stories and anecdotes are given much as Reynolds first recorded them. She made alterations to Miller's work and suggested additions or changes as the two reworked the memoir. The final typescript includes some of these additions or changes in her hand, which I have incorporated into this first published edition of *American Cocktail*.

The manuscript had various titles beginning with "The False Spring Violet," followed by "The Tan Experience," and then "Caramel: Autobiography of a Drop of Burned Sugar." On December 11, 1978, Anita Reynolds wrote a formal affidavit signed by herself, Howard Miller, and Jean Loesch and witnessed by two others, stating that the book jacket should carry the line "With Howard Miller under my name as author." Four days later she added a footnote to this affidavit, saying that the title of "Miller's version" had been changed to "American Cocktail." After considerable effort on Miller's part to interest trade publishers, and having been out of touch with him for several months, on March 28 of 1980 Reynolds wrote Jean Loesch, still a treasured friend, "If you can get it ALL back from Howard Miller do so and carry on as you wish."[11]

Before she passed away in December 1980, Anita Reynolds gave a copy of the autobiography to her cousin, Otey M. Scruggs, then a history professor at Syracuse University. On her instructions, he

American Cocktail

Foreword

I scarcely noticed the group of German tourists sitting at the table next to mine on the hotel terrace overlooking the Caribbean until one of them leaned over to me and asked in English: "How long did it take you to get that wonderful tan?"

I gave out just the slightest sigh and answered by rote: "About four generations."

My questioner turned back to his companions and translated. In the ensuing conversation, I thought I heard the word "Nigger" tossed about.

At that particular time, I was fuming over calls to impeach the black United States ambassador to the United Nations for daring to suggest that our country was less than ideal in its handling of human rights issues here, and I was not in any mood to tolerate any racist remarks.

However, I bit my tongue and said nothing; they were, after all, guests at my husband's hotel. But it did enter my mind to tell them of the fate of the last white man who called my father "Nigger." He was killed by a blow from a shoe.

The mind wanders to pleasanter times. Paris in the 30s. Montparnasse and St.-Germain-des-Prés, where the artists and writers flocked in never-ending numbers. I was an asteroid then, in orbit about the brilliant stars: Breton, Derain, Matisse, Picasso, Brancusi, Max Ernst, James Joyce, Hemingway, Carlos Williams. Perhaps, I thought, some of their genius would rub off on me. Perhaps a word of encouragement.

Moments savored: Man Ray suggesting a career in stage; Matisse sketching my portrait; Picasso asking me about my experiences in the Spanish Civil War. If the truth be told, I believed my only talent to be that which had been uncovered in an aptitude test a few years earlier at Columbia Teachers College—an ability to recognize spatial relationships. Not much call for that. Still, that did not stop me from trying to imitate those about me, and there were triumphs.

An article in *The Messenger* reviewing a new F. Scott Fitzgerald work from the point of view of a flapper won for me an invitation to visit the author's Long Island home, an invitation I must confess I had little interest in accepting. (My friends were upper class Negroes and the Greenwich Village crowd which included Eugene O'Neill and Edna St. Vincent Millay. The newly rich Irish and arriving Southamptoners in the mid '20s did not attract me at all; rather dull and unintelligent, I'd heard.)

Then there had been my work in clay, and dancing with Denishawn and Norma Gould, whose devotion to the "Greek" style of barefoot dancing made famous by Isadora Duncan led me to be hired as an exotic-type extra (earning $10 a day) in such Hollywood epics as *The Thief of Bagdad* and *The Four Horsemen of the Apocalypse*. I was also cast as the "star" of the first black-produced movies made at that time.

It is true I was encouraged to write the history of my family by William Aspenwall Bradley, editor and agent for most of the English-speaking writers in Paris, but life was too short then to invest the time and concentrated effort to develop this or any of my talents. Rather, I contented myself with enjoying the wit and beauty surrounding me. And on occasion, the star-gazer would be elevated to the upper stratosphere when photographer / artist Man Ray would ask me to join him for lunch at *La Closerie des Lilas,* or when sitting with André Derain, listening to him speak of Michelangelo, Da Vinci and Botticelli as if he had lived and worked among them.

The scene fades and reality intrudes as the German tourists get up to leave. No, best not say anything now. Save it for another time.

This story is another time. It is a distillation of my memories of growing up a "colored girl" in the United States, Europe and North Africa. It is the people I have known and the sights I have seen. The facts are as I recall them and may sometimes differ from the way others might remember. This is the nature of memory, and I make no apologies for mine.

1

The Civil War was in full bloom when my maternal grand-mother, Medora Reed, fled Virginia and a life of servitude in 1862, at the age of twelve, and made her way to Boston working as a cabin girl on a ship. On a later trip back South, she picked up her Cherokee Indian mother (her father, who had not been interested in marrying her mother, was a "Mr. Reed," a white man in whose house she had worked as a serving girl) and returned to Boston. Her illegitimacy was a sore point with Grandmother. When I learned that my maternal grandfather, her first husband, had also been born out of wedlock, as a Jerome Bonaparte bastard, she said most sternly: "When in the hanged man's house, do not speak of rope!"[1]

Despite her lack of formal schooling, Medora used her natural intelligence and stubborn ambition to educate herself. She memorized virtually all of Charles Dickens, whom I can remember hearing her quote incessantly during my childhood. Along the way, she met and married Bertrand Thompson, a Union Naval officer aboard the wooden warship *Eutaw*.

A man who became one of her most influential teachers was abolitionist Charles Sumner (after whom my brother was named), and she and Bertrand became active in the abolitionist movement in Boston. They joined the Essex Club, whose membership was drawn from the population of freed and escaped slaves and persons of mixed blood, many of them fair-skinned enough to "pass" and melt into the general population of America. There were doctors, lawyers, teachers, clergymen, tradesmen and domestic servants, all dedicated to the abolition of slavery and helping freed or escaped slaves to find a new life in the North.

Shortly after my mother was born, in 1873, my grandparents moved to Denver. (Grandmother was always "heading West," and dreamed eventually of moving to South America, though she never made it that far.) A son, my Uncle Clarence, was born in 1888, and my grandfather died just as the twentieth century was rounding the corner. The tug west pulled my grandmother all the way out to California, where she settled in Los Angeles, along with her children and her still-living mother. One of my earliest childhood recollections is that of being lifted to the edge of a bed in which a very old Indian woman with a hooked nose and long black braids lay. Her thin fingers reached out and touched the top of my head. "So this is the little girl," she said. That was the last time I ever saw my great-grandmother, but her daughter, my grandmother, looked like a white marble statue of her.

We all lived in Grandma's big house at 22nd and Los Angeles Streets, at that time a good distance from the center of the city. There were fig trees and orange trees in the back yard, and huge pepper trees and hitching posts for horses in front of the house. Living there in 1906, along with my grandmother, were her second husband, a handsome Creole gentleman named Mitchell, out of New Orleans, their two daughters (stepsisters to my mother), my brother Sumner, two years my junior, my mother and me. I was five at the time.

Father remained for a time in Chicago, where I had been born. He was doing quite well as a diamond broker (as evidenced by my mother's beautiful multi-diamond engagement ring and sunburst brooch), and he was reluctant to move out West until he could be sure of a good job there.

Mother and Father had met in Denver in the Gay '90s. Mother had a college education and worked as a bookkeeper in the Colorado state treasurer's office, spending her days standing behind a desk that came almost up to her shoulders. On her own time, she played the organ in the colored Episcopal church. Although my mother was of mixed blood (apart from her Cherokee mother, there also was the mulatto Bonaparte mistress), she could have easily passed for white (as her brother did), but she chose to think of herself as Negro.

My father, as I said, was working in Chicago as a sales representative for a German jewelry company. Part of his job at the time required him to bring his firm's clocks and jewelry out West. It was on one such trip to Denver that Samuel William Thompson met Beatrice Sumner Thompson, the woman who was to become his wife and my mother.

They met at the Episcopal church, and it was apparently love at first sight. The details of their romance were successfully hidden from me for many years but I learned from an aunt that Mother had been very much in love with a man of Pennsylvania Dutch descent. They had been more-or-less engaged for nine years, since she was sixteen, when she met my father. That relationship, however, had been doomed to failure, according to my aunt, because this long-time suitor had a severe drinking problem, which Mother finally decided could not be cured by love.

My father, then, did not so much come between them as he did hasten the end of an unhappy relationship. It is not difficult to imagine that my mother was playing out her heart on the organ when she first caught sight of the dapper young newcomer. As Dad was always elegant in his manner and dress, I can picture him wearing a cutaway and striped trousers, with shiny shoes, a derby perched on his head, a white flower in his buttonhole and carrying a walking stick.

As for Mother, her ivory skin and golden hair caused heads to turn wherever she went. She, too, enjoyed expensive clothing and jewelry. (Her father had worked as a jeweler in Boston after the Civil War.) Her style of dress ran towards laces and satins, her exquisitely coiffed curls set off with large plumed hats.

As I said, love at first sight. They were duly married in August 1900 and moved to Chicago. I was born March 28, 1901 in Chicago's Provident Hospital, Dr. Dan Williams (later to gain fame as the first surgeon to operate on a human heart) attending. An early photograph of Mother shows her holding her smiling three-month-old baby, called by a friend of hers: "A glad dog in a meat shop."

A scene enters my mind. My father's jolly brother, Noah, and his lovely wife Lilly (whose family owned the *Baltimore Afro-American* newspaper) are in our apartment, dancing to the music on the phonograph. (That Uncle Noah had been secretary to Booker T. Washington meant nothing to me then.) The four adults are whirling all about me, and I sit among the red roses on the carpet, happy in their happiness, laughing and filled with a great feeling of love and joy.

Father's family was enormous; there were lots and lots of cousins, all seeming to thrive in each other's presence. There were always family get-togethers, parties, dinners and picnics, characterized by lots of good food and laughter. I was so protected by their warmth, it never occurred to me that any of us was different from the majority of people in Chicago, or that we belonged to a "minority group." We belonged to St. Thomas Church and to each other. That the church was colored, the local YMCA was colored, Provident Hospital was colored and Dr. Dan was colored never gave me any cause to wonder or protest.

2

What did give me cause to both wonder and complain was the birth of my brother, Sumner, when I was two and suddenly no longer the center of all the attention. My protests were stifled, however, in the presence of all the fuss that accompanied the event, and so I went along with everyone else to say what a beautiful baby he was. I learned quickly that one sure way to hold onto my parents' love was to take care of him, the beginning of what was to become a lifetime of devotion to "little brothers."

When Sumner (I called him Tada) was two, we moved, as I said, to Grandma's house in Los Angeles. I can remember once sitting on the floor beneath her huge grand piano, listening to my Uncle Clarence playing a pleasant piece of music. When I asked him the name of it, he told me, "L'après-midi d'une faune" and translated for me.[1] I couldn't imagine just what it was that a faun did all afternoon, so I asked him. Now, my uncle was a dignified gentleman, a tall, fair-skinned man with auburn hair and a freckled face. But for me, he let loose his dignity and danced across the room, flitting here and there, jumping over the furniture and having a delightful time answering my question. To me he was a perfect faun.

A student at Harvard then, Uncle Clarence was visiting his family for a few days. I liked him every bit as much as I did my relatives in Chicago, but he showed his affection in a quieter way, with a sly smile, never sweeping me up in great rollicking hugs like Dad's family. (We were not a hugging and kissing family. In fact, I have no recollection of any overt display of affection between mother, father, sister and brother. Perhaps this is why I so vividly recall an early sensuous experience. Recovering from an attack of scarlet fever at the age of four, I was given olive oil massages by a pretty, young nurse with golden hair. She was very tender with me, and her hands all over my body, rhythmically, smoothly, firmly pressing, caused the nearest a young child could have to an orgasm.)

Like most of Grandma's family, Uncle Clarence was very sharp and amusing. He, Grandma and my mother laughed heartily over their jokes and stories about the "passing" members of the family. He was married then to Maravene Kennedy, a cousin to Governor Cox of Ohio. Although she knew all of my family and liked my grandmother very much, they did not advertise my mother's colored marriage. I had no idea of what any of their stories meant then, but I did know there was something secret and hidden about them, and that the stories had a tone that was ironic beyond anything I could hope to understand or appreciate. Still, I hoped that someday I would be able to laugh with them at the same jokes.

Gradually, these nuances began to seep through to me, and by the time I was ready to go to kindergarten, I was very curious to know how I would be received in the great big world out there, where my dark skin might attract unfavorable attention and cause me the discomfort I'd thus far avoided. A needless worry, as it turned out. I will always remember my first day at school as a public triumph.

In the kindergarten class, we were given some clay and told to make anything we like. I decided to make my favorite toy, a sailor-suited teddy bear who, despite having only one leg intact, won from me more love than any of the two-legged, long-haired rosy dressed-up dolls in my five-year collection. Apparently my clay rendition won my teacher's approval, for she took me by the hand to each class in the large building to show me off. Standing proudly before the bigger boys and girls, I lifted my clay teddy bear for them to see. I was greeted by friendly laughter, more likely attributable to their pleasure in having their routine interrupted than their admiration for me, but I relished the role of prima donna. I have enjoyed going to school ever since my most auspicious debut as the only brown-skinned girl at the Washington Street Grammar School.

At the end of that first delightful week, I took my clay model home. My family's comments were somewhat more restrained than my teacher's had been, however. Grandma said, "That's fine," and Mother said, "Quite good." (Mother did not want me to become conceited. Whenever someone complimented me on my pretty curls, she would twist my ear and scold, "pretty is as pretty does," leaving me feeling hideous, with all the many "trespasses" on my young conscience.) Still looking for a pat on the head, I took my clay teddy bear to Maude, Mother's step-sister, who was only ten years older than me. She smiled but said nothing particularly gratifying, only grunted. Dolores, Maude's big sister, was not at home (she was at her job translating French and Spanish stories into English to make movie plots for the Hollywood studios). Only her crazy Cuban husband, Meseo, was in. He mumbled something in Spanish—"loco"—then closed the one eye he had opened to look at me.

Undaunted, I headed toward the laundry rooms (Grandma ran a hand laundry in her home), where the Negro women were washing and ironing the delicate stuff of her customers. I loved the smell of hot starch, the sound of flat irons slapping on the side of the coal stove, the pretty linens and the friendly laughter and songs of the workers. They treated me with false dignity, but I could feel the warmth that came through their teasing. They made a ceremony of sitting on the soap boxes and chairs in the room to closely examine my small sculpture. At last, I felt, here was the attention I'd been looking for, until one of them snorted: "Is that sailor dead? This for his tombstone?" Terrified, I grabbed my model and fled outdoors.

I found Grandma's second husband, Mr. Mitchell, sitting in his shed concentrating on his life's pride, a perpetual motion machine made from a cigar box and watch parts. I had long before decided against trying to understand either the machine or Mr. Mitchell. He just seemed to be pleasantly daft, with a sweet smile always showing on his soft, frail face. He was very tall and slender, and he walked with a slight stoop when he got up to go indoors, which was only to eat or sleep. Showing him my sculpture was only a courtesy; I did not expect him to say anything, and he didn't.

So, then it was over the back fence to see my best friend Yupie, a round, rosy boy about my age, whose Dutch parents shamed all their neighbors with their cleaning and scrubbing habits, but delighted us all with their homemade cookies, distributed by Yupie about once a week. Yupie was not in much of a mood to give me the compliments I was looking for. He grabbed my clay figure and held it high over his head, as if to smash it to the ground. I screamed, and he relented.

"Come," he said, "let's see if he has a tassel."

This was a typical observation from my friend, a sex-curious "roly-poly," which is what I called him at home when it seemed necessary to emphasize my distaste for him, lest someone guess I was a little fascinated by his attempts to see if I, too, had a "tassel." (At six, he presumably would have known that I did not, but that didn't stop him from trying to explore my well-hidden parts.)

I mustered up all my five-year-old dignity and replied with disdain: "You wouldn't see it in his clothes."

"Sometimes you might," he tossed back, laughing.

Finally and truly disgusted, I wrinkled my nose at him and went back through the fence. I was just in time to run into Mother, who was about to go over to Luna Park to listen to the band concert. "Like to come?" she asked. After placing my clay model on the highest shelf I could reach, making sure my real teddy bear could not see it and get jealous, I raced down the street after Mother to hear the German band.

The music was fine and brassy, not at all like that of the Germans who came with violins and cellos to play Bach, Mozart, "real music," at our house. As I sipped my favorite drink, a strawberry sodapop, I paused between the oompah-pahs to comment in a loud, bratty tone: "Oh, there's the 'Poet and Peasant Overture' again." Meaning, with contempt: mediocre or "semi-classic" as my Grandmother would say. A lady in the row ahead of us turned to look at me, and my mother gave me a pained glance that silenced me better than a thunderbolt might have. I knew very well the suffering that my misbehavior caused her; she had no need to say, "stop showing off."

From our earliest childhood, my brother and I knew well the hurt expression that was Mother's only form of punishment. It was worse than a spanking might have been. After all the "suffering of childbirth" and the "struggle to make ends meet" and the "sadness of unhappy people," we found it easier to be good than to suffer the consequences of that look. My brother carried this burden all his life; I dropped it and ran when I went East to College.

Back at Grandma's, the house was in an uproar. It seems that "Loco" Meseo had poured carbolic acid into our butter and some of the other food and had flown the coop. The odor of carbolic filled the house; nobody would have touched any of the tainted food. Dolores was furious: "I should have divorced him years ago!" Grandma and Mother laughed heartily. Tada and I were intrigued, but scared. Mr. Mitchell did not change his ever-present tender expression, but he looked a little puzzled and embarrassed over the whole thing.

Only Maude seemed sorry to see the lunatic leave. "His farewell note is so sad," she said. It was she who got us all settled down again by scouring out the kitchen and cooking us all a lovely, unpoisoned dinner of lamb chops, peas, mashed potatoes and homemade ice cream. After dinner, Maude, Dolores and Mother got together around the piano, Mother playing, and sang for us. (Only Maude could really sing well.) After some Schubert, they launched into such favorites as "Don't You Remember Sweet Alice, Ben Bolt?" and "The Big Red Shawl," along with some Williams and Walker ragtime numbers. I was asleep before the end of the concert, little dreaming that the storm cloud of a murder charge would soon darken our lives.

3

Dad's arrival from Chicago the year I was in kindergarten was a joyous occasion, indeed. I can remember his rushing into Grandma's house, dropping his tan leather satchel and kissing everyone. It was the first and last time I can recall ever seeing my parents embrace openly. Mother smiled when he complimented Tada on having grown so much, and frowned when he ruffled my curly hair (all grown back after my bout with scarlet fever) and said I was "pretty as a picture." We all gaped with excitement when he told us about his plans for moving into our new house at 23d and Normandie Streets. What a house it was! It cost $6,000, a fortune in those days, and I heard about the extravagance for years and years after we moved in.

It was a two-story frame mission-style house with a large porch running along the front and two sides. A grandfather's clock from my father's old Chicago employer graced the hallway. The stairway to the left formed one side of a "Turkish corner," decorated with an oriental silk tent roof, divans covered in the same material and a small ivory telephone table. The exotic look was completed with a brass and stained glass lamp hanging from the ceiling and a scimitar on the wall. It would make a most romantic spot as I grew older and began to receive personal, private phone calls—adolescent romance.

To the right of the hallway was the parlor, used only for company, with its formal set of stiff, carved mahogany chairs and a gold and turquoise silk brocade sofa. In one corner of the room was the piano, and in another was a mantelpiece, on which were displayed treasures Uncle Clarence had brought back with him from China. A Chinese rug in gold and blue covered the floor.

Behind this show-offy room was the library, where we spent a great deal of our time. One wall was lined with books, and it was here, beneath the funny-looking square wood-and-stained-glass lamp, that I read my first copies of *American Mercury* and the most deeply hidden book in the library, something called *Three Weeks*. It was written by Elinor Glyn, and it was full of something that was supposed to be very exciting about a woman who had a love affair on a bed of rose petals.[1]

Next to the library was the dining room, with a large bay window covered with honeysuckle, the scent of which filled that part of the house. The dining room table could seat as many as twelve, and there were matching chairs, a sideboard containing the Haviland china and a cupboard to hold the engraved silver settings. There was also a small cabinet which held bottles of champagne, never touched and probably turned to vinegar before anyone opened one. On top Mother displayed her Wedgwood and her delicate collection of tea cups.

Behind all this was the kitchen and breakfast room, where we had our family meals. The main feature of the kitchen was an ingeniously designed icebox, with a door opening to the outside at the back door and kitchen door so the iceman could make his deliveries without coming into the house. The breakfast room was a burst of colors, with beautiful flowered wallpaper and bright, cream-colored rattan furniture.

On the way upstairs to the bedrooms, one had to go by the large, life-sized oil painting of Mother. The painting hung over the landing, and the west window threw an almost ethereal light on it. The painting captured all of Mother's youthful beauty and elegance, and its presence dominated the house, and our lives, like a golden Madonna.

Upstairs, the women and men were strictly segregated, with my bedroom and that of my mother on one side of the hallway, and those of my father and brother on the other side. I found out many years later that my mother, Elinor Glyn notwithstanding, had long ceased to sleep with my father out of fear of pregnancy and another painful delivery as she had had with my brother . . . birth control unknown. Although Dad was absolutely gallant at all times, this undoubtedly was the source of the tension Tada and I could feel in the air. They were both too well brought up to quarrel in front of us, but the silences and sarcastic remarks filled the house like stalactites and stalagmites, and my brother and I wandered through them with a torchlight to get safely to our own quarters upstairs . . . a screened porch that ran the width of the house and connected Tada's room and mine.

Running through the Stephen Foster opera of my childhood was a syncopated counterpoint of color prejudice. Even before Dad left the Chicago jewelry business to come West, blacks were beginning to lose their middle class jobs to immigrating whites. Only the Negro doctors, lawyers, undertakers and others who could make a living among the colored populations could continue to work as they had. But the expanding railroad travel in need of ever more luxurious services and expensive accommodations was wide open to "smart" blacks needing employment. Mr. Pullman was the Great Provider.

Although Dad had worked as a seller of jewelry, there was no room for him to continue in this business in the changing world. But he still had to continue to support his family, even if it meant taking menial jobs. It never occurred to him, apparently, to try to pass for East Indian or Mexican. He was an American Negro and had to piece together a life for his family out of whatever the racist majority would allow him to do. A cloud of resentment hung over our heads as Dad struggled to swim upstream against the muddy currents of obstacles thrown in his path. He could only work in lowly jobs or lose his shirt in business ventures for which he had no experience, and little helpful advice. But still, nothing could have prepared us for the trouble that hit us in 1910, when Dad faced a charge of murder.

Working as a redcap, Dad had been involved for a long time in a running battle with a white conductor whom he found particularly rude and overbearing. Finally, one day, the conductor turned on Dad in a fury, called him a nigger and attacked him with the wooden steps used to board the train. Giving in to the anger and pressure, Dad took off his shoe and hit the conductor on the head, knocking him out. The man never regained consciousness and died in the hospital the next day.

The household was in an uproar, of course. Tada and I were terrified about what might happen, but Mother took it all in her stride. She was always on the warpath against any form of discrimination and mistreatment of blacks, Jews, Mexicans, Indians, Japanese, women, children and any other underdog she could find to fight for. This very personal case of injustice was made to order for her battling instincts.

So certain was Mother that Dad would be exonerated, she did not even call on her brother (who had graduated law school at the age of 18) for assistance. Instead, she rallied together her political and influential friends, Governor Hiram Johnson of California and Charley Schwab, president of Bethlehem Steel, who had been a boyhood friend of Father's in Chicago.[2] Together they found a witness to the "murder," a Pullman porter who testified that Father had only been defending himself. After a quick hearing before railroad officials, the case was dismissed.

It was all rather like the Jack Johnson–Jim Jeffries fight.[3] While everyone else was screaming for Jim Jeffries to knock out the "Black Monster," we secretly cheered for Johnson. By then, I believe, I had concluded that it was easier to be the white man's burden than to carry it.

4

The Johnson-Jeffries fight took place just before the outbreak of the First World War. It demonstrated well the streak of stubborn independence in my family that often saw us on the opposite side of public opinion in general.

During the war, Grandma displayed on the wall by her bed a magazine photo of a German submarine, its captain and crew, sighted off the shore of Norfolk just before the United States declared war. Grandma greatly admired the Germans as highly cultured scientists, scholars, and musicians, like the chamber music players who performed at our house. When they came over, they pulled out a map of Europe to follow the progress of the battles. Grandma gave them a room of their own to use, and as I passed by, I could hear them whispering in German. It was an exciting secret to carry to school: "My grandmother's house is full of German spies." Of course, no one believed me.

I did not much care for the Kaiser nor his helmeted troops. From the stories I heard, I pictured them trampling their horses over pretty French peasant girls and laying waste to the poor skinny Belgian children for whose sake we dared not waste a single morsel of food. I sang "In Peril on the Seas" in church on Sundays and wept for the sons of our family's friends who looked so grand in their uniforms.

Grandma wept, too, but for her own reasons. "Barbarians at each other's throats again," she would rage. "Money and lives wasted that should be spent on improving the life of each country. Let the Kaiser teach them a lesson!"

Politics was big in our lives, with Mother campaigning for her friend Hiram Johnson and Uncle Clarence's involvement in the Cox-Harding race for the Presidency. Clarence was in town during the big campaign for his wife's cousin, Governor Cox. He spoke on Cox's behalf at the Harvard Club in Los Angeles, where Clarence was guest of honor. (Ironically, one of the waiters at the dinner was my father.)

As it turned out, of course, Cox lost the election. Years later, he wrote that he believed he had been defeated because someone had said he had Negro blood. Our family found this especially amusing, since most of us thought that Harding was colored; that is, as "colored" as my grandmother was, and that he was related to a highly esteemed colored family in Philadelphia, to whom I will leave the honor of claiming him as one of their own. These were the kinds of stories Grandma relished. Sharing them with me seemed to be her way of passing on the tradition of laughing at the American culture. She was old enough to see the joke, and I was young enough to learn it.

Though I had been named Anita, after Anita Garibaldi, the feminist wife of the liberator of Italy whom Grandma had known in Boston, she always kept from me the weight of responsibility the name carried and called me "Jazz-Baby." That name suited me well into the depressing 30s.

As a youngster, I may have begun to appreciate the ironic humor that delighted Grandma so, but we children laughed more readily at our own stories which pointed up the foolishness of the adults around us. Walking with me to school, my friend Arlene Peck told me a jolly story about Mr. Sullivan, a man who had been hired by the neighborhood to act as a guard against the bootleggers and mobsters who were infiltrating the Los Angeles area. It seems that Mr. Sullivan had seen a light in the Pecks' basement and went down to investigate. He found a man stooping over something and yanked him up by the scruff of the neck. It turned out to be Mr. Peck, who was busily making moonshine and quite annoyed to find himself being collared by the very man he was paying for protection.

This was the kind of story we liked, and we laughed about it all day. When we got home from school that day, we found Mother chuckling over another kind of story, the ironic kind she and Grandma enjoyed so much. She had just gotten off the phone with a friend of hers, Mrs. Blodgett, a round, good-looking brown woman who lived with her contractor husband and two children in an expensive home. That morning, Mrs. Blodgett had let into the house a maid from an employment agency. The woman worked vigorously all morning, and Mrs. Blodgett was pleased with her. Later in the day, though, the maid turned to her and said, "what kind of people live in this house, anyway? You know, these clothes are dirty enough to be nigger rags!" To keep her energetic helper, Mrs. Blodgett shut her mouth and pretended to be the housekeeper for the owner for the rest of the day.

As I said, this was not our kind of humor. Tada and I had other, more important things on our mind. Leaving Mother to share her story with others who might appreciate it more, we changed into our play clothes to fix wheels on our soap box coaster. We were very proud of the coaster. We had built it ourselves and kept it in tip-top shape. Every morning, it served as our newspaper delivery wagon. I would push the paper-laden wagon with my foot, and Tada would run alongside, rolling up the papers and slamming them against the front doors as we raced by, waking up the entire neighborhood at 7 A.M.

After school, however, the coaster was strictly for fun. We would take it to Harvard Boulevard, a long, curving hill which attracted lots of coaster riders, and occasional collisions. One day as we whipped down the hill, I swerved to avoid a crash. But it was too late. My leg was struck by the wheel of another coaster, and I suffered a deep cut. It was very painful, of course, but the thought that filled my mind was not the pain but how we would manage to hide it from Mother.

Tada helped me limp home, and we dashed down into the cellar, mumbling something about fixing the coaster. Tada sneaked upstairs for the iodine and sticking plaster, and he patched me up as best he could. We waited until the bleeding stopped and the bandage looked quite casual so we could nonchalantly make an appearance upstairs. While waiting there, we discovered in a hidden corner of the basement a book belonging to my father, describing the secret rituals of the Freemasons. We read it with great fascination, and were awed by all the signs and handshakes and ceremonies of Father's secret organization. After reading it, we carefully returned the book to its hiding place and made a pact never to mention any of the things we had discovered, as though we two were now initiated into the organization.

Upstairs, no mention was made of the cut on my leg. Everyone was busily preparing for our dinner guests, Mr. Abbott, owner and editor of the Chicago *Defender,* and his lovely, tall and elegant blonde wife.[1] Mr. Abbott was one of the very few African-type friends of our family, but he was so rich and important, he could have been a Zulu or a wild man from Borneo and still have received the greatest respect from us.

When Mother and Father had guests, Tada and I were banned from the dining room. We were fed in the breakfast room and then sent upstairs. But any interesting conversation would send us to the top of the stairs, our ears tuned in to pick up every word. Conversations with Mr. Abbott, or with James Weldon Johnson, Field Secretary of the National Association for the Advancement of Colored People, or A. Philip Randolph, founder of the Pullman Porters Union, or Dr. W. E. B. Du Bois, editor of the NAACP magazine *The Crisis,* always focused on "the problem," that is, the problem of the Negro in America.

"The problem" was discussed with great intensity, often centering on the difference between the philosophy espoused by Booker T. Washington, that the Negroes should stay in the South and work hard, and that of Dr. Du Bois, who urged them to get as much education as possible and be integrated into the mainstream of American society. Although my father's brother, Noah, had been secretary to Booker T. Washington, and Washington himself had been a guest in our home, our family sided with Dr. Du Bois and the efforts of the NAACP to get the Dyer anti-lynching bill passed and to guarantee equal rights and opportunities to the colored people of America.

I had my own private talk with Dr. Du Bois one day shortly after the end of the First World War. He and I walked around the neighborhood after lunch, he admiring the old dusty palms, the yuccas, geraniums and other things so common in California, and I solving the Negro problem. "I don't understand," I said, "why the Negroes, having just come back from war and having learned to use machine guns, are not using them in the Southern towns to which they returned to such degradation. They ought to be making the South safe for democracy."

Dr. Du Bois smiled softly and gave out a chuckle. "You must learn, little one, that the world doesn't run by the 'oughtness' of things but by the 'isness.' And not only the South, but all of the Western world has to learn the value of tolerating its colored, its Asian and African populations, and to live in harmony with everybody, however different racially or politically they may be."

At home, he told my mother, "I'm afraid you have a little Bolshevik on your hands."

Mother smiled and said, "Oh, she'll dance it out of her system eventually," and I ran upstairs to finish my latest flapper article for *The Messenger,* the radical magazine of Philip Randolph and Chandler Owen.

5

The "Negro problem" by no means dominated the whole of our lives. My parents had a full and active social life, from informal card parties to elaborate, formal dances. The former began with games of whist and ended in elaborate "Dutch suppers" of sausages, ham, cheeses, all kinds of fish—salted, smoked, in cream, in oil—several dark breads, pickles and lots of beer to wash it all down.

At other times, formally dressed and smelling of lilac vegetal and bay rum, Mother and Dad would bid us goodnight and be off to one of their gala evenings. The elegance of a white net dress with a full skirt appliquéd with lavender flowers still appears in my dreams of Mother, as does the lingering scent of the lilac vegetal. It was the perfume preferred by refined women; it was "ladylike" and isolated her in my respect and love, as did her Boston accent, acquired in her school days in Cambridge, Massachusetts and spoken in the family only by her.

Most of their gatherings were prim, decorous and rather formal, members of a minority group trying to outdo the majority in behaving "properly." Mother despaired, however, at my ever becoming a proper lady. I laughed too loudly and too often and danced with far too much enthusiasm to be a true Boston bluestocking or feminist. Too much of the Thompson in me, not enough of the Bertrand. "You are just like your father's Creole sisters," she would complain. "Skinny legs, from spending their whole lives with their feet higher than their heads and being slaves to their men and homes."

I could not quite figure out the kind of life I'd enjoy with my feet higher than my head, but I got the idea. Women should have their feet planted solidly on the ground and have "champagne bottle" legs like Mother's; they should not enjoy doing housework and trying to please their rough, lascivious husbands. Since Dad was the gentlest and least selfish man in the neighborhood, Tada and I would laugh at this nonsense. Tada would take off his shoes and demand very imperiously: "Slave, go fetch my house slippers and dressing gown." I'd run upstairs with the shoes and back down with the slippers and batik coat I'd made for him, laughing in a most unladylike fashion at all of our silliness as I bowed low before him. Feeling guilty, but enjoying it, I did not at all mind being like my aunts, who loved their homes and their men, spoiling them with affection and good food. We all knew that once out of Mother's sight, I would do exactly as I pleased.

If Mother despaired over her failure to transform me into a proper lady, she must have choked over my battles with the church. Early into puberty came my first communion at St. Philip's Episcopal Church, which my parents and some of their friends had founded. Dad was a vestryman and Mother played the organ, and as soon as I was big enough, I joined the choir. And even if I did wear my hat over one eye and walk with a slightly syncopated step in the processional, I took that first communion very seriously. When Bishop Johnson laid his fat fingers on my head, I barely noticed the lace ruffles held by a purple ribbon around his wrist. I was definitely transfigured, ready for the nunnery.

Our priest then was Father Cleghorne, from St. Kitts. My family was partial to West Indians, with their soft accents and what we thought were their English ways, so Mother and Father Cleghorne got along just fine. He and I, however, were in conflict anytime he tried to convince me of things that I didn't understand and was unwilling to accept on faith. So, after my initiation into the adult world with my first communion, I decided it was time for Father Cleghorne to explain to me the mysteries of the church. For instance, I said, I had already figured out the explanation of the Immaculate Conception. This information far from delighted him, and his eyebrows hit the roots of his hair as he asked in a scathing tone: "And just what can that be?"

I explained most logically that what made the conception immaculate was that it was the creation of one person alone, just like a play by Shakespeare or a flash of intuitive genius from Einstein or a symphony by Beethoven. The only thing a couple or a committee could conceive would be brats and confusion. He was shocked at my brashness, but perhaps not as shocked as I was when I learned his vows of celibacy let him off the marriage hook when there was gossip of hanky-panky between him and one of the ladies of the congregation.

I decided I wasn't ready for the nunnery after all. Sex was beginning to enter the picture for the first time, and this sort of changed things, too. I wasn't exactly well prepared for these matters by my mother. In fact, the entire discourse on the subject at home consisted of one discussion in which Mother asked me, "Do you take a cold shower every day?"

"Yes," I answered.

"Every day of the month?" she pressed.

"Do you mean while I'm menstruating? Why, of course!"

"Oh," she said, "well, please see Dr. Nelson about it."

That was the beginning and end of sex education at home. But at school, Miss Reed brought out her wax models and explained all the parts and their functions. Nothing about love, though, only anatomy. (In retrospect, she must have been very brave to handle even that much for a mixed class of boys and girls aged twelve to fourteen.)

One bright spring day, I ran out across the lawn to meet our mailman, an old friend. "I'm fifteen years old today," I informed him proudly.

He stood still, looking at me with real concern, and said, "Baby, I'm sorry to hear it. You're going to have a hell of a life with those bedroom eyes." Deflated and puzzled, I took our letters from him and turned back slowly, afraid to ask what he meant because I sensed the answer.

My first sexual experience, apart from my friend Yupie's childhood gropings, occurred that year, not in a bedroom but in a bathroom. In a bathtub, to be more exact, with my friend "Myrto," two years my senior and tall and blonde as I was short and dark. Her real name was Dorothea Childs. Myrto was the orphan of Scottish missionaries who had died in a jungle of some tropic disease, leaving her to be raised by an indifferent aunt in California. She had her own apartment and did exactly as she pleased, which included taking a lover, a cameraman in Hollywood, who sometimes took us to Charlie Chaplin's "anarchist" bull sessions.

Myrto, then, was as experienced in matters sexual as I was naïve. She and I would often stroll through the woods close to Los Angeles High School, cutting classes and reading Edna St. Vincent Millay. Occasionally she held my hand while crossing a brook or put her arm about my shoulder. This was the extent of her display of affection until the day in her apartment when she suggested that we bathe together.

I suppose I must have been somewhat shocked, but not too shocked to risk it. After some wild water-play and brutal back scrubbing, she began to massage me, slowly taking control while I submitted to the sensual experience, until, of course, I reached the climax she had been planning for me. Confused but delighted, I rested just long enough to try her technique on her, with the same success. While we never repeated this experience, we remained close friends for as long as I was in California.

My introduction to the "real thing" at the age of twenty-two was far less agreeable, brutal in fact. It served me right because I allowed an "intellectual giant" to persuade me that "virtue is its own and only reward," and that "flirting and spooning if you don't mean business is beneath the dignity of a liberated woman."[1] Of course, being a liberated flapper of the lost generation (no wonder it was lost!), I fell for this ludicrous line. Afterwards, however, I retreated from experimentation and remained pure by seeing only the tender young men of our group, friends and brothers of friends, all nicely brought up and willing to stop when I said stop.

While sex was at best a mixed experience in my life then, one of the absolutely pure delights of my adolescence was that of sitting out under the stars at the Hollywood Bowl. We would take newspapers and blankets and spread them out over the side of the hill facing the orchestra. There were no seats then. With me would be my mother and brother, and often a beau, holding my hand and sharing a deeply felt romance of music and love. I can recall most vividly a colorful presentation of *Carmen,* with gypsies and campfires and wagons spread out over the hills around us and the principals performing on the lighted stage. After the performance, we went back to visit the impresario, Mr. Beheimer, who was a friend of my mother's and became a true friend of mine by getting me into Norma Gould's School of Dancing.

Dance and movement filled my life with a marvelous joy. It might have begun when I was a toddler, just learning to walk. I can remember Mother sitting on the green grass of a knoll, her red plaid woolen shirt spread out in the large circle in front of her. She glanced up often to watch my progress as I tried to stand, then walk, then run across the lawn. I was inspired by my wish to catch a pigeon.

"You must put salt on his tail to get him," Mother said.

I sat down with a bump. We had no salt. But afterwards, I walked and ran proudly, nonetheless, and years later sailed into dance.

It began when Ruth St. Denis placed an ad in the L.A. papers calling for youngsters to appear in a municipal pageant the city of Los Angeles had commissioned the Denishawn company to put on. We all arrived at Denishawn for the selection process, and Ruth St. Denis, singling me out for my brown, "exotic" looks, decided to train me to be her resident nautch dancer.[2] She taught me to move my body and arms in a sinuous, snakelike style of an East Indian dancer, tinkling tiny pairs of cymbals. I, of course, was thrilled; Mother was appalled. "You are not going to be a belly dancer," she declared and dragged me off to her friend,

Mr. Beheimer, to find a more respectable outlet for my dancing urge. And so it was that I attended Norma Gould's School of Dancing.

It was a very pleasant place, with lots of delightful adolescent girls. Norma Gould was an admirer of Isadora Duncan, and we all danced barefoot, with a bit of *crêpe de chine* hanging over our shoulders and draped in front with a cord under the breasts. I was chosen for all the exotic solos, being the only brown girl in the school. Since the school didn't admit blacks or Jewish girls, Miss Gould told the others I was Mexican, thus foisting on me my first "passing" role. To play the part more fully, I took on a pseudonym that I was to use later on in Europe, that of Matelle, the family name of my father's stepfather. The spelling was probably phonetic Creole for Martell.

In the summertime, we went out to Santa Anita Canyon and had a grand time living in log cabins and dancing like nymphs among the trees.[3] My roles as an Egyptian or a Spaniard ultimately led me to Hollywood. The studios often went to the school looking for students to take part in Greek or Roman sequences or other dancing roles. I was chosen to be one of the attendants to the princess in Douglas Fairbanks' *The Thief of Bagdad.* That was a lot of fun, because Fairbanks and his wife, Mary Pickford, were working on the same set, he doing *The Thief of Bagdad,* and she on the other side in *Mary, Queen of Scots.* Of course, we tried not to get into the wrong picture; Anna May Wong and I would have looked strange in Scotland.[4]

Douglas Fairbanks was a nice man to know. Long after the filming of *The Thief of Bagdad,* he still remembered me, and when I asked him if I could take W. E. B. Du Bois out to see the studio, he made the arrangements for the visit.

The only other "spectacular" I worked in was *The Four Horsemen of the Apocalypse.* I was an extra dancing with Pedro Valdez, who had taught Valentino to tango. During the filming of this movie, I met Noble Johnson, one of the "four horsemen." He was an Indian-and-black cowboy who owned a large ranch in Colorado. He taught me to handle a pony, which I rode as the "star" of a number of small films that were being produced by a black company formed by his brother.[5]

Sometimes I played an Indian girl, but in one film, I was supposed to have grown up not knowing that I had any Negro blood. This was possible because the camera made the golden color of my skin look white. The climax of the story came when I had to face the shock of learning who I really was. I had to pull on my face most dramatically and utter with astonishment: "My God, I'm a Negro!" It was difficult to stifle the giggles.

I don't know how seriously I took any of the dancing and acting in those days. It was just fun. I remember going with Norma Gould's school to see Pavlova and Nijinsky dance, or with Mother to see her favorite, Otis Skinner, playing as an Arab beggar in *Kismet,* or Sarah Bernhardt, marching around the stage with the French flag, singing the *Marseillaise* with one wooden leg as she leaned on the staff.

That was all well and good, but my mother firmly dampened any ambitions I might have had about becoming a serious dancer or an actress. She thought Hollywood was immoral and the next thing to appearing in a circus.

6

The Chicago riot broke out in the summer of 1919.[1] We learned of it while Mother, Tada and I were on our way there to visit Father's family. He had stayed behind in Los Angeles, and wired us to get off the train in Omaha until things quieted down.

The riots dismayed Mother's friends, the dues-paying Episcopalians and NAACP members. They couldn't understand the outrageous behavior of those who seemed to think that ten percent of the American population could successfully take up arms against the majority. But the young people were exuberant. All those we met, including some of my own cousins, had taken part in the riots. They hadn't been shot at or done any shooting themselves, but they had been running arms from one end of Chicago to the other. They had also gone into Gary, Indiana, where things were also hot, and distributed ammunition to those who were fighting.

Some of them who could pass for white had acted as spies, and infiltrated the Ku Klux Klan and some of the unions whose members were fighting to keep the Negroes out of jobs. They were all excited about this, and I rejoiced with them. It was time, I felt, that the underdog stopped yapping and got ready to bite. Not since the largely futile slave uprisings of the eighteenth and nineteenth centuries had the black man showed himself willing to take up arms in his own defense.

Mother, Tada and I were not in the midst of any of this, however. We did get off the train in Omaha. We didn't know anyone there, so Mother asked the taxi driver to take us to the best hotel. At the Fontenelle, we were comfortably installed, that is as comfortably as possible in the heat of Omaha's summer. While we waited for things to settle down in Chicago, the bills began mounting up, and Mother became concerned that we'd have to cut short our trip without seeing our relatives. So, she called the nearest "relative" she could think of, the clergyman of the Episcopal Church, to ask if there were a less expensive hotel we could stay at. When he learned we were at the Fontenelle, he suggested that we move to his house as soon as possible because the hotel did not welcome colored guests. "Only Booker T. Washington has ever been there," he told us, "and he went up in the service elevator to see some big shot donating to Tuskegee." Before we checked out, we decided to have one final fling in the hotel dining room, Tada and I speaking our Mexican Spanish, and Mother just nodding and saying, "Si, si, si," not understanding a word we said. It was a lovely time, because we made her say yes to absurdities.

We moved into the home of the Episcopal clergyman, saving us money and any embarrassment we might eventually have had to face. Our stay was short and enjoyable. While there, we were joined by a young man, several years my senior, named Andy Singleton, who later became a Nebraska state senator. (I ran into him fifty years later in St. Thomas. He was accompanied by his beautiful wife, twenty or thirty years younger than he, and when I reminded him of our meeting in 1919, he exclaimed, "Why, I was a mere babe in arms then," and his jolly laugh rang out over the Caribbean Sea.)

Eventually, we made it to Chicago and stayed the summer, enjoying the warmth and joviality of Dad's large family. I kept one eye on my father's two sisters, my "Creole aunts" as Mother called them, to see if I'd ever catch either of them with their "feet higher than their head"; I never did. One kept house for her son and daughter, and the other, I suppose, was the perfect example of a husband-pleasing slave that my mother always sniffed at. She was sixty-three years old and had recently married a man of forty-two, much to Mother's dismay.

After the summer, it was back to Los Angeles, with the comfortable familiarity of my dancing, occasional movie role and flirting with beaux. I also worked for a time at Siegel's—the Bergdorf-Goodman of Los Angeles at the time. It was a thrill for me to handle all the beautiful clothes that had been tried on by stars—Mary Pickford, Pola Negri, the Gish sisters, Pearl White, Gloria Swanson. I remember being especially impressed by one I considered to be truly a great lady, Clara Kimball Young. The others seemed rather coarse to me.

The comfort and familiarity began to be a strain, however, and the tightness of Mother's protective reins frustrated my efforts to grow up. I had a crush on the son of our dentist, Alva Garrett. Alva had been a soldier in the war, and it was for him that I had sung "In Peril on the Sea" in church. He returned safely and even more handsome than I had remembered. He must have known I admired him, and one day he asked my mother if he could take me rowing on the lake at West Lake Park.

Well, I was thrilled. I wore my taffeta suit with the wide pleated skirt and took along a blue parasol that I twirled over my shoulder as my gentle cavalier rowed me across the lake. It was the most romantic thing I could possibly imagine. Alva, I suppose, must have been amused, but he carried on with the suitor's role nicely. However, as we got to the corner of my street, just as the sun was about to set, he suddenly grabbed my hand and pulled me along at a dash for the last two or three blocks, saying, "I have to get you in the house before sundown or your mother will really give it to me." So much for growing up. I was twenty-one years old. When the opportunity arose for me to leave Los Angeles, I was more than ready.

In California in 1923, I thought I was a pretty sophisticated "Jazz Baby." I had, after all, associated with the intellectuals at Charlie Chaplin's "anarchist" meetings, meeting many of the avant-garde thinkers of the time, Edward Weston, Tina Modotti, Robo and Sadakichi Hartmann. We all knew about Freud, knew Adler and Jung, and we talked freely about the current political issues.[2] I remember vaguely now that we were all in favor of "no government at all." Perhaps I alone knew nothing of syndicalism, trade unions or even exactly what it was the "anarchists" had in mind for us, I was with a group of charming companions. That was enough for me, and they seemed to enjoy my "exotic" presence among them.

Socially, too, I felt at ease. I had been trained in ballroom dancing with my brother for benefit shows and felt confident in "society," where I was always popular with young women (I never flirted with husbands and other girls' beaux) as well as with young men who filled my dance card with their claims within minutes of my arrival at a ball. One of the last dinner parties I gave in Los

Angeles was done in Chinese style, with the guests sitting on the floor and eating with chopsticks. As an extra touch of class, there were *Violet Milos* on the table for us to smoke. Any self-assurance I may have had, however, disappeared when I arrived in New York to be a bridesmaid in the wedding of Mae Walker, the adopted daughter of a wealthy black woman who had made a fortune creating and selling hair-straightening pomades.[3]

We met Mae through Madame Walker's daughter, A'Lelia, who had come to our home seeking a place to stay while in Los Angeles. There were no respectable hotels for colored people, and the white hotels did not welcome them no matter how well off they might be, so we often took in friends or friends of friends from the East. A'Lelia had come to introduce her mother's products into the Los Angeles colored beauty parlors. When she called from the train station, I answered the phone and invited her to come over. When she arrived and heard Mother was not there, she was reluctant to accept the hospitality offered by "a little girl like you," but she did come in and settled in for a long stay, with Mother's hearty approval. She took over my room, as was the custom when we had guests, and I moved into the playroom for the duration.

I was fascinated by A'Lelia. She was the first really African-type person I had known so intimately, and I adored her luxurious habits. While Tada and I would be gulping down breakfast ("you must not go to school on an empty stomach," Mama insisted) of an orange or apple, oatmeal, bacon and eggs, A'Lelia would be stretched out on her chaise longue like Goya's *Maja,*[4] dressed in a lavender-chiffon or white-lace negligee, sipping heavy cream with a spoon dipped from the small bottle before her. Smiling good-naturedly at our envious glances, she would wish us a happy day in class.

After breakfast, however, she got busy turning the kitchen into her workshop, boiling petroleum jelly, adding some perfume then ladling the concoction into little cans labeled *Madame Walker's Hair Straightener.* Each time she tipped the ladle, she would amuse us by saying, "one dollar, one dollar." I thought that was certainly an easy way to get rich.

I never understood how A'Lelia and Mother got along so well, their worlds were so far apart. While A'Lelia would be sipping cream in her negligee, Mother might come into the breakfast room, sending Anna May, the "poor unfortunate" she had brought home from reform school to "educate" and "civilize," scurrying for her cup of tea and toast and marmalade. She'd be all business as she got ready to go to work, auditing the books of several small orange packing companies. She'd be fully dressed in her business suit of gray wool, perfectly tailored, with a white ruffled blouse, a long gold chain and gold watch attached to her suit belt, and her hat tilted slightly over one eye. As Grandma had taught us "a lady does not leave her bedroom without her gloves," Mother's gray kid gloves would be lying beside her black leather briefcase. After a terse, "good morning, is your homework well done?" to Tada and me, she would turn to A'Lelia with pleasantries.

Outwardly, Mother disapproved of A'Lelia's "sporting ways." She "played the horses," for instance, and refused to give a dime or a damn for the NAACP, the Urban League, the church, the Negro colleges or anything except her own pleasure and comfort. Yet Mother laughed with her, and they were great friends. For A'Lelia's part, she seemed to love and respect Mother. She often asked advice about the proper way to do and say things so as to be acceptable to educated people, and Mother enjoyed helping her. For instance, there was the time that someone in Greenwich Village had palmed off a coat of arms on A'Lelia that was decorated with a *bar sinister.* Mother was quick to let her know this meant she came from a family of bastards, and so, A'Lelia went to great expense to have all the coats of arms changed in her cars, the silver and gold service, bookplates and everywhere else she had so lavishly displayed the embarrassing symbol. In a sense, I suppose, Mother and A'Lelia enjoyed vicariously living each other's life.

When A'Lelia's mother died, leaving her a vast fortune, she returned East and eventually married a physician, Dr. Wiley Wilson, an enterprising rogue who left her after a short time. For a wedding present, she gave him the southwest corner of 138th Street and Seventh Avenue in New York for his office and clinic, and for his honeymoon traveling case, a solid gold shoe horn. They came to Los Angeles for their honeymoon, and we saw them often. When A'Lelia was planning Mae's wedding, I was asked to be a bridesmaid.

It was to be a September wedding, to be held right after the annual convention of the National Association for the Advancement of Colored People in Kansas City in 1923. All of our serious friends were there for the convention: Dr. Du Bois, brilliant and suave and magnetic as ever; James Weldon Johnson, so gallant and deeply intelligent; and Walter White, with whom I flirted quite openly. The wealthy Herbert Seligmann and I ate sherbet at a side table, and he ate so much of it, I nicknamed him "Sherbert Heligmann," and this became a running joke between us, although I saw him only once in New York.[5] On the night of my arrival he took me to dinner and dance at the old Waldorf-Astoria. Just where I belonged, I thought, feeling glamorous in an accordion-pleated pale yellow chiffon dress.

But there was little room for levity at the convention. The subject of the "Negro problem" dominated most of the talk. We made a trip to Leavenworth to see a group of colored soldiers who had been sentenced to the federal penitentiary after someone was shot in a Texas bar where they had been refused a drink. No one would expose the guilty soldier, so about 25 were dishonorably discharged and sent to prison for thirty years.

Arthur Spingarn, the NAACP president, and Dr. Du Bois and Mother all made speeches encouraging the men to "behave decently," promising that the NAACP would fight to get them out of prison, which was accomplished eventually. It was a good thing they didn't ask me to speak. I would have urged every black man in a United States uniform to "shoot 'em up. The Army can't put you all in jail. Better to die fighting for your own rights than to kill Germans to 'make the world safe for Democracy!'"

This sort of thing caused quite a battle within my personality. Just as Mother's friendship with A'Lelia showed another side of her, I, too, was torn by conflicting feelings. Dancing and flirting were all well and good, but they didn't mix too well with social problems, nor could they unburden me from the cloak of guilt I bore, engendered by repeated references to my many flighty "sins." They rang in my ears: "Pretty is as pretty does;" "Forgive us our trespasses;" "God bless everybody, and make me a good girl, for Christ's sake, amen." My failure to be a "good girl" caused me many uneasy feelings as we left Kansas City, Leavenworth, the prisoners and the business of the NAACP behind to attend Mae's wedding. The cost of the wedding would have been usefully applied to civil rights cases and support of the anti-lynching legislation.

7

A'Lelia's home at Irvington-on-Hudson was a palace. It had once been the home of Enrico Caruso, and A'Lelia easily kept it in the style to which it had been accustomed. There was an enormous hallway, like the lobby of a grand hotel, a library, a salon with Louis XV furniture and an Aubusson carpet and tapestries on the wall. Off the salon was the conservatory, containing exotic potted plants, a collection of delicate summer furniture and a pipe organ. The dining room was huge and contained complete silver and gold services as well as the "everyday" Limoges china. All the servants were liveried, of course, and each morning the butler would go into the conservatory and waken all the bridesmaids by playing on the organ a bugle-like "When Hearts Were Young."

Preparations for the wedding were in full gear when we arrived. We were to be dressed, at A'Lelia's expense, in lovely lace Enfanta dresses, with a tight bodice and enormous skirt. Since the wedding was to be held at St. Philip's Episcopal Church, we would be required to have our heads covered, so each of us had a little silver-braided crown to wear. Our shoes were silver lamé and made to order. This made for a lot of happy confusion as the women ran around getting measured for their outfits. We carried an ivory-colored leather prayer book and each was given, as well as the entire outfit, a necklace of small pearls.

When we weren't dashing around trying on clothes, the women would spend time playing cards in the playroom on the floor above the bedrooms. There was a billiard table and tables for gambling and card games. A separate rumpus room the size of a small nightclub was the location for a party almost every night. The popular musicians from New York would be there, from Sissle and Blake to Duke Ellington.

Outside the estate was as grand as inside. There were garden terraces that led to the Hudson River beyond the swimming pool. There was also an enormous garage housing, among other cars, two Stutz roadsters that were a joy to me since I had learned to drive in a Stutz in L.A. at age 14. My mother preferred the stables. A'Lelia had two or three horses, and Mother always enjoyed a good horseback ride. Once in a while I could be persuaded to get on one, although my experience with horses in the movies hadn't given me much pleasure, and I was still fearful of falling off or being kicked sky-high. But with a nice tame mare, trotting through the lovely woods was colorful, calm and exhilarating. Washington Irving countryside.

At that time, I was more or less engaged to Charlie West. He had been the star of the Washington-Jefferson team that had come out to California to play in the Rose Bowl, when the winning Eastern school played the best Western school at the New Year's Day event. The other team that year wanted to knock Charlie out of the game, but it wasn't so easy. Although they knew he was supposed to be a Negro, his father was Irish, and Charlie so light-skinned that cries to "get the nigger out of the game" went unheeded; they couldn't find one.[1]

I met him through a mutual friend after the game. I gave a dance for him at our house in Los Angeles because he was a visiting celebrity "All American" player, and we fell for each other like a ton of bricks. He had a beautiful physique, and he danced with dignity and grace, my ideal of a perfect athlete. He was devoted to me from the start.

In September of 1923, Charlie was starting his courses at Howard Medical School in Washington, D.C., and coaching the Howard football team. Sometimes he could get away and come up to New York. Our "engagement" consisted of my wearing his Alpha pin and his gold football on a chain around my neck. It was always a pleasure to have him visit me for the dances at Irvington-on-Hudson.

Most of the bridesmaids at Mae's wedding were friendly and outgoing. We had been selected from different parts of the country where A'Lelia had traveled. Most of us had never met before, but our parents knew each other since we were among America's small percentage of relatively affluent Negroes. In contrast to her bridesmaids, Mae was retiring and quiet, but we all liked her very much. She was a doll, short with a lovely brown complexion and beautiful hair. She looked like, and may have been, an Indian. With her long, silky hair, it would not have been unlike old Madame Walker to have adopted her to show off the "wonders" her hair treatment had done for Mae.

While we liked Mae, we were not too crazy about the groom. His name was Gordon Jackson. He came from a "good family," that is, one that had lived in Chicago for several generations and had acquired property and money as the city expanded. His sister was highly respected, a dignified, prim, correct school teacher. Gordon's family were members of St. Thomas Church and of the high stratum of colored society in the Middle West, but Gordon himself was something of a spendthrift and a playboy, older than Mae and looking slightly uncomfortable over the prospect of marrying such a nice girl. We felt sorry for Mae, felt as if she were being married to this man only to satisfy A'Lelia's need for social prestige, but none of us was willing to say anything until I discovered that Mae was smitten with one of the young men who came to the dances each evening. He liked her but was still in college.

One morning I got her alone in the library and whispered conspiratorially, "Mae, you know if you'd like, I'll arrange an elopement so you and Sol can go off together before the wedding. It will be a great disappointment to a lot of people, but it may mean your happiness." It all sounded like something out of one of my old bad movie scripts, and Mae was terrified of even listening to me. My wild scheme was not followed, and the wedding went through in great style.

The church was filled with the social and rich colored people of the eastern seaboard and Chicago and probably the largest collection of expensive fur coats ever assembled. The ushers were all professional men; my escort was a gallant young lawyer from Baltimore. Father Shelton Bishop presided over a moving, terribly correct, ceremony. When we left the church, the streets around St. Philip's were packed as though for a Marcus Garvey demonstration. It seemed like all of Harlem had turned out to see the wedding. It was a great day for A'Lelia, if not for Mae.

Having brought up the name of Marcus Garvey, I am reminded that Harlem at that time had many different faces to it, the "back to Africa" movement espoused by Garvey being only one of them. My interest in Garvey was directed chiefly by my father's brother Noah, who worked with him as his public relations counselor.[2] My own feelings were not oriented towards his philosophy, however. I couldn't see much sense in taking half the black population of the United States and moving with them to poverty-stricken Africa.

My interests lay in many directions. I had, for instance, a cousin at Lincoln who came to New York at times, Langston Hughes. He and I agreed on so many things. There was his world also to be appreciated, with the writers and artists of the time, Claude McKay and Paul Robeson. Then, too, there were the athletes in my life, not the least of whom was Charlie West.

The world in which I immersed myself was not confined to Harlem. Many of the people I admired and enjoyed being with were in Greenwich Village. I was taken there by Abbie Mitchell, an actress, and her husband, Will Marion Cook, a concert violinist, who were friends of my father. We went to one of the local cafés, Lee Chumley's, where I met Eugene O'Neill and Edna St. Vincent Millay. I found it hard to believe that Miss Millay was someone who "burned her candle at both ends;" she seemed to be such a nicely brought-up young woman, I imagined she went to bed at eight o'clock with a volume of Tennyson. O'Neill struck me as a typical journalist, a slender man and pleasant to chat with. Many "greats" frequented Chumley's but I was too ignorant to know them.

The group that hung out at Lee Chumley's and other places like it were hospitable to those blacks who were in the Village at that time. There were few of us, but I believe they would have welcomed more. But colored people suspected all whites of being so prejudiced, that those who welcomed them were considered to be hypocrites. Even I, who might have known better, avoided certain situations. I was brought up to believe that a white man might want to have a sexual affair with me, but that he would not respect me afterwards. Now I know there are gentlemen among all races, just as there are cads among them all. I think that "kiss and tell" would have perhaps been more characteristic of some of the insecure blacks I knew than it was of most of the white men I associated with. But the fear of being taken for a "high yaller easy lay" inhibited any notion I might have had about an inter-racial affair.

There was nothing simple about what respectable colored people thought were their moral standards. The women, especially, were so prudish, at least so it seemed to me, I got the impression they were afraid to be mistaken for an "easy lay" even by their husbands. Everything in colored society was formal. I remember that some women were called Mrs. Doctor Smith or Mrs. Lawyer Serotee, basking in whatever profession her husband was active in. I found this all very different from my life in Los Angeles, where we talked freely about birth control, the Lucy Stone League, and the advisability of women keeping their maiden names after being married.[3] But there were very few professional black women. My mother helped an intelligent and splendid woman in Southern California become a physician, but she was considered most unusual. Women did not become physicians. Mrs. Bass, who ran a newspaper, was considered unusual. My mother, who became one of the first women certified public accountants in the country, was considered unusual. If I hadn't been so inhibited by the ideas of what women can and can't do, I might have studied architecture, but there was no such thing as a woman architect.

So, New York offered me a myriad of new experiences and people. I began to recognize that my Los Angeles sophistication was no match for life in the East, but I was young, enthusiastic and curious, and everyone was kind to me. I seemed to be welcomed in all the different worlds, and I enjoyed it very much. Charlie West notwithstanding, there were many charming men in my life. Lee Chumley took a shine to me as did a chap named Throckmorton, a stage designer who threw a "Cleopatra Party," where he was Antony and I was Cleopatra and everyone came in costume.[4] It was there at the party that I realized that all the pleasure, the stimulation, the newness and excitement that I felt meant that I belonged in New York. I decided to stay.

8

Mother left me in New York because that's where I wanted to be. She left me in the charge of friends, the Austins, who lived at 237 West 139th Street in a handsome block of homes designed by Stanford White. It was in a part of Harlem called "Strivers Row," although certainly the Austins were not striving, nor did I see anyone in the block who was. Mrs. Austin kept an elegant home. Her husband, an estate lawyer, was passing for white along with his brother in offices on Madison Avenue. Among other things, their work called on them to appraise antiques, and the Austins' home was filled with a fine selection of antique furniture, prints and a library of fine books.

No one was about to keep me for nothing, however. When I told my father I planned to stay in New York and go to Columbia rather than the University of California, he told me "make your own living then." "You bet I will," I answered. I told Mother not to worry and sent her home, fairly confident that I could come up with something. Thinking quickly, I crossed over 139th Street to the home of Mr. Miller, a comedian who was currently appearing in the Negro musical show, *Runnin' Wild,* which followed *Shuffle Along* as a big hit in New York.[1] The big number in *Runnin' Wild* introduced a new dance known as the Charleston. Mr. Miller asked if I could sing. I told him no, not unless he wanted to hear my feeble imitation of my mother's church choir voice. Very well, then, could I dance?

Dance? Of course! What kind did he want? Flamenco and castanets were my speciality, I said. Unfortunately, they weren't casting for Spanish dancers in *Runnin' Wild.* They wanted tap dancers and people to do the Charleston. So Jack Carter, one of the young men who attended the parties at Irvington-on-Hudson, volunteered to teach me the Charleston. And Mr. Miller sent me to see Bill ("Bojangles") Robinson to learn how to tap.[2] Many an afternoon was spent in the rumpus room in the basement of the Austin home with Bill Robinson trying to change my flamenco into a proper tap dance and Jack working with me on the Charleston. Eventually I was good enough at both dances to be hired as the "pony" at the far end of the chorus line of *Runnin' Wild.*

We were a good looking bunch of girls, I must say. For the Charleston number, we wore white tutus, i.e. ballet skirts and tight black patent leather bodices, and white wigs. With our brown skin, it was certainly a striking combination.

My father, who had thought I'd never be able to make a living, decided to come to see what sort of living I was making. Unlike the movies where the father has a fit at seeing his daughter with "theater people," Father noticed there were many respectable people connected with the show, including my two Boston friends, Esther and Dorothy Bearden, who were certainly just as nicely brought up as I had been. Satisfied that I was behaving respectably, he came backstage, like a stage-door Johnny, and met me for dinner. Of course, he let it be clear that any time I wanted to return to school, he would be glad to finance my studies—in California.

I decided to take half his advice and return to school, not in California, but at Columbia. Convinced that no one could ever make a living as an artist, I registered at the teachers college for courses in methods of teaching art and child psychology. I did not leave *Runnin' Wild,* however. By day I was a prim, respectable student, at night, a wild chorus girl. It amused me greatly that the college boys wanted to date the showgirl, and the show-boys wanted to take out the college girl. The former would pick me up after the show to take me to the Cotton Club to listen to Duke Ellington and dance the night away. But the boys who came to see me after classes at Columbia, to share a soda in a drug store at 116th Street, were the show-boys. Taking a tip from Edna St. Vincent Millay, I was burning my candle at both ends. However, when it came time for *Runnin' Wild* to go on the road, I decided it would be better for me to stay and finish my studies at the teachers college.

I spent a lovely summer vacation in Atlantic City and the other beaches where our friends gathered, but when September came around, I found I had to change my plans. There were no other jobs to be had in New York, and if I expected my father to help support me, it would have to be someplace he would approve of. Father had a sister in Baltimore, and since Charlie West was attending school in nearby Washington, I decided to move in with my Aunt Edith.

Compared to New York, Baltimore was very provincial, and Washington, D.C. wasn't much better. The life of the colored people in the Washington area was lively enough but even more formal than anything I'd experienced up until then. I found the whole scene to be stiff and uncomfortably segregated. I remember trying to get permission to bring H. L. Mencken to an Alpha dance in Washington that was one of the social events of the season.[3] I had met Mencken through Arthur Bragg, the son of the Episcopal priest of Baltimore. When Mencken learned I was going to the Alpha dance, he asked if he might be invited, so I passed along his request to my hostess, Muriel Milton. She was absolutely appalled. "Why, we don't have white men at our parties. We don't have white people at all. But if we did, they would certainly have to be our social equals, and no journalist would ever fit in our parties. Unless you know white people in the diplomatic corps, don't ask to invite them." Thoroughly rebuked, I apologized to Mencken and told him the guest list was filled.

To continue my education, I enrolled in a normal school in Baltimore.[4] I found it to be dull and not at all challenging, but I stuck with it for the two years it took me to become a teacher. While attending school, as I said, I was living in my aunt's house on Druid Hill Avenue. It was a comfortable, three-story affair. The kitchen had an enormous coal stove, on the back of which there was always a tub of dough which could be whipped into Parker House rolls on the spur of the moment.

My aunt was a pretty woman. She had the deep-set eyes of my father's family and my color. She had a sweet face and a sweet disposition. Her husband, Ed, was maître-d' at the most expensive hotel restaurant in Baltimore. He liked good food and nice service, and he could cook as well as my aunt. And if I wasn't too crazy about living in Baltimore, I couldn't complain about the food, the soft-shelled crabs, terrapin and above all, the hot bread. As my aunt said, "it made the butter fly."

I had my own room on the top floor, nicely furnished, with a mahogany four-poster bed and a large secretary desk. The house was a pleasant place to receive my friends in Baltimore. There was Rita McCarthy from across the street, and the Colemans and the Whartons from around the corner, and my aunt's family, the Murphy's, who were all friendly and kind to me, especially Frances Murphy, who taught child psychology at the normal school. Even though she was much older than me, in her sixties, we were very close friends. I taught her to drive. We would drive out to the country in her Essex and talk about all sorts of things. She was a high-strung, unmarried woman with a keen sense of curiosity and sharp wit. She was probably my favorite person in Baltimore. Aunt Edith was very kind to me, but I always found her a little strange. I would have called her a "country cousin," and I suppose I acted like a "city slicker" in her presence, although she always seemed proud of me and welcomed my friends visiting.

During the summer, I went to the country house in rural Pennsylvania of my cousin Albert, who had a daughter about my age. Lots of people in the area were related to my aunt, my father and grandfather, and they all took me in as part of the family. I was happy about this, but I still felt out of place, a wild chorus girl in a world too genteel for comfort. The segregated aspect of this life was strange and discomforting to me. I broke out once in a while with Arthur Bragg and a few others like him, and I continued to see his friend Mencken and others who might have been called "bohemians."

I began working in my uncle's restaurant. I went in every night to sell cigarettes when the band was not playing for dancing. That was a fun job! I went through the place with a Spanish shawl over my shoulder, calling, "cigars, tobacco, cigarettes." When the customers danced, I went into the manager's office to do my homework for school the next day.

One night, when most of the customers had gone, a man sitting alone called me over and asked me to have a drink with him, a glass of champagne. I was tired enough to sit down, and I certainly wasn't afraid he was going to try anything in the middle of the restaurant while I waited for my uncle. I had seen him there before, usually with large parties. My uncle had told me he was one of the richest men in that part of the world, the head of a large business. He stayed late often to talk with me during that season in 1925, and I enjoyed his company. I imagine my uncle must have thought I was running around with the man, but I was never able to let myself get involved in an affair with him. I was still afraid that a white man, no matter how rich and gentlemanly, only wanted a "brown-skinned baby" for his backstreet mistress. I was certainly much too stuck-up to take part in a relationship like that. So I danced with him, accepted his company, rides to his hunt club and little presents now and again. He offered to set me up in a place in Philadelphia if I liked, and if I'd been as sophisticated a "jazz baby" as I thought I was, I might have taken him up on it. But although I had departed from the Episcopal Church shortly after my first communion, its influence, along with that of my Boston Puritan mother, served to keep me poor but respectable.

My split with the church had left a void in my life, and I still looked to fulfill my need to have the mysteries of the universe explained to me. In seeking the answers, I had become involved in the Christian Scientist church. I had worked after school in Los Angeles for a man who was a Christian Scientist. He had me read the daily lesson to him every day, and the logic of putting the whole puzzle together in the way his religion taught him appealed to my reasoning mind. Although it may not have made much sense in hard fact, it made wonderful sense to my spiritual side, and so in Baltimore I attended the Christian Scientist church.

Going there gave me a sense of ease and confidence, and when it came time to take my examination to allow me to begin teaching in the public school system, I felt relaxed, certain that my intelligence would carry me through, reflecting as it did the intelligence of the universe. I came out with a score of 99 percent.

By a stroke of good fortune, the head of the art department in the Baltimore school system, Leon Winslow, was a good friend of several of my teachers at Columbia. I was encouraged by him to apply for the job of supervisor in the art department, and with his help, I studied for the supervisor's exam and passed. So I entered the school system, not as a teacher, but as a supervisor, working with one of the greatest art educators I had ever known.

Winslow believed that since every child was not likely to become a great artist, he shouldn't be burdened with the task of learning to draw and make pretty pictures. Rather, he should understand the principles of art and be able to apply them to his everyday life, to see art in food, clothing, shelter, tools and machines. The system worked beautifully, and I was thrilled to be part of it. The children took great joy in doing artistic things with all the everyday things with which they lived. They were delighted with the small doses of art appreciation we gave them.

Dad was proud of my accomplishments and insisted that as a supervisor, I should have a car to visit the schools in the district. I lost no time in searching the Baltimore showrooms, and I picked out a brand new 1927 Dodge Roadster. Oh, it was a dream! It had wire spoke wheels and a canvas top held up with wooden braces, and a rumble seat. All my friends would pile into the car, as many as eight at a time, to go to football games and dances.

I had been asked by some of the girls to join a sorority, but I declined. The sisters looked too prim for me, and I felt they would do nothing but censor my behavior. Had I been asked to join a fraternity, however. . . . The fraternity dances were the brightest part of that period for me, and the brightest of the stars was my own Charlie West. When I danced with him, I felt so proud; he was the finest of the fine. I loved to dance, and the men seemed to like to dance with me. My dance card would be invariably filled as soon as I entered the room, as in earlier L.A. balls. Of course, as my escort, Charlie danced the first and last dances with me, as well as all the waltzes. One of the young men, Roscoe Lewis, liked to try to get Charlie's goat by cutting in when we were waltzing, especially when the band played "I Know You Belong to Somebody Else, But Tonight You Belong to Me." Roscoe didn't really threaten our relationship, but something happened in the summer of 1927 that very nearly upset the apple cart. I went to California to visit my family and to attend summer school at UCLA, and there I met Ralph Bunche.[5]

We were immediately attracted to each other, so much so I forgot everything and everybody back East, including Charlie. We had a beautiful summer together, meeting on the campus at UCLA and going to my home, where we sat on the veranda holding hands as the sun went down on our young love. The only thing that kept us from falling into a serious engagement and immediate marriage were his youth and the fact that I wasn't ready to think about it yet. Who knows where that summer might have taken us had I stayed? But I didn't stay. In September I returned to Baltimore, and found a nightmare waiting for me.

I was no longer living in my aunt's home. Instead, I had a large apartment in the house of a woman I thought was a friend. Ruth was a good-looking woman, though not especially bright or articulate. Her husband was much older than she, and he enjoyed arguing politics and social problems. He would encourage me to get into debates with him, mostly so he could hear himself talk and to show off how much he knew. Our chief bone of contention, as I recall, was over whether Negroes should be Democrats or Republicans. I would argue that "Lincoln was a Republican," and the South is Democrat, and he would counter with, "therefore the party takes you for granted, fool!"

One day, during one of our altercations, Ruth interrupted with, "You talk about everything to Anita, but you never say anything to me."

"Well," he snapped, "you're too dumb." Not exactly the response she had been looking for. I walked out of the room and tried to avoid having any discussions with him after that. But living in the same house it was kind of difficult. Apparently, he must have said something to arouse Ruth's jealousy, because she started counting every egg that went into my apartment, every gallon of gasoline that went into my roadster, and came to the conclusion that her rich husband was contributing to my "extravagant living" and that there was "something going on" between us.

The fact of the matter was that I thought he was one of the ugliest men I'd ever seen, sort of a dirty yellow, old and probably arthritic, as far as possible from the kind of man I admired, with the brains and charm of Ralph Bunche or the physique and sound common sense of Charlie West. He didn't have nearly the polish, charm or intelligence of my own father, who was about his age. However, this didn't deter Ruth from launching a campaign of slander against me that went flying all over the Eastern seaboard among everyone we knew. It seemed that within a short time, even my own uncle and aunt were questioning me, and Charlie must have had a devil of a time defending me against this woman. I moved out of their house and back into my aunt's home, but this didn't do anything to stop the attack. Finally, I decided I couldn't bear it any longer, and at the end of the school year I quit my job and fled Baltimore, feeling like there was a pack of hounds yapping at my heels, not to mention a large number of bitches.

I fled to the only place I could live comfortably on my own, New York. I moved back to the Village and settled into a life in which I surrounded myself with people I could understand and who could understand me. Ralph continued to write brief, deeply affectionate letters, and Charlie came up from Washington to see me. I also spent time with his family in Washington, Pennsylvania, and I was especially fond of his sister, Ethel, who often came to New York to visit with me.

But my feelings for Charlie were no longer the same. Now that he was a doctor, he seemed to be treating me like a patient, just wanting to take care of me, protect me and guide me. I resented that type of care, and although I was still fond of him, my passion was rather dampened by this condescending attitude towards his "wild baby." So, I began to encourage him less, and by the end of the summer of 1928, I decided to get away from the Negro college fraternity crowd altogether and asked Father if I might attend Wellesley College. He agreed, and I began making preparations to enter in the fall. But then I met a group of students who were going to Paris in September. When I asked myself, Wellesley or Paris, there was no contest. So, keeping my plans to myself, I quietly accepted the tuition for Wellesley, sold my car, and on September 28, 1928, I took off for Paris.

9

I felt while crossing the Atlantic a great sense of going home, to a place where I really belonged. Away from the lynchings, away from the Negro problem, away from the polarization, away from all the disagreeable aspects of my life in the United States.

I was not running away from American Negroes, however. Countee Cullen and Yolande Du Bois were coming soon to Paris on their honeymoon. There were others, too, whom I had known in the Village, who would be in Paris. Harold Jackman and Roscoe Bruce and Nora Holt were all either in Paris or going there about that same time. There was a cousin of my father, a jazz musician who had stayed in Europe after the war and married a Belgian woman. There was a couple named Mitchell who had a nightclub in Montmartre that we all knew about. Bricktop was there and the Blackbirds were going over.[1] So had I wanted to have a segregated group of friends in Paris, I might have found it, although the blacks in Paris saw each other either by chance or when they wanted to, not by virtue of living in the same place. They lived where they pleased. There was no discrimination against them, nor did they think of discriminating against whites, French or American.

I never met Florence Mills or Josephine Baker, who were great stars in Paris at the time, but I was proud to have known Ned Gardine, whose physique was shown off in all the subways in a clearly recognizable portrait of him as a specimen of modern manhood, the great athlete. I liked Ned, and it was fun to meet him in the subway each time I took a trip. Of course, my parents would have to find out eventually that I had not gone to Wellesley after all, but I thought I could reconcile them to my going to Paris for one reason. My mother's brother was there.

Uncle Clarence's marriage with Maravene Kennedy had broken up some time earlier, and he had since been commissioned by the French government to help reorganize industry there. He was married to a German woman, Lizbeth von Heimen, and they lived near Saint-Philippe-du-Roule in Paris. That would be my first stop after settling with all the rest of the scaredy-cat American students at the Hotel Continental.

We didn't have much money to stay at the Continental for very long, but the kids were all afraid to go to the Left Bank. I was no exception. I thought the Left Bank was probably covered with Apaches, with all sorts of wild things going on, and I was as leery as the rest. We stuck to each other like glue, riding together from the boat train to the hotel and looking together over the Tuileries, wondering what really was going on over there while we were supposed to be in school.

I was registered at l'École du Louvre, where I was to take an art history course to be given in English through the auspices of New York University. With it came the history of France and trips to all the appropriate monuments.

I explained my course of study to Uncle Clarence, but I don't think he much approved of my being in Paris. For one thing, he didn't care for my appearance. I thought I looked elegant in a low-waisted crepe and satin dress that came well above my knees, as did all the fashionable dresses of that year. I was most proud, too, of my handmade shoes of black patent leather and lizard and my matching lizard handbag, cloche hat and seal coat trimmed with red fox. I thought I looked rather like Gloria Swanson. My uncle just gave me a disapproving look, but later he wrote my grandmother to say that I had shown up at his home looking like "an actress." Grandmother was distressed, for even though it was she who had dubbed me "Jazz Baby," she hardly expected me to be so much of one as to shock my uncle. Still, I wasn't dependent upon him. I had my friends, and we eventually got up the courage to move to the Left Bank, to the Boulevard Montparnasse and into the Venetia, a hotel frequented by artists and writers.

Oh, how great that was, to be in the middle of things, right across from the Jockey Club.[2] Now we were ready to take in the artistic life, to get a working knowledge of French, to dance through the night in Montparnasse or Montmartre, and, yes, to study as well, for we were all ambitious and were going to be doing great things eventually.

I met Louise Bryant, widow of John Reed, author of *Ten Days that Shook the World,* and she took me under her wing and introduced me to her friends, among whom were Pierre Loving, the Seldes brothers and Ernest Hemingway. Sometimes with Louise at the Select I would meet Man Ray.[3] He looked like an owl, all serious and wise. He was so protective of me when we met, I called him my Dutch uncle. All these friends would be around to intervene whenever any of the writers or journalists would get fresh with me. They called me "the yellow peril" and "Tondelao," and seemed to think of me as a sex object. Louise would have none of that, however. She was high-strung and nervous all the time, having been told by some specialist in Berlin or Vienna that she had only five years to live. This stress seemed to make her a little irrational, and she and her roommate, Eva Le Gallienne's sister, Gwen, took it upon themselves to see to it that no one got fresh with me. I can remember Louise taking someone's arm off my shoulder and reprimanding him, "You get your filthy hand off that innocent girl's shoulder." I thought this was kind of her, but a bit funny since I didn't think he was being fresh at all.

Man Ray was especially helpful and kind to me. He told me that Montparnasse was probably not the place where I would be able to learn the most. He invited me to go to Saint-Germain-des-Prés to meet his friends, some of the surrealists and other artists. I was most flattered to be taken to Les Deux Magots and meet the *crème de la crème* of the art world. I followed very closely through the gossip the careers of Aragon, Breton, Max Ernst, Giacometti, Arp, Tanguy, Derain, Matisse and Picasso.

One afternoon, Nora Holt took me to Carl Van Vechten's apartment. He had a large suite in the Bristol Hotel.[4] There I met Virgil Thomson, Maurice Grosser and Kristians Tonny, the start of a long and beautiful relationship.[5] Tonny was a good-looking Dutch chap, a surrealistic painter. He knew about as much English as I knew French, so he had a hard time expressing the feelings he seemed to have immediately on meeting me. He followed me closely with his deep blue eyes as I moved among the guests. Carl seemed most displeased about this obvious "crush," and he stood against the grand piano with his teeth bared. I was quite embarrassed.

Later in the evening, I sat on a divan and started to read Tonny's palm in my primitive French, and Maurice and Virgil came over to have theirs read, too. It was a parlor game I had learned in Hollywood, just for fun, but everyone likes to hear about himself, so I had a captivated audience. Except for Carl. Nora had gone off with Carl's wife, leaving me alone with these three young men and Carl's angry stare. Finally, to break up the quartet, Carl practically grabbed Tonny, Maurice and Virgil and said they would be off to dinner at the Place d'Alma. Tonny turned first, then Maurice and Virgil, and they all pulled me to the door with them and insisted that I was coming along, too.

I didn't know what had happened to Nora, but I was certainly annoyed enough at Carl's discourtesy to want to make him uncomfortable by going with them. We all piled into a taxi and went to eat, at Carl's expense, of course. Carl, Maurice and Virgil quickly forgot that day, I'm sure, although it was an amusing one. We became friends with no recollection of my difficulty with Carl. But I never forgot it, for it marked the beginning of my time with Tonny.

He came to see me often and would sit and just look at me. Although I was flattered, I couldn't figure out what ailed him. Finally he confessed he had a fascination with American Indians. Somehow, I had become in his mind a Pocahontas or some character out of Fenimore Cooper, whose works he knew better than I. He hadn't known many girls before, and being timid, he hadn't approached many. However, his approach to me was very direct. He seemed to think he was some sort of a cowboy taking charge of the American Indian in Paris.

I never tried to pass myself off as an Indian. Usually, when asked, I said I was an "American cocktail," for among the French that included Indians, Negroes and everything else that made up a different kind of American. Parisians who didn't care much for Americans usually found the métisse, the person of mixed blood, or the Negro or Indian, to be attractive. The "cocktails" were often welcome in many places where white Americans were not.

As I got more and more involved with Tonny and *"la vie bohème,"* Uncle Clarence took it upon himself to rescue me. He invited me to dinner and introduced me to a handsome young German baron. He started calling on me quite regularly, no doubt with the encouragement of my uncle, who would have much preferred to see me safely married, out of the Left Bank chaos and into the Right Bank bourgeoisie, but horseback riding in the Bois de Boulogne, getting dressed up to go to expensive restaurants, going to the opera and being dragged to the home of some stuffy matron didn't hold much appeal for me.

My chance to extricate myself from the situation came one night as the baron brought me home. Tonny lay in wait for us. He snatched a knife out of a pumpkin in front of a grocery store and started chasing after my escort. It not only got rid of the baron for me, but the *histoire du couteau au potiron* became quite famous along the Left Bank, made Tonny quite the hero and discouraged any other suitors.

I stayed away from my uncle, and I imagine he was delighted I did. Father, too, washed his hands of me. He and Mother had separated, and he wanted nothing more to do with my foolishness. Mother, though, scrimped money from her allowance to send to me.

I didn't very much mind Tonny's chasing away any suitors because I wasn't about to fall in love with anyone at the time. Perhaps Tonny was in love with me, but I felt like a sister to him, although that didn't stop us from being lovers for a time. Tonny was young and handsome, and a successful artist. He had a one-man show of his work, and I was very proud of him. He had delightful friends, and we all ran around together, singing and talking and dancing in the streets and through the Luxembourg Gardens.

I enjoyed every minute with Tonny, even in his most erratic moods. He certainly had some wild ideas and would dash around doing the most bizarre things, but it only made me laugh. We moved into an apartment together, and I don't doubt I might have married him except that I felt he was really not very stable.

Man Ray advised me that marriage is only a contract to protect property and children. Having neither, it made little sense for me to be married, so I fell very comfortably into the "vie bohème" with Tonny, continuing my studies at l'École du Louvre, and, when I knew enough French, going to the Sorbonne for courses.

Our studio was a lovely place in a modern building, with a modern bathroom and kitchen. Tonny and I had the same tastes in furnishings and everything, although I must confess the studio was always in a state of chaos because of his work. There was paint everywhere.

Tonny was an extraordinary draftsman, very gifted. He used to draw over a sheet of paper that had oil paint on the opposite side, like carbon paper. He would fly fast over the surface of what appeared to be a blank sheet of paper, whistling and tapping his foot the whole while, occasionally lifting it to see how he was doing. It was always beautiful in design, reminding me of the work of Hieronymus Bosch, especially when he went into monsters and little people and things flying over the page like a delicate tapestry. I enjoyed watching him work and marveled at his dexterity.

We had many friends in the neighborhood whose work I liked. Pavel Tchelitchew and Allen Tanner lived across the street, and Eugene "Genia" Berman lived not very far away.[6] They and our other friends enjoyed Tonny's daredevil stunts, particularly when he drank. He would run across the street in the middle of traffic or hang onto an automobile or bus as though he were about to fall off it. These gestures, vaguely suicidal, both amused and frightened me.

Many of our friends went to Jean Cocteau's or André de la Rivière's evenings to smoke opium. I didn't smoke with them, but I enjoyed turning the opium over the burning olive oil, using what seemed to be long knitting needles. It smelled lovely. While André accepted opium smoking readily enough, he was most distressed over his girlfriend, Françoise, who would sit rocking back and forth in his American rocking chair sniffing cocaine. She would rock endlessly, reading a book and periodically take out a small package of cocaine, dip her index finger into it and sniff it into one nostril or the other. It didn't change her appearance or behavior, but it upset André because he believed it to be very harmful. When he took Françoise to Brittany to visit his family, he took her cocaine away from her.

Another of our friends, Robert Desnos, neither smoked opium nor sniffed cocaine, but he was addicted, in his own way, to spiritualism.[7] We would often sit around the oldest, most exotic table we could find, with our hands touching, trying to make the table tap out messages. One evening, we began receiving messages in Dutch. A French girl, who didn't understand Dutch, took down the message letter for letter. Tonny, the only one among us who could understand it, translated. The message was from his grand-mother, telling him to come down from the apple tree.

A more somber experience occurred shortly after Desnos told us about a "vision" he'd had after the death of two young women. The death had been witnessed by André Derain, who had been racing the women's car in his Bugatti.[8] He successfully completed a sharp turn, but the other car didn't make it, and the women were killed.

After the accident, Desnos claimed one of the women was his mistress. We didn't believe him, and the trance was supposed to prove it. He stood, looking over the transom of the door in An-dré's studio, and talked very excitedly about what the dead woman was supposedly saying to him. Then his voice changed and he said, "I see, on a hill, a tree alone, the only tree in sight, and under the tree is the body of a young woman, nude, who has a burn hole in her chest and not a drop of blood on her skin."

Then he fell down and everyone crowded around him saying, "That's enough, stop this foolishness." We lighted the candle that he had knocked over and tried to forget about what he had said. We were only mildly shaken by the prophecy, but we were truly frightened and dismayed a few weeks later when Françoise, who had gone to visit André's family, was found dead under a tree, a bullet hole in her chest and not a drop of blood on her skin.

10

In the summer following Françoise's death, a group of us decided to make a pilgrimage, going to Toulon first and then on to Venice. "Bébé" Christian Bérard had organized a pilgrimage to the tomb of Diaghilev, the Russian ballet impresario, who was buried on an island near Venice, and this gave our trip a purpose.

In Toulon, we saw "Douggie," who had been Isadora Duncan's secretary and filled us in on all the details of her life. William Seabrook, the Hearst writer, was there, too, along with his wife, a delightful companion.[1] I enjoyed hearing some real American gossip, especially about Americans in Paris.

Carl Van Vechten was in Toulon. One night he and Seabrook got into a long discussion over the difference in meaning between the words "sensuous" and "sensual." Mrs. Seabrook and I listened, bored. She was trying to persuade me to accompany them to Africa; her husband had just written a sensational thing about black magic in Haiti, and he wanted to continue his research into Africa. I wasn't interested. Voodoo and magic were much more exciting to me in the form of the art objects we were all interested in at the time, for instance, the masks and fetishes that Tristan Tzara was collecting. Everyone had a piece if he could afford it. So, wishing the Seabrooks luck on their African trip, we moved on to Venice. Tonny joined the others to visit the grave of the impresario. I stayed behind to watch some glass blowers; although I had been just as caught up as everyone else in the cult of the *ballet Russe,* I really didn't have any desire to visit a grave.

Venice, though, was lovely and romantic, undoubtedly the ideal place for a honeymoon, but it was hardly that for Tonny and me. Our efforts at romance weren't too successful. We did try, however. We went for a ride in a gondola, and it almost captured for us the elusive mood. We were drifting slowly under the Bridge of Sighs, heading towards an enormous moon, feeling the spell of Venice, when another gondola approached us. The voice of one of the occupants drifted towards us in strong Midwestern sing-song. "You folks got a match?" So much for romance.

Giving up on Venice, we went back to Paris and then made our way to Tonny's home in Holland where we spent the month of September. We stayed with Tonny's parents aboard their yacht, named *La Belle Poule* for one of Napoleon's ships. It was large enough to sleep six comfortably.

Tonny's father, a small, nervous man, was a painter. His mother was what I would call a typical Dutch woman, large and round and full of energy. She was quite attached to her son, and an undertone of jealousy sometimes made for an awkward moment between her and me. For instance, one evening after dinner, we were down to our last cigarette, and no one felt like going ashore to get more. Tonny's father offered it to Tonny, who in turn broke it in two and gave me half. His mother burst into tears and said, "You would never have done that for me."

These outbursts were few, fortunately, and most of the visit was pleasant. The autumn was lovely, with the chrysanthemums hanging over my head as I walked the path along the shore. The flowers often had cobwebs between them in the early morning dew. Tonny's mother called them "the veil of the Virgin." I found it rather unpleasant to have those saintly cobwebs on my face, but then all of Holland seemed to have a spooky feeling for me. "Spook" is a Dutch word, and from the stories I heard, each and every windmill came equipped with its own spook.

One thing I found it hard to get over was the insistence of everyone we met that I join them for a "cup of tea." Invariably, the tea was served with all kinds of breads and cakes, cheeses, fish of all kinds, salted, creamed, smoked, and a huge variety of cold cuts. I suppose I was the skinny Indian every Dutch friend wanted to fatten up.

I attracted a lot of attention in the village. The Dutch men, especially, would come up to me when I would be walking alone and speak in snatches of whatever exotic language they had learned, from Java, Sumatra or wherever they had run into brown girls. They were very cordial and sweet in their attempts to find a language in which we could communicate, but when I answered in French or English, they would turn away, disappointed.

I was charmed by the rich country, the small square farms and the great flat expanses that made all of Holland seem geometrical. The people were friendly and good-looking, and everything was in full blossom. But ultimately it got to me, the rows of wooden shoes at the doorsteps that could not be worn on the scrubbed floors inside, the systematic dikes and all the heavy, orderly atmosphere. I was quite content to return to Paris in October.

Tonny was painting a portrait of Gertrude Stein, and he was also working very hard on illustrations for James Joyce's *Ulysses*.[2]

I always felt the Bosch-like figures he liked to draw would be perfect for the book. He would go to the Joyce home evenings and describe to me later how the writer looked at everything through a jeweler's glass with his impaired vision, having about one-tenth of normal vision in one eye. Although I didn't accompany Tonny to the Joyce house, I did occasionally meet him and his family at Les Deux Magots, where they sometimes invited us to sit with them.

Gertrude Stein frequently invited Tonny to her home, and I enjoyed tagging along. Tonny was only one of the many young artists she would have over at her home on the Rue de Fleurus. Almost everyone we knew went—Allen Tanner, Eugene Berman, George Huguet, Virgil Thomson—at least once a week. She talked to me sometimes, often about Baltimore, and she told me some interesting stories. Even though she was most cordial to me I always felt she was being polite because Tonny was doing her portrait.[3] On the other hand, her companion, Alice B. Toklas, wasn't in the least friendly towards the young people who came by at Gertrude's behest. She sat in a corner of the salon the whole time doing needlepoint. The sound of the needle popping in and out reminded me of an operation I had observed in Paris, like the sound of the needle sewing up the skin after surgery. Gertrude's notes to Tonny bore her seal, imprinted with, "A rose is a rose is a rose," going around in a circle. I have kept some of those "rose" notes, which I always thought was the nicest thing about her.

Of course, every night wasn't spent at James Joyce's or Gertrude Stein's, but there were a great many parties nonetheless. I remember one party held for the Blackbirds at a grand *hôtel de ville*. While the whole company danced below with French aristocracy and rich and / or brilliant Americans, a girl on the balcony wearing an apricot-colored chiffon gown looked down in joy, quite beautiful, smiling and dignified. Suddenly, she threw her arms into the air and shouted "Hallelujah!" A few "amens" went back up to the balcony. She came down the stairs with a slightly dizzy dignity. The party went on until the roof very nearly caved in.

Another delightful party was given by Caresse Crosby when the pond froze at her home, a mill on the property of the Count de la Rochefoucauld.[4] She had invited most of the Paris crowd, and those who could ice-skate enjoyed it a great deal. I didn't skate, but I liked watching Tonny, who was quite marvelous on ice skates. Later in the evening, the count, Armand, came over from his chateau to join the party. He was accompanied by a tall skinny man who was introduced as the Duke of York. The duke had had quite a bit to drink, and he climbed to the roof of a shed. It was not very high, but he found it most difficult to get down, and a great fuss was made over rescuing him, with everyone pretty high on champagne and laughing hilariously. A few years later he was the King of England and father of the present queen and very serious. The Prince of Wales had not yet found "the woman I love."

Caresse and Harry Crosby owned the Black Sun Press that published a lot of the avant-garde material that was being written at the time. One of their magazines, *transition,* carried reproductions of Tonny's paintings along with the first chapters of *Ulysses,* Kay Boyle's writings, and many others. I liked Kay very much. She was married to Lawrence Vail at the time, and they had several children to whom they gave easy attention. There was a son named Sinbad, I believe, and a daughter named Apple. Kay told me one day over an aperitif at the Deux Magots that she didn't know which she enjoyed more, writing stories or having babies. She was such a creative person, she just bowled me over.

Djuna Barnes, another highly gifted writer, asked me over sometimes, but the one who really looked out for me was my fairy godmother, Louise Bryant. She took me to the home of William Aspenwall Bradley the first time I had luncheon with him. Bradley was an American, the editor and agent for most of the Americans and Englishmen who wrote in France.

His wife was a delightful French woman who helped me in many ways to understand her country. At their luncheon table, I met many of the well-known writers of the time, Carlos Williams, Claude McKay, and Ford Madox Ford. Mr. Bradley was one of the finest gentlemen I had met, a cosmopolitan scholar. He once told me he would not publish a manuscript that had been rejected by Louise Bryant.

In that atmosphere, and with the encouragement of Bradley and Louise, I was tempted to write, but my standards for excellence had been highly elevated since the days when I wrote for *The Messenger*. I tried one or two little things, an Anita Loos, *Gentlemen Prefer Blondes* type of piece based on my experiences as a chorus girl. I thought it was rather funny, but I didn't dare show it to Mr. Bradley or Louise, and I wound up tearing it up.

In a more serious mood, I wrote a story about a lynching. I put my soul into the skin of a girl who was supposed to have been raped by the man who was lynched. Without showing it to my friends in Paris, I sent it off to a literary magazine in London. It was accepted, but the editor wanted me to make it part of a series and asked me to send more immediately. I had no more to say.

That was the last contribution he ever got from me. How could I explain that the story had been an inspirational thing that came off the top of my head when someone asked me to explain about lynchings in the United States? I couldn't work up my interest beyond that one story, and so the project ended. The fact of the matter was that I had pretty well forgotten the disagreeable facets of American life which had led me to go to France. I was not reminded of the horrors of American lynchings every day, nor did I care to be. One must feel deeply to want to write about these things, but at the time, I wanted to be living in a light, gay way, not feeling deeply about much of anything.

Mr. Bradley and Louise had a way of pricking my conscience, though. They insisted that I get busy and, if nothing else, write the history of my family. I said I would get to it just as soon as I could get away from the wild whirl of one *vernissage* after another, from the dates and the cafes and dancing at the Boeuf and l'Ange Bleu and my courses at the Sorbonne. In response to my long list of "important" things waiting for me in Paris, Mr. Bradley suggested that I leave and go to North Africa, to Tangier, where I would be able to work without the distractions of Paris. He said Claude McKay was quietly working there and Aaron Copland had gone down recently.

I was tempted to go, but first I had to talk it over with my surrogate father, Man Ray. I told him I was too short of funds to travel. I was getting about $50 or $60 a month from my mother, who was separated from Father and couldn't afford to send me any more than that. Father was so disgusted with me, he wouldn't send me anything. Once in Tangier, I figured I could live on my small income as well as I had managed in Paris, but of course getting there was the problem. Well, even though Man Ray was one of the few surrealists who managed to make money from his work (he, Picasso and Derain were about the only ones with large cars), he wasn't about to finance my trip. He did, however, introduce me to his friend, Arthur Wheeler, a wealthy stockbroker.

Arthur and Rose Wheeler were a great couple to know, warmhearted, intelligent people. Arthur was a square man with a round belly and a hearty appetite for good things. One afternoon he took me to lunch at Maxim's (where I'd been only once before, with Gertrude Stein's nephew) and asked me about my projected trip to North Africa. I told him as much as I could, which wasn't very much since I didn't know exactly what I was planning to do beyond working on the history of my family. When I told him of the stories I had written, about the chorus girl and the lynching incident, he seemed to disapprove and suggested that the sooner I forget the problems of the Negro, the more comfortably I would live.

Well, that was easier said than done, as I well knew. I suppose there was some counterpoint of feeling that was much deeper than I realized at the time. I told Arthur that I had always felt a guiding passion to try to improve racial relationships, to get people of different nationalities, colors and religions to understand and appreciate each other. Talking about it had no effect one way or another on my dedicated interest in that mission, the dedication which I accepted as a heritage from my family, stemming from basic conflicts which had not been satisfactorily resolved.

Arthur knew I had been accepted in France; the French were more apt to accept my being part Cherokee or Negro or Métisse than they were an American. But while the intergroup tensions didn't affect me personally, I was very aware of their existence around me, when someone was referred to as a Jew or a *sacré Jesuite* or a Puritan Protestant. The French and the English continued their non-ending enmity; the Battle of Waterloo would be re-fought at the drop of a hat. Fear and animosity towards the Germans were also widespread, and even in 1930 there was a fear of war from all directions. Fascism was starting to show itself, communism was well established by then and the "master race" was feeling the pinch in Asia and Africa. It looked like any or all of these conflicts might explode at almost any time.

I was personally convinced that they could all get together and stop this nonsense. They all needed each other, particularly the undeveloped nations that seemed too anxious to throw off their colonial status and thus throw away the opportunity to build up their nation. Arthur listened to all my talk and raised his eyebrows and a glass: "Here's to the year 3000 when your dream comes true."

He seemed to have a more immediate dream on his mind. As we were leaving Maxim's, he said, "You know, I'll be very happy to give you the money to go to Morocco and help you in any way necessary in the writing of your book, but today it'll be worth an extra thousand dollars to you to spend the afternoon with me in an apartment that I rent just the other side of the *Madeleine*."

"Thanks a lot, Arthur," I said, "but I'll try to get along without the extra thousand."

He sighed, then laughed. "I don't know what you women want. Just exactly what is it you like? It's pretty obvious that you don't like sex."

Didn't like sex? Well, maybe there was something to Arthur's remarks. Most of the men I had known seemed to feel that their satisfaction was a woman's satisfaction. If a woman showed pleasure in a caress, the man would mistake it for sexual excitement. He would go along his merry way and leave the woman wondering when she was going to have more satisfaction or if she was ever going to reach an orgasm.

My experiences led me to have little expectation of enjoying sex to the fullest. Before Tonny, the men I had had relationships with were young college men from among family friends. One was a student in Paris about whom I was quite mad in the first few weeks after my arrival, before I got to know more civilized people. I had an affair with him that resulted in the only abortion in my life, which proved to be nearly fatal. I soon learned that he didn't really care for much of anything in Paris. He spent most of his time in Montmartre, listening to jazz bands, throwing away all the money his parents had sent him to go to school. He didn't even bother with school at all but slept most of the day away and became friendly with the Montmartre crowd. To one of these "friends" he lent a revolver with which one musician shot at another on the streets. The intended victim was uninjured, but several pedestrians were hit. Since guns were registered in France, the young man got into deep trouble with the law. I went through that and several other crises with him until he finally ran back to stay where he could live the Harlem life of his choice.[5]

This and other experiences, equally unpleasant, soured me for affairs. Arthur Wheeler's proposition held no appeal for me. In any event, I had never known a white American, and I had no intention of starting now. I was certain they left the earth littered with Madame Butterflys. What did I like? Arthur had asked. "Well," I replied, "I enjoy dancing."

That seemed to tickle him beyond anything he'd ever heard, and he chuckled about it as we started toward his hotel, where we were going to see Rose, his wife, who was ill with the flu. On the way there, we stopped at a jewelry store on the Rue de la Paix, and he ran in and bought several gifts, both for Rose and for me. One of the things he dumped in my lap was a mother-of-pearl cigarette case and lighter that I kept for as long as I smoked.

We arrived at the George V Hotel suite where we found Rose in bed, looking almost as green as the crêpe de chine pillow on which she was propped. But she was in a jolly mood, nonetheless. A young man was playing the phonograph and dancing for her in the middle of the floor. Rose welcomed us, and Arthur lost no time in telling her about his proposition of the extra thousand dollars and of my "ridiculous" reply. Instead of getting annoyed, Rose burst out laughing. "Why," she said, "I don't blame Anita. I wouldn't sleep with you for a thousand dollars myself."

The young man and I danced away the rest of the afternoon in the Wheelers' suite, and eventually they ordered oysters and champagne, and I left the hotel feeling just a little tipsy, still loving both Rose and Arthur Wheeler.

THE
MAY
CRISIS
1917

1. Anita Thompson, three years old. Moorland-Spingarn Research Center, Howard University.

2. Anita, age sixteen, on the cover of the May 1917 issue of *The Crisis*. At the time, the magazine noted, she was dancing under the direction of Ruth St. Denis in a Los Angeles production of Samuel Coleridge-Taylor's opera *Hiawatha*. Moorland-Spingarn Research Center, Howard University.

3. Anita Thompson as female lead in *By Right of Birth*. Lincoln Motion Picture Company. Archival film from the collections of the Library of Congress.

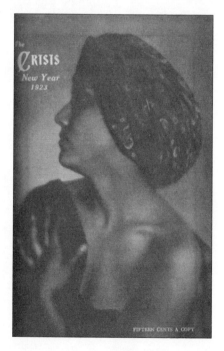

4. On the cover of *The Crisis*, January 1923. Moorland-Spingarn Research Center, Howard University.

5. "Kindest regards to Mr. Harry Austin / Cordially, Anita." Circa 1923. Anita stayed with Austin's family on Strivers' Row in Harlem while attending Columbia Teachers College and dancing in *Runnin' Wild*. Moorland-Spingarn Research Center, Howard University.

6. Looking like a flapper, ca. 1923. Moorland-Spingarn Research Center, Howard University.

7. Anita Thompson (center) as lady-in-waiting to the princess in *The Thief of Bagdad* (1924). Used by permission of Kino Lorber, Inc.

8. Portrait of Anita Thompson signed "Greetings to Dad from Anita / 'Runnin' Wild,' April 1924." Moorland-Spingarn Research Center, Howard University.

9. "To my dear Mrs. Austin / Sincerely, Anita." In orientalist garb. Moorland-Spingarn Research Center, Howard University.

10. Kristians Tonny at the easel. Circa 1928? Moorland-Spingarn Research Center, Howard University. Used by permission of Sylvie Salgues Kristians.

11. Transfer drawing by Kristians Tonny dedicated to Anita Thompson. An example of the technique Tonny perfected at this time that became his signature mode of composition in the early 1930s. In the dedication he refers to the posh Right-Bank apartment he shared with Thompson, paid for by Gertrude Stein. The inscription begins, "Pour Anita mon premier dessin dans ce sacre apartement." (For Anita, my first drawing in this sacred apartment.") Used by permission of Sylvie Salgues Kristians.

12. Photograph of Anita Thompson with Kristians Tonny and her Moroccan servant Wamba, Tangier, Morocco, ca. 1931–1932. Moorland-Spingarn Research Center, Howard University.

13. Photograph of Anita Thompson with Kristians Tonny and friends in Morocco, ca. 1932–1933. Moorland-Spingarn Research Center, Howard University.

14. Anita Thompson with her first "husband," the English aristocrat Charles Seller, in London. Moorland-Spingarn Research Center, Howard University.

15. Man Ray portrait of Anita Thompson, dated Paris, March 11, 1934. Copyright © 2012 Man Ray Trust / Artists Rights Society (ARS), NY/ADAGP, Paris. From the collections of the Moorland-Spingarn Research Center, Howard University.

16. Man Ray portrait of Anita Thompson, mid-1930s. Copyright © 2012 Man Ray Trust / Artists Rights Society (ARS), NY/ADAGP, Paris. From the collections of the Moorland-Spingarn Research Center, Howard University.

17. Anita Thompson modeling a Chanel evening dress while dancing with a male model, 1938. Moorland-Spingarn Research Center, Howard University. Photographer unknown.

18. Anita Thompson in a Chanel evening dress, 1938. Moorland-Spingarn Research Center, Howard University. Photographer unknown.

19. Anita Thompson modeling
her favorite Chanel dress, ca. 1938.
Moorland-Spingarn Research Center,
Howard University. Photographer
unknown.

20. Anita Thompson with her
friend Rose-Monique Bazin de
Jessey, at Le Montmarin, ca. 1939–
1940. Moorland-Spingarn Research
Center, Howard University.
Photographer unknown.

11

April 14, 1931. Alfonso XIII, King of Spain, abdicated and spent his first night of exile in Marseilles. I spent the same night there abdicating St.-Germain-des-Prés. I planned what seemed to be a pleasant route to get to Tangier. I was going to take the train from Paris to Marseilles, spend a restful night there and then catch the boat to Tangier in the morning. As it turned out, I got little rest due to an ugly encounter with an ugly little man who left a nasty taste in my mouth for a long time to come.

I was sitting in my compartment on the train, reading *The Well of Loneliness,* when I noticed a young, blonde German leering at me, apparently trying to attract my attention to his most unattractive self.[1] I tried to ignore him, but each time I glanced up, there he was staring at me. Finally, he came and sat beside me and asked what I thought of the book. I told him I found it interesting enough, but I couldn't see why the two women lovers in the book wanted to get married.

That seemed to be the end of the discussion, and I paid little attention to him. He did mention he was going to Algeria and asked if I knew of a hotel in Marseilles. Since the hotel where I was staying was certainly big enough to hold even the most repulsive of guests, I gave him the name. The name of the Hotel Nautique slipped out automatically because almost everyone we knew had stayed there. It was an old Trader Vic sort of home-away-from-home on whose walls hung paintings of some famous artists who, when broke, left a picture in lieu of the missing cash payment. I knew that some guests had left messages and jokes on the walls of the men's toilets. One of these Tonny was proud of because his patron Saint Parcin had signed it in answer to the owner's notice, "Do not pee on the floor" with "No! Pee on the ceiling." Of course, no "prophylactic American," as I was called (because of my tidy ways and refusal to experiment with opium, for example) would frequent the Hotel Nautique were it not known to be respectable and sanitary despite its private bathroom jokes.

I thought that had ended our conversation, but as I left the train station in Marseilles to look for a taxi, he ran to catch up with me. He put a hand on my shoulder, calling my attention to a young, handsome French woman who had a little boy by each hand, one about four and the other perhaps two years older. They were chattering away with great animation and were obviously a lovely family.

This horrible blonde monster grabbed me, pointed to the boys and said most lasciviously, "aren't they wonderful? Aren't they beautiful? I could just eat them alive." Thoroughly repulsed, I knocked his hand off my shoulder and went in another direction as fast as I could. I was so terrified of the obvious pederastic overtones of his remarks, the inference that since I had read *The Well of Loneliness,* I could understand anything, that when I got to my hotel room, I pulled the huge chest across the door. I could barely sleep that night, fearing the monster would come through the transom after me. Why I thought he would want me after drooling over the little boys, I don't know, but the whole idea was so frightening, I couldn't close my eyes. As I later discovered, Morocco had its share of European men chasing after Arab boys, but little of what I saw there ever disgusted me so thoroughly as my encounter in Marseilles.

In any event, I arrived in Morocco unmolested. As planned, I went to the house of Claude McKay, where I intended to stay until I could get a place of my own. His house was typically Arab in style, a square building around an open court built of native stone or adobe brick covered with plaster. Ceramic tiles covered the floors and ran halfway up the walls. The furniture was very simple. Mattresses on the floor were thrown out into the open air daily by the houseboy, who would scrub the whole house and then dump the dirty water out into the street.

Sitting on one of these mattresses, one would clap his hands and the houseboy would roll in a table, usually only a foot or so high, made of white wood, scrubbed like the top of a butcher's table with sand and tomato or lemon until it had a kind of peach fuzz finish, as clean as you could possibly imagine.

I enjoyed this new simple life. There was no electricity, so we used candles. Water was brought into the house from a common well in the neighborhood. The kitchen had a charcoal stove, and the cookware was made of baked clay. All the food was slowly and carefully prepared and was usually delicious.

Particularly appealing was the smell of fresh round loaves of bread baking in the charcoal ovens. The bread, leavened by allowing a clove of garlic to germinate in a small amount of flour before forming the loaves, when needed would often be carried on a board balanced on the head of a servant to the community oven. The servants would all wait in line and pay the man with the oven a few sous for the baking charcoal. The odor of burning charcoal and baking bread filled the air with a delightful scent that mingled with that of the many flowers in the patios and climbing walls.

The Arabs encased themselves in bulky clothing to protect their skin from the hot sun. The women in particular would be completely hidden in what appeared to be a bedspread, with only their eyes peeking out over a soft handkerchief. Their hair was covered by a silk scarf and the kaftan could not be seen. The men wore a djalaba, a hand-woven long woolen costume with a hood that could cover their heads. If the weather was particularly bad, they might cover this with a burnoose. On their head, they wore a fez. If the fez was wound around with a turban, my fatima told me, it meant the wearer had been to Mecca.

Claude McKay said he planned to become a Moslem, and though he continued to wear European clothing, he did sport a fez and took on many of the Arab customs. His decision may have been influenced by the fact that he had a wife in Jamaica whom he seemed unable or unwilling to divorce. It certainly didn't prevent him from proposing right and left to every woman he met, possibly hoping to follow the Arab custom of having up to four wives, providing he could afford to set up four separate households. Although Claude was a nice person, I was not attracted to him as a man. Aside from his being too fat for me, I felt that perhaps there was a deeper reason for his being in North Africa that had nothing to do with his writing, that of many of the other European men there, an interest in boys.

While he and I got along during the few weeks I stayed with him, we disagreed as we had in Paris over our attitudes towards blackness. He felt most strongly that anyone who had black blood should be Africanized. In Paris, for instance, anytime we went anywhere together, he asked me to mat up my hair, which was about the only way I could have looked African. That was his idea of how to take care of the "problem." It was not my idea. I argued in Morocco as I had in Paris that there were already too many different races and nationalities, and it was far past time we all got together to be one family. The debate between us was never resolved, and after three weeks I found a house of my own in the Arab neighborhood between the Grand Soco and the Petit Soco, not far from the Minza Hotel.

There I copied from my neighbors the Arab style of furnishing and cooking. I tried to learn as much as I could, and I became quite friendly with the women, even though we were obliged to communicate in sign language and smiles. I went into their homes for all their celebrations, feast days, marriages, circumcisions and other ceremonies. I enjoyed their company very much.

Sometimes I dressed in the Arab woman's manner to go shopping with my fatima. It is great fun to amble about town, through the spice-scented narrow market streets, past the sidewalk cafes— enjoyed by men only—in and out of shops, gazing at everything and everybody from behind the veil that revealed only one's eyes, so heavily shaded with charcoal that no one could guess one's identity. Any woman in native dress but wearing no veil was recognized as a prostitute. Men spat on the sidewalk when she passed. I was told that no more than one out of three of them was Arab—they were mostly Spanish.

Children ran through the streets, around the café tables—hid sometimes under the chairs and tables—then reported the conversations that were not heard by their mothers or other women interested in business transactions or gossip exchanged among the men. Women's "lib" always has and always will exist!

I enjoyed the anonymity of the veil; it is more pleasant, more comfortable, than being gaped at, singled out and judged—often criticized for "that old (or new) dress or hairdo" in the minds of friends I met in our "modern, civilized" thoroughfare. But there is more than costume involved in changing cultures. No chance of my becoming an Arab.

There weren't many Europeans there at the time. Those that were, mostly retired English colonists, often got together at the bar of the Minza after collecting the mail in Petit Soco. It was there that I met an acquaintance of Edward Westermarck, the noted anthropologist, who was in North Africa gathering material on Arab customs, myths and stories.

As it was, my own writing was not going very well. I was working in a haphazard way to get together the story of my family. Having no documents to work from, I was forced to fill in what was going on with my own impressions. It was turning out to be a stream of consciousness thing that was so baffling it would have put both Gertrude Stein and James Joyce out of business. It didn't make much sense, even to me, so I was quite ready to drop the effort when I went to meet Mr. Westermarck.

We got along splendidly. I was able to help him in his work by bringing him information I gathered from my Arab neighbors. In exchange, he let me borrow from his great library books I had always meant to read, many of which had been recommended to me by friends in Hollywood or New York. There was Marx's *Das Kapital, Varieties of Religious Experience* by William James, Spengler's *Decline of the West,* and Freud's basic works. I became a voracious reader, devouring all the books I'd never had time to read before and turning myself into a "real scholar."

Of course, this scholarly interlude was not destined to last very long. The peace was disrupted most explosively by the appearance of Tonny, who dashed into Tangier with a great burst of energy. He was in and out of the Minza, tearing Paul Bowles and Aaron Copland from their work when he could and having a great time in the exciting atmosphere among the Arabs in the Socos. As if to further prevent me from working, a young man came up to me one day while I was waiting for Tonny at the Minza. He introduced himself as a friend of Djuna Barnes and said she had asked him to look me up. "Ah'm Charles Henri Ford," he said with a pretty Southern drawl.[2] So another American expatriate joined the club.

At home, my fatima was rather unusual. She was over six feet tall and strong as a soccer player and she never spoke a word to me but took the money she needed for the market, cooked what she liked (always good) and—when she scrubbed the house—she simply picked me up from the mattress where I was often stretched out reading, dropped me onto another sofa, washed the floor, replaced my mattress and threw me back onto it.

And so, there I was again in contact with the St.-Germain-des-Prés crowd. From then on, my life in Tangier was complicated by the involvements, the gossip, the activities, the old and new friends, echoing my life in Paris and putting an end to both my scholarly and writing aspirations.

One of my new friends was Angelita Sarcas, an attractive little middle-aged woman with blonde hair and blue eyes. Her father owned the Grand Hotel, the first large hotel in Tangier, and her husband was a wealthy French naval officer whose family had lived in Morocco for many generations. He owned, among other things, the fields, the wheat that grew in them and the mill that ground the wheat for the entire community. This left Angelita quite well off, and she had a delightful, gay life. She loved to show off her Patou dresses, some of which dated back prior to the First World War. She also had a fine collection of Persian rugs, but when she unrolled them for me to see, I couldn't make out the design for the millions of fleas living in them, jumping up and down in clouds that deformed the patterns.

She told me she owned a palace, too, although she did not live in it. She said she had acquired it from a young Arab who had inherited it from his father and then ran up huge gambling debts in Monte Carlo. He gave her the palace in exchange for paying off his debts.

I decided I had to see this place for myself. It turned out indeed to be a palace. The front part had large arched windows looking out on Gibraltar. The floors were covered with large squares of black and white marble, and the walls were covered with inlaid mosaics of many bright and beautiful colors. To the rear of the main section was a patio with a fountain and delightful night-blooming flowers. There was also an apartment that had been the quarters of the man of the house, quite as large as the house itself, over a conservatory. The women lived in the seraglio in the front.

The apartment was also paved with marble blocks, as was the connecting terrace that looked out over the straits. The building was on a high peninsula called the Marchand leading down to the Straits of Gibraltar. There were forty acres in all of the estate, and tenant farmers living on the property grew everything from potatoes to artichokes and all the many kinds of fruits that grow in that part of the world. Well, I always wanted to live in a palace, so I persuaded Mrs. Sarcas to move there and rent me the back part that looked towards the town. Our quarters were connected by a corridor running the length of the patio across the second story. I was always delighted when our paths crossed. Angelita had been born in Tangier and knew a great deal about Arab life. I also learned a lot from the tenant farmers, the fatimas and the gate-keeper, Awami, whose little house was right under my bedroom window.

My fatima was very young and left in my charge by her mother, who told me to discipline her. One day I saw her cross the ravine that marked the west end of the property with a small stream. Aisha had all her clothes on top of her head to keep them dry. I noticed a shepherd on the opposite hill, tending his sheep, play-ing a flute and watching my 16-year-old charge. When she ap-proached me in the patio I just smacked her face and said she must have known the man saw her. Frightened, surprised, horrified, she cried through her tears: "That doesn't matter! All derrieres look alike. He didn't see my face." I was ashamed of my reaction but did not understand her point of view and told her so.

Awami and his wife Aisha (another Aisha) had three children. From my window I could watch them as they went about their daily routines. Aisha spent a great deal of time sitting outside preparing the food. She would sit on a straw pad on the ground, grinding couscous or making bread, all very slowly, with the children running all about her.

We lived on the outer edge of town, near the Arab cemetery. This was a source of constant fascination to me. Burials were al-ways accompanied by loud singing, and afterwards, food was left at the graveside. This attracted beggars who, having no place else to sleep, spent their nights in the cemetery, eating the food and sleeping by the graves. We had to cross the cemetery to get into town. This was a little frightening, especially at night, because one could suddenly stumble on a sunken grave or be assaulted by

a beggar seeking a handout. In their white robes, they were quite
spooky.

Usually we went into town on one of Awami's donkeys, across
the cemetery and down the hill past the enormous mosque. The
mosque was attended by most of the townspeople on Fridays, the
Arab Sabbath. One of the members of the congregation was
Abdul Aziz, a son of the late sultan of Morocco, Moulay Hassan,
and his arrival would be heralded with great fanfare. Horsemen
with beautiful red and gold robes preceded him with their trum-
pets blaring. Then his car, perhaps a 1930 Dodge touring car, appeared, with black Senegalese guards hanging onto the running
board. He was seated alone on the back seat, with an immobile
face looking straight ahead, wooden-looking yet nonetheless
handsome in his white robes, red fez and dignified air. When he
left the car, the crowd pressed in to kiss the hem of his djalaba. He
would not slow his progress to the mosque, but he touched each
admirer and suppliant on the shoulder as they came up to him. If
he spoke to any one of them, one could not know it by a movement of his lips in a carved amber mask.

With three religions and thirteen nations ruling over the lives
of the people of Tangier, it seemed that almost every day was a
holiday of one sort or another. Every week there were three Sab-
baths: Friday for the Arabs, Saturday for the Jews and Sunday for
the Christians. We celebrated the Fourth of July for the Americans, the 14th of July for the French and every king's and queen's
birthday and a multitude of fasts, feasts and celebrations. We never
knew when we got onto the donkey to go into town if the banks
would be open or not.

Not that it was all that important. Nobody had much money,
and nothing cost much either. The $50 to $60 I had to live on

each month was a small fortune. I paid only $4 a month for my apartment, fifty cents a week for a fatima to help me and fifty cents a week for all the meat she and I could eat. Gauloises Bleu cigarettes cost five cents a pack and Scotch $1.25 a bottle of the best from Gibraltar, within rowing distance.

Most of the native population was very poor, living mostly by barter. They loved bargaining so much that a good part of the shopping day was spent arguing over prices. I became quite adept at this and soon was joining in with the others, listening to the salesman ask for twice what he expected to get and offering half what I expected to pay, arguing and snapping our fingers in each other's face, until we finally came to an agreement at the middle. When the argument was over and the settlement reached, we both laughed, touched our right hand to our forehead, lips and heart, and salaamed. We'd then be great friends, all ready to start over again the next day.

Whatever money the Arabs did get, they put into precious stones, gold, or silver, which they kept locked up in chests. The poorest would have a nickel teapot, while those a little better off might have several of these and perhaps some brass trays. This was wealth to them, and the women spent hours shining their metal objects and showing them off to visitors. The middle-class women's bracelets, anklets and necklaces showed off their prosperity.

The Arabs were forbidden by the Koran to charge or pay interest on money, which was one of the reasons they kept their wealth in tangible goods like the brass trays, jewels, rugs, land, horses, clothing, et al. This prohibition against interest was one of the sources of disagreement between the Arabs and Jews of the community. The Arabs did not hesitate to borrow money from the Jews, particularly since they had no intention of paying interest.

The Jewish lender, knowing this, had the Arab sign a promissory note, including the interest, each of them knowing full well there would be a big fight when it came time to pay. And there were plenty of these fights, with horrible cursing and snapping of fingers to the end of each other's nose: "Your mother was a snake!" "Your father a donkey!" If the Jew won, he got his interest, often as much as ten percent. If the Arab won, he gave back only the principal. In these fights, neither touched the other's nose.

Moroccans lived as much as European laws permitted by the laws of the Koran. They also had to obey the laws of the countries governing them. Tangier was truly an international town, governed by thirteen legations, thirteen different countries. There were British, American, French, Italian, Spanish, Dutch, Belgian and more. I can't remember them all. They had what they called a "tribunal mix," a court in which four or five judges sat for crimes against European codes. Crimes against Islamic law were tried in the Mendubia / Arab court.

Slavery, too, was a very real part of life, though quite different from that of slavery in the Western world. The concubines were purchased by wealthy Arabs from dealers who brought them up from Senegal and black Africa. At the time, a girl brought 400 francs, a boy, 800 francs. These youngsters grew up in the homes of their masters. Their treatment and their lives were governed by Islamic law. Unlike slavery in the West, the Koran dictated that these slaves were to be part of the home. They ate the same food and, like other members of the family, had a complete change of clothing on each of the eight big feast days of the year. Grown up, the girls sometimes became concubines of the male members of the family, giving the impression that the men had many wives. In fact, Mohammed was the only man who ever had more than four wives at one time, so my neighbors told me. The children of any slave women and the men of the family became legitimate children, and the treatment of all the workers was supposed to be kind and merciful. A slave who felt he had been mistreated had only to go to the mosque or to the Mendubia—court of Islamic law—and complain to the authorities, who would see to it that either the mistreatment were ended or would free the slave or turn him over to someone else.

Yes, things were quite different from the life I had known, but I wanted to immerse myself in the Arab way of life. The rich Arabs I knew were genteel and dignified, the poor often childlike—all friendly and jovial. I became friends with a group of young men in Hailal, an organization composed mostly of older men, well-established merchants, lawyers and other professionals, who had the responsibility of teaching younger men in the arts, business, the professions and sports. They taught theater, drama and literature as well as their jobs. They also trained a soccer team and a polo team. Courteously—in my presence—they spoke French or Spanish.

Speaking, supposedly out of my hearing, they mentioned Abd el-Krim, and I understood that they expected to free from his confinement in Madagascar their hero of the mid-twenties of the Rif war against Spain—whom they defeated from the cliffs near Ceuta—and against the French who came up behind them and captured their leader.[3] Some of the young members of Hailal (which is the Arab name of Morocco) were being educated in European and American colleges. I trust one of them has become Morocco's Yamani. Under the surface there was indeed a political movement growing, particularly among the young men who were looking to be free of the French.

My involvement with Hailal was non-political, however. I was invited to help out with a production of Shakespeare's *As You Like It*. When the costumes arrived from Egypt, they couldn't tell the men's clothing from the women's because they looked more or less alike to them. The skirts were obvious, but the hat and other details were hard to distinguish. They asked me to separate the costumes for them, to help everyone dress for the show and particularly to help make up the young boys who would be playing the female parts. Girls were not allowed in the theater, much less on the stage. (One day years later, when I was walking home with W. H. Auden after his class at the New School—I passed his house in Cornelia Street to reach mine in Morton Street—he told me that in Shakespeare's time the same custom prevailed.)

As a result of my work with them, the men declared me to be an honorary member of Hailal. They didn't treat me as they would a woman, they treated me as they would a young man from a strange land, but my membership was considered to be satisfactory to all. They didn't even find me attractive, and those who liked me called me "sugar cane" (canne à sucre), others just "cane"—too skinny to contain any sugar.

My oldest Arab friends were the Snoussis, who lived near us on the Marchand, our plateau that had once been a village, I guess—a large square with its own mosque and four sides of mansions (or small palaces) now occupied by rich Arabs and a few Europeans. We became friends quickly because all of the family spoke French. It was a very distinguished family. The father had been counselor to Mullay Hassan, the last sultan of Morocco. The father of all these Snoussis died at the age of 95, leaving a multitude of widows / wives and a whole tribe of children, ranging in age from fifteen to their seventies. His last widow was thirty-seven years old and came from Damascus—"home of the loveliest." She was well-educated and spoke better French than I did.

She invited me to take part in the many ceremonies at the Snoussis' home. I was there for the party celebrating the circumcision of one of their grandsons. The little boy sat in a huge brass bed with silk brocade draped all around it. While he recovered from the shock, the women sang to him and carried him tidbits of food, and slaves danced on the patio. Most of the slaves were Senegalese and there was much shouting and banging on drums.

There was another marvelous party to celebrate a wedding. On these occasions I dressed in my Arab silk dress and sat with the others around the edge of the huge room, my legs folded under me. The bride entered, resplendent in white satin and twenty to thirty strings of pearls that started at her neck and went down in rows to her waist, forming a breastplate of pearls. The belt of her silken dress was at least five inches wide and embroidered in pearls, diamonds, rubies and emeralds. She was not a young woman, and I think perhaps this was her second or third marriage, but she was greeted with great joy and the usual "yi-yi-yi" cry of all the women present.

Marriage was another custom which differed greatly from the American notion. The Koran allowed each man to have four wives. The only stipulation was that in order to have them all at the same time, he must keep them in separate houses, as the woman is mistress of her own household.

None of the complexities of marriage rules was understood by one particular American woman who arrived with her heart set on marrying a handsome Arab, probably with some crazy notion she had gotten from watching Rudolph Valentino in *The Sheik*.

The first handsome Arab she saw was the guide she hired to take her out as far as possible into the countryside. There she let him know she was willing to be his mistress, but she would also like to be his wife. She was a retired nurse and told him she had enough money to take care of both of them. The guide, a young man who, like the other Arabs, was not attracted to European or American women with their naked faces, open dresses and masculine behavior, declined the offer.

Knowing that I had many Arab friends, the woman cornered me and explained that perhaps the man didn't understand what she wanted. She wanted me to make it clear to him she knew he had a wife but she was willing to buy the second house so she could be his second wife. I explained to her that maybe he had turned down her offer because he didn't want her. This made her indignant, and she stormed to the office of the American consul, Donald Bigelow, and told him the man had attacked her. The consul called me in and asked if I knew about the case. I explained what I knew about it, and he called the nurse back in, told her to stop her foolishness and said if he heard of any more such stories she would have to leave Tangier.

Americans weren't the only thorns in the sides of the North Africans. Complaints against the French were frequent. Although many French colonists had lived there for generations, they weren't all from the best of families. Many were poorly educated and acted about the same way uneducated people do anywhere. I often heard complaints from Ibrahim Snoussi, a young handsome man who was intelligent and spoke French well. He was a judge, the youngest at the Mendubia, the Arab court.

Ibrahim came into contact with French civil servants all day at the Mendubia. He complained of their rudeness and their "bar-

baric" behavior. A Frenchman, he said, would come into the office in the morning and say something like, "That wife of mine made awful coffee this morning. I don't know what I'm going to do with her." Then he would proceed to talk about other women members of his family in a derogatory manner that an Arab would find positively heathenish. An Arab never mentioned the name of a woman in his family. Even if you knew someone's mother or wife or sister were ill, you could only say, "how is your household today?"

The Arabs found plenty of reasons to dislike the French in many of these day-to-day details, and the French, in their turn, considered themselves superior to the Arabs and acted in a condescending manner. So, my never-ending attempts to get people together were once more a failure. I was never able to convince any Arab that the French had something to offer or vice versa. All I could do was to immerse myself in both cultures and hope they wouldn't break out in open warfare while I was there.

During the last few months that I lived in Morocco, I accepted the devoted help of a slave. Her name was Wamba and I guessed that she may have been the daughter of one of the Snoussi men whose large house was indeed crowded with legitimate and illegitimate women and children. Giving her and her four-year-old daughter to me—beside the friendly intention of the gift—may have been motivated by the desire to lessen the cost of the household.

Wamba came into my home like a newly adopted happy puppy and became so entirely mine that I was as reluctant to send her back to the Snoussis—when I returned to Europe—as she was to let me go without her. How could I explain owning a slave to questioning strangers?

At the bar of the Minza, there was an ongoing discussion about Arab customs among the retired Europeans. The bartender, Dean, who called himself Egyptian but laughed more like Harlem, would always tell the visitors that I was the authority on the subject. "Who knows any Arabs?" It was a source of great pleasure to me because it gave me a chance to advance my cause of explaining one group to another. I would go on in great detail, trying to make them understand the customs, the four-wife system and the relationship of the young men to the older men. This always interested them, for they seemed to think there was a constant homosexuality going on of a sort that would have been considered vicious at home.

It was not so. In Tangier at the time, the boys went to school from the age of five to about thirteen, getting their basic education and learning the Koran. But at the time when European boys would be going to high school, the Arab boys would be made apprentices to the trades they would be following for the rest of their lives. If a boy was to become a cobbler, then a shoemaker would teach him the trade. If he were going to be a lawyer, then he went into a lawyer's office. Whatever the job, trade or profession, he would start to learn immediately from an older man.

It was quite possible for the relationship between the older men and their apprentices to include more than teaching a trade. Women were not considered as sensuous objects but rather the bearers of children and the mothers of families. The men who were training boys took it for granted that if they wanted to fondle them, it was permissible, much as it had been in ancient Greece or Rome. But this relationship changed as soon as the boy became a man and started his own trade. I never saw an adult Arab acting in an effeminate way. I never saw one over the age of twenty who would be mistaken for what we would consider to be a homosexual, a gay boy. Whatever passivity they had in them was pretty well outgrown by the time they were out of their teens. The former apprentices would become teachers of new boys, and whatever fondling went on would be initiated by them.

Although the Arabs in general were disgusted by the European patterns of homosexuality, there were always a few depraved or hungry young men who would be willing to accommodate the Europeans for money. One of them was a guest at one of my parties. I had made the mistake of inviting a Britisher who said he was a naval officer interested in the mores of non-Europeans. When he asked to be allowed to come to one of the parties I gave for my friends in Hailal, I let him join us. Later, when I thought everyone had left, I went to see if Awami had closed the porte-cochère. I found my Britisher coming out of the conservatory, where he had spent some time with one of my guests. Both were rather embarrassed meeting me. I suppose there must have been more young men than I knew of who were willing to go with the European men. Otherwise the Europeans would have found themselves without partners.

Abdul, one such young man suspected of being a prostitute, drew the attention of an American writer who had found him in Fez being "terribly mistreated" by the French owner of the pension where he was staying. The writer, Paul Bowles, a friend of mine, decided to adopt Abdul and take him back to France. He brought the boy to my house and asked me to put him up until the papers were prepared to allow Abdul to come to Paris. Abdul was a nice looking boy, fifteen or sixteen years old and very polite. I took him in until I heard that my friend was ready to receive him. Abdul then went off to Paris where the American showed him off as his prize.

For a while, I heard that everything was going well. But then Abdul began bringing home gifts he said had been given to him by a "very nice old man." The "very nice old man" was a source of great concern and a puzzle to Paul, but he didn't find out who it was until he took Abdul with him to a photographic exhibition. Abdul dashed across the floor of the studio and pointed to a portrait of André Gide, saying, "That's the nice old man who has been giving me presents. He has asked me to come and live with him and be his doorman."

I no longer pursued Paris gossip with much interest, as I was quite busy working as a guide for tourists who stopped in Tangier and wanted to know something about the country. This allowed me to travel to the interior, at their expense, and see much of the land. On one such trip, I took an Englishman, his daughter and business partner to Fez. We stayed at the Palais Jamais and saw Fez during the latter part of the fast of Ramadan. Fez is a beautiful city, set in a saucer with a wall around the edge. The Palais Jamais was one of the palaces built on the wall, and from there one could look down over the city where there were some three hundred minarets.

During Ramadan, Moslems cannot eat, drink or smoke during the day. They have to wait until the sun goes down. So every evening, we could hear a little melody being played from every minaret in the city to let the people know the fast was over for the day. Immediately after this, one could hear the sound of doors slamming and the pitter-patter of bare feet as the children ran through the streets carrying food to their fathers in the shops or offices where they had been all day without eating. Sometimes feasting and music went on all night. I don't know when anyone slept. When the new moon appeared on the horizon, ending the fast of Ramadan, the cry of "yi-yi-yi" went out all over the town, as a chorus of birds singing for joy.

But even in Fez there was something foreign to cut through the charm of the city. On another trip with an English woman, we spotted a dead cat in the street, which was a river of dirty soapy water because of the Arab custom of washing out their homes and emptying the water onto the street. This sight didn't bother us, but as we passed a group of American tourists, a voice with a Midwestern accent boomed out: "Fez would be such a beautiful place if it wasn't for all these dirty A-rabs." I pretended not to hear, and my client waited until we were out of earshot before turning to me and chiding, "Your compatriots!"

Being a guide was not my only occupation. In Tangier I had a little business. I ran a small shop right on the street that passengers from the cruise ships had to pass on their way to the Petit Soco. I found it interesting and very rewarding to go to the Arab market and buy everything I could find that was nicely shaped and colored. It could be leather or clay or hand-woven materials, anything I thought would make a nice addition to a European home. The shop was decorated like an Arab room, with mattresses on the floor, which was covered with a Moroccan rug. Mosaics ran halfway up the wall. There were several chests and a few large shelves to hold whatever I had picked up at the market. At a round table in the center of the floor my fatima sat to brew mint tea all day long.

When the tourists came by, some peeked their heads inside to say, "What's in there?" I thought it was pretty obvious it was a shop, since there was a beautiful wrought iron sign with an Arab on horseback holding a gift over his head. The name of the shop was El Hadia, which means The Gift, and there was a translation in many languages on the side of the wall. Finally, a few courageous ones would come in. They would sit on the mattresses as best they could and sip tea and ask to see the merchandise from the chests or the shelves. I had learned well how to conduct a business transaction. There were no prices on anything, and I told all my customers they could pay whatever they felt was a fair price. This always seemed to please them, so they offered what they thought were ridiculously low prices, and I always grabbed them up because they were at least a hundred times what I had paid on the Arab market.

One of my first customers was a newlywed couple from England. They were not very rich, but they had enough money to buy the materials to furnish an Arab room in their Norfolk home. I sent miles of hand-woven material and good rugs and brass trays and leather poufs very simply decorated. They wrote to me as the things arrived and told me how successful the decorating was. They also sent me customers, and so my shop thrived. But it was also the kind of business that I could always leave, shutting it up for a week to go off to the interior and act as a guide again. Great variety and great fun.

I remember two experiences in particular while I had the shop. One was the passing of the Graf zeppelin.[4] It went over Tangier, so low that standing on the street in front of the shop, I could see people in it. It was a very exciting moment. Another less agreeable experience, one which frightens me still when I think of it, clearly illustrates the difference in moral attitudes of different cultures and how deeply one is prejudiced in sexual matters. I stood by my closed shop one evening, leaning against the door waiting for a young friend, Idriss. He was going up to the house to have dinner with Tonny and me. It was dark, but there was a street light and I could see fairly well. Before Idriss arrived, a little boy who was perhaps five or six years old came out of nowhere and greeted me politely. I answered him as I would a child, but he kept getting closer and closer and finally put his head against my hip and started stroking my thigh in such a way that I became frightened. The sexual element in his behavior was strong and terrifying. I gave him a whack and sent him on his way, probably with a little money and undoubtedly quite bewildered by my reaction.

I was so upset, I didn't tell Idriss or Tonny or anyone else about the experience. It reminded me of my encounter with the leering German on the train to Marseilles, and neither episode has ever left my mind entirely. The only comfort I could get came when I heard that an Englishman who had sexually assaulted a little Arab boy who was not a prostitute had been caught by the boy's father. The father called out all the men of the village to punish the Englishman by going over him one after the other in a manner that left him uncomfortable and not anxious to go after an Arab boy again.

It wouldn't have helped any for me to speak with Tonny about my feelings. He laughed at me because of my scruples that made me disapprove of pederasty. Although he never spoke of it, it was quite possible he had experienced some homosexual activity in his adolescence, though I don't think he ever returned to it. A few years later he married a delightful young woman and they lived "happily ever after." He laughed at my high moral tone just as he laughed at most bourgeois customs. Certainly he did not like the parties at the legations that I enjoyed, and if he would go with me, he would spend the whole time jumping around the floor and making fun of the whole idea of social dancing. So it wasn't until Tonny went back to Paris that I could enjoy the parties, usually in the company of an Italian officer who was handsome, a beautiful dancer and a gentleman of the old school.

Vincenzo had been a cavalry officer before Mussolini came into power and was working in Tangier as the education officer at the Italian legation. He had exquisite manners and I found him to be a most agreeable partner. When he was in a happy mood, Vincenzo would sing a song in Italian. Not speaking the language, I can only guess that the song had something to do with a woman's heart quickly forgetting and returning once more to love. But I can assure anyone who thinks all Italians can sing like opera stars, that they most definitely do not! Vincenzo was strictly a johnny-one-note whose voice rang out with great gusto and no musical quality whatsoever. Anyway, he was always gallant and we had a lot of fun together, but we were not in love, and, as with the German baron in Paris, as soon as Tonny arrived, usually unannounced, Vincenzo flew out of my life.

My love life was like that then, lots of variety but no real substance. Yet I was not unhappy about it, and I did not even resent my mother's writing that she had told Ralph Bunche, when he said he was going to North Africa to get me, that I was in Algeria instead of Morocco. There was no point in resenting anything my mother did anyway. She did whatever she wanted to do, which included interfering in my life and in my brother's life. He had just married an Irish gal with whom he had lived for several years, a poorly educated movie extra of whom my mother most heartily disapproved. They finally married and moved to San Francisco just to get away from Mother's continuous interference.

I was far enough away to do as I pleased, and I certainly could not control anything my mother did or said in Los Angeles. Probably it was better in the long run she hadn't told Ralph where to find me. Certainly if we had married, his public life would have been far less successful than the life he had with Ruth, who was the perfect wife and companion to him. I would have been quite opinionated and argumentative, I am sure, and he would have wound up as Ambassador to Russia or serving time in the federal penitentiary for having killed a willful, strong-headed wife!

For a short time I was in love with Mrs. Sarcas' son Raymonde. He was in the military service and seemed to me to be the epitome of a Foreign Legionnaire. I was drawn to his poetic nature and far-away expression, just as I was always attracted to men I felt I was going to be able to save from drowning. Mrs. Sarcas, who boasted of a large number and variety of lovers, nonetheless clung to the idea of her son marrying someone much purer—and richer—than me. While she and I were great pals, she didn't want me as a daughter-in-law. Of course, her opposition only served to make Raymonde and me feel our romance was much heavier than it probably was.

I was very fond of many associates in Tangier. I cannot describe them all but it was among them that I discovered counterparts to many I had known in other countries, learning that fez, fedora, derby, straw boater, or cap only distinguish nationalities, not personalities. I found the same characteristics in an L.A. high school student, a tap dancer in New York, a shopkeeper in Rabat. I concluded that there may be a limited number of personality types scattered all over the globe. One might guess that body shapes define individuals more than do family or national influences.

I had no trouble forgetting Raymonde, Vincenzo, Tonny, or anyone else for that matter, the day my Prince Charming arrived. He showed up at my shop, sent there by the newlywed couple whose room I had decorated. He was all that one imagines as the perfect British officer. He looked very much like James Bellamy in the "Upstairs, Downstairs" television series. He had been an officer, Sandhurst 1917, in the Indian Army and had spent ten years in India.[5] He now lived in London, a retired captain. When he came to Tangier in 1931, he was, I believe, a political agent. That may have been why he was sent to me, as he asked me to tell him everything I could about Arab life. I was very willing to oblige, and our friendship went along on intellectual lines for some time before we became conscious of a strong mutual attraction.

Charles was good looking in the movie-star version of an English officer. He certainly was attractive to me because of his breeding, the way he spoke, the tone of his voice and his bearing. He was tall, slightly stooped, and walked slowly, usually with his right arm swinging in front of him. I always thought he was hearing bagpipes play when he walked with such dignity and charm. He had deep blue eyes, dark hair and an olive complexion. He was somewhat Italian in appearance, though he was a Yorkshireman. He dressed very carefully, but without any special show of the care. His linen was starched where it should be and his ties were always inconspicuous regimental and school ties. His shoes were always shined, and he said all he had learned at Repton, his public school, was how to shine shoes.

It was his irreverence and opposition to jingoism that attracted me to Charles in the first place. That plus his discomfort with the military life and a desire to be a poet or a writer appealed very much to me. He was interested in literature, had read all the Russians in his youth (in 1931 admired Ernest Hemingway), but his mother had forced him to go to Sandhurst. He had graduated in the class of 1917 and given the option of going to France or India, he opted for the latter, joining the 37th Dogras.[6] It was a vein of sadness that I felt in him that attracted me, as ever the big sister willing and wanting to take over such a glamorous little brother. And somewhere in my unconscious was the assurance that my mother would have considered him the perfect match, the perfect "gentleman" although public school men did not use the term for themselves and each other but "educated men." Oh, had she only married him instead!

12

It is probable that among the "civilized" people of the world, compatibility is determined by what the French call the "cerebral" in sex. When one imagines himself to be with the perfect partner, for whatever rational or neurotic reason, one relaxes and cooperates, so that the result is one of mutual satisfaction. My role in my relationship with Charles was that of the exotic woman. Perhaps he had wanted an East Indian girl and hadn't been able to have one, or perhaps his experience with dull white women had given him the impression that an exotic woman would be the perfect sex partner. As for me, I responded to my need to be respected, to the knowledge that Charles was chivalrous and that he would protect me when I needed protection. These were the gentlemanly attributes of my father and my brother that I had always sought in other men. In them, Charles did not disappoint me. I went into his arms, his bed, with complete confidence, and he handled me as he would have a precious Stradivarius, playing the tunes we both loved.

Our lightning affair, progressing from our first meeting to our marriage, took all of three weeks. Charles had unburdened himself from his first wife, an Irish Catholic girl he had met in India, in a Reno divorce. They had quarreled over many things, apparently, but the split came over her insistence that they have as many children as possible. This was anathema to Charles. His income was only 1,200 pounds a year, and it would be quickly exhausted. Of course a man of his background and education could not be expected to work and get more income, and thus, the divorce. As a Catholic, his wife, Sally, was unwilling to recognize the divorce. I was perfectly willing to recognize it, however, and we found an Episcopal priest (or someone who claimed to be one) in Tangier who agreed to marry us. So we took him at his word and were wed.

At Christmastime in 1932, I was off to London. Charles had gone on ahead of me to open the house while I remained to pack up and say goodbye to my friends. There was one particular sad note in leaving. I had become quite attached to Wamba and her lovely daughter. When I was leaving for London, however, I had to take her back to the Snoussis. I thanked them but explained I couldn't take her with me. They in turn explained the situation to Wamba. But when my luggage arrived at the ship, out jumped Wamba. She insisted that she belonged to me and that where I would go, she would go also. I had a great deal of difficulty getting hold of Ibrahim Snoussi to take her home, and my heart was deeply touched by the separation.

While I was living in England, I often heard the story about the headline in the London newspaper that read: "Fog on Channel; Continent Isolated." The insular attitude really struck me when I landed, laden with brass trays, hand-woven woolens for drapes and many of the things I had liked in Morocco. The customs officer looked over my wares and said, "Where's this stuff coming from?"

"Morocco," I explained.

"Where's Morocco?" he wanted to know.

"It's in Africa."

"Well," he said, waving me on, "take it along. Africa
belongs to us." My return to civilization.

I felt from the start that time was playing funny tricks with me.
In Morocco, I had been living in a world that was much like
Europe in the Middle Ages: the adherence to the laws of religion,
the feudal socio-economic system, the absence of machines, the
family roles, with the female as breeder and tender of the hearth
and the male as warrior, provider, lord and master.

All these were different in Europe, much different, and I had a
lot to learn, even perhaps how to speak again. Charles was always
accusing me of speaking too softly. It seems that many Americans
have a tendency to talk quite loudly, so that a "refined" American
speaks as softly as possible to appear more civilized. By now, my
speaking had apparently been modulated to the point of inaudi-
bility, for Charles would constantly shout at me, "For God's sake,
stop mumbling!" Being in love helped. Actually, the hardest thing
to get used to at first was the cold. Although it had been much the
same in Paris, the years in Morocco left me feeling all the more
chilly on my return to Europe. The houses were not well heated,
and there was quite a bit of dashing from one room to the next,
going from fireplace to fireplace.

Charles' home was a large, three-story house on Gloucester
Terrace between Lancaster Gate and Paddington Station. One
entered the ground floor, past the Doric columns over the marble
steps that characterized the facades of all the homes in the area.

On one side of the hall were the drawing room and the library, furnished just as his father had left it, in heavy leather, with a large Persian rug on the floor and red velvet drapes at the bay window over the street. Behind the library was an informal room that Charles allowed me to furnish to my own liking.

I had that room painted a cream color and added yellow chintz drapes, with wide stripes connected by ostrich plumes that went flying up the wall. The furniture I picked was light and gay, and the room took on the air of a sun parlor. The pictures I had brought from France were framed and put up on gold backgrounds. Before the fireplace in that room Charles and I spent many an hour playing chess. We could look out to the garden at the back of the house, a walled rectangular-shaped area with a hedge and ivy and a few flowers. It was home for our dogs, two Sealyhams, Sally and Peter, and a terrier, Jane.

The dogs were a delight. They were not often allowed in the house, but anywhere they were they were adorable. The Sealyhams had been purchased for me just before I came. Sally was bowlegged and not too bright. Peter had very straight front legs, and he was no whiz kid either. But they were loveable. Jane, an "Aberdeen Terrier," as the English called the breed, was much older. She had been in the family for a long time and was often in the house. She had belonged to Charles' father who had died several years previously.

The English had a great love for dogs, contrasting sharply with the indifference for animals in North Africa, where one could see English women running around trying to save dogs, donkeys, horses, sheep and goats from the cruelty of their owners. The British adored their pets, as characterized by a little dog cemetery in

Kensington Gardens a short walk from our home. It had little tombstones, and quite often one could see bunches of violets left on a grave by a grieving master or mistress.

In time, I grew to enjoy the English. There was so much for me to admire in Charles' "English" traits: his deep loyalty, his integrity, his insistence upon the truth and fair play. I also found out there was a great deal of pragmatism behind those ideals. It made sense, for instance, when Charles would say it pays to be honest. After all, when one pays one's debts, one gets more credit. He was even able to make an absurd sort of sense out of paying taxes, one which the French would have laughed at. Even as students in Paris we understood that it was simply "not French" to pay one's taxes. But the English dashed to pay their taxes as soon as possible.

I was surprised early in January soon after I arrived that we were going to the post office to pay our "radio tax." These and all other taxes Charles would rush off to pay when they came due, without waiting for a bill. He explained that it saved the government money. "They don't have to send out bills for the taxes. We all would wind up paying for the billing and the interest lost anyway. So it makes better sense to pay immediately and save money for everybody." Profit with honor from almost the only people I knew who truly respected their government.

My life soon fell into a comfortable routine. At about eight in the morning, there would be a knock at the door and in would come Stewart, the butler, a tall man who looked exactly like a movie butler. He was an ex-soldier who had been hired by Charles's father and was still part of the household. He was every bit the professional, in polished shoes and a green baize apron, carrying in the early morning tea, opening the curtains and delivering the newspapers and mail. Charles and I would sit in bed and have our tea, then get up to bathe and dress. Then we would answer the morning mail. I had to learn whom to call "Esq." and whom to address merely as "Mr." "Esq." was reserved for "educated men," those who had gone to a "public school," what we would call a private school, of which there were a great many in England. Much of the mail came from the solicitors telling about various matters of the estate. They helped govern Charles' money and made many of the decisions about what should be done with it.

I was delighted when they allowed me to convert a house that had been left to Charles into an apartment building. I had great fun working with the carpenters and other workmen who redid the house, dividing it into four apartments. In doing so, I ignored the fact that the house wasn't really ours. Charles' father only had a ninety-nine year lease on the place. It belonged to the Ecclesiastical Commissioners, who forbade converting their houses into apartments. But I went ahead anyway. We put a Welsh couple into the basement as tenants and rented all the floors above as apartments. They were rented to young couples, mostly professionals and civil servants. It worked out rather well.

The mail did not contain many personal letters. Charles' circle of friends was rather limited, mostly retired Army men. One of his best friends was Admiral Locke, who was much older than we. He was living in Portsmouth, where he had returned with his family. He had seldom seen his children in his service days, and he amused us with stories of his confusion in telling them apart now that they were grown. Another caller who dropped in often with his wife for Scotch and a chat was Colonel Hardy. He had been in the Indian Army with Charles.

Another dear friend was the woman who had been Charles' mistress during the time he had lived in the house by himself, from the time he retired in 1928 until now, 1932. She lived with her husband, who was home only at night, so she and Charles often spent their days together. Her name was Kay. She was a handsome, tall woman, almost as tall as Charles, who was over six feet. She had soft golden hair and a lovely English complexion. She knew that I knew she had lived with Charles, but we got on quite well. She even gave me delicate little hints on how to make him happy.

Sometimes the morning mail would contain a letter from Charles' mother in Yorkshire. She and Charles had never gotten along very well. She was a domineering woman, and he had been a reticent, sensitive young man. He was still rather shy, and his father had been of similar temperament, so his mother, who had been the superintendent of a hospital and was terribly efficient at running things, had enjoyed pushing them both around. For some reason she decided she liked me. She would pump me with questions that showed she thought her son was a nincompoop and wanted me to prove it. Since I was as headstrong as she, Charles let me read and answer her letters. She recognized that I was almost as much of a battle-axe as she, so we got along quite well. When we were together, Charles was out of danger of being devoured by either of us; we were busy devouring each other.

After the mail had been read and answered, it might be eleven o'clock and time for our "elevenses," more or less a breakfast of kippers and bacon and toast and tea and fruit. After that, we would go out to mail the letters and take the dogs to Hyde Park. We would walk until about one, then stop at a pub for meat pies and beer. Some days there would be shopping trips, with arguments over getting me dressed up in English tweeds and flat shoes. We would go to Harrods or to Charles' tailor or wine merchant or to Fortnam and Masons for delicacies to nibble on the way home.

Back home, it would be time for our afternoon nap. Our love-making was often in the afternoon. It was such a pleasant time. For me, Charles' love-making was like being played by a violinist, delicately. He was sensitive to my vibrations, and being not very aggressive, left open the possibility of my taking the initiative when I wanted to. Altogether, he was the most satisfactory lover I had ever had.

By four, it would be time to get up again, to have tea at one of the fireplaces. There was an informal living room that took up all of the second floor of the house, and we would often receive our guests there, have our tea, play chess, read or relax. The room was furnished with big comfortable sofas and chairs of no particular style. Some of them were covered in chintz, others in canvas. There were a few antiques, my brass trays and yards of hand-woven wool from Morocco to complete the décor. At six or so the butler would come in to find out our plans for dinner and the meals for the next day. He would bring with him our Scotch and sodas. Dinner would be at seven-thirty or eight. Afterwards, alone or with guests, we would return to the Scotch and soda, read, play chess or go out to the theater or the dog races.

Racing—horses and dogs—was the single sport of our leisure days. The races were important to Charles. Men of his class were not allowed to work, only invest their inheritance. To Charles, "investing" meant betting on the horses or the dogs. When we went to the continent, we would often go to Monte Carlo, where the betting would become really hectic, especially on roulette. And so I approach the less pleasant side of this ideal marriage. The gambling reminded me of the discomfort in my own home, the emotional strain of my mother's suspecting my father of betting. If it wasn't on the horses, it was on the stocks that he knew nothing about or the "Chinese lottery," a sort of numbers racket followed in Los Angeles.

Even more disagreeable than the gambling, however, was Charles' drinking habit. It seemed to have been part of his life since India. He once said that no officer was considered worth his salt if he could walk to bed. He had to be carried by his "boy." If that was a myth, it gave Charles grounds for drinking constantly. While it didn't affect his ordinary behavior much, there were times he would sink into a deep depression, almost suicidal. He would lock himself into a room and play sentimental music on the phonograph, listening and talking to himself. This would happen about once a week, and I found it frightening, especially since it seemed I couldn't do anything about it.

Charles had an underlying strain of regret and fear that stemmed from his having opted for India in 1917 after graduating from Sandhurst. Most of his graduating class had gone to France, and many of them were killed in the war. Charles had been forced by his mother to enter the military. He had never wanted to be a soldier at all. Certainly to have opted for India in 1917 was a proper choice, but his mother had so broken his self-esteem, he feared he was not strong and brave enough for France's trench warfare. So Charles, in India, survived, but he carried with him the guilt of all survivors.

Among his classmates was his best friend, whom we shall call Dell. Dell had been reported missing, and we didn't know if he was dead or alive. Charles was consumed with guilt over what might have happened to Dell and what had happened to some of the others.

I argued, as I always had, echoing my grandmother's opinion, that those who make war are criminally insane. But Charles had been so brainwashed in his cultural patriotism that he resented my arguments. He used them as an excuse for getting tight.

Often this sense of honor would be undercut by my cynicism. On entering Westminster Abbey, for instance, I failed to notice the Tomb of the Unknown soldier in the floor of the aisle and walked right over it. Charles was greatly distressed. He simply could not understand how I could do such a thing. Considering all the arguments I had made against war and my usual attitude towards most things considered sacred, he would not be convinced that I had not done it on purpose. I argued that there should have been a fence around it or an eternal light or something to keep us from walking on the poor unknown soldier right in the middle of the church aisle. He assumed that I was ridiculing everything English.

It takes a great deal of compatibility of taste to overcome incompatibility of educations as different as ours. Our relationship was chiefly physical. Sexually, we enjoyed the same wavelength. I thought he was handsome and he thought I was beautiful. I thought he was an elegant English gentleman and he thought I was a pretty East Indian girl. Actually, neither of us was particularly good looking, so there was always a brewing storm waiting to hit our marriage.

One aspect of our life together that did appeal to me very much was traveling whenever the season changed. In the spring, we would go to Paris. In the summer, Monte Carlo or somewhere else along the Mediterranean. In autumn we had to see the white cliffs of Dover, and Christmas would either be spent with Charles' mother in Scarborough or, more hopefully, in North Africa where we had a house in Hammamet. The only pleasure in going to Scarborough was in crossing the country and seeing the beautiful fields. Every inch of England, every river, every woods, seemed to be tended with the same care that the cultivated fields and gardens were given. The elegance and beauty of it all touched me deeply.

Christmas at Charles' mother's home was usually mirthless. We did manage to get a laugh out of her presents to us, such as new woolen underwear for Charles. For me, there would be money, which I confess made splendid good sense. While at his mother's, Charles would spend much of his time walking on the beach or going to a pub alone. I would be left with her. I don't exactly know what it was supposed to mean, but we always had separate bedrooms there. While Charles would be out wandering, I would sleep quite late. His mother had only one servant, and so I would lie in bed, undisturbed until about eleven or so when my mother-in-law would come to the door and say, "Come and have some nice tea." Then I would scramble out to find that at perhaps six or seven that morning she had made an enormous pot of black tea, which had been sitting there all the time getting colder and colder. She couldn't throw it out, though. She was such a penny-wise, pound-foolish person that she could write a check for a hundred pounds without blinking, but then she would make you drink that cold, cold tea.

Often she would question me about Charles, trying to confirm "what an idiot" he was in every way she could think of. She even asked me if I thought he was homosexual. When she wasn't hounding me about Charles, she would throw about all sorts of gossip about the royal family. She "knew" the Prince of Wales was homosexual, for instance, because "he went to France to see Georges Carpentier."[1] She also "knew" the Prince had five Scotches before lunch and that Edward VII used to cheat at cards. These tidbits seemed to be of the utmost importance to her, though I rather suspected she had never known or even met any of the people she so freely talked about.

Finally, there was her passion for riding, which she tried to foist on me, urging me to follow the hounds with her at her hunt club. Well, I wasn't about to get back on horseback. I had been quite scared out of my wits when I was in Hollywood making movies on horseback, and the ones in England were much bigger than the ones I ever rode in California. Once I did go to a hunt breakfast with her just to quiet her down a bit. She went off following the hounds and later let me hear every detail. She was an accomplished rider, I must confess, and she undoubtedly thought I was a nincompoop like Charles because I refused to ride.

She seemed rather amused by my fears and looked down on me for them. She didn't really have too far down to look, by English standards. She was from a lower middle-class family, while Charles' father was upper middle-class. These distinctions were most important in England. I was certainly middle-middle class. Anyway, she persisted in trying to convert me to Anglo-Saxon standards, just as I tried to push Charles into a more cosmopolitan outlook on life.

One of her Anglo-Saxon notions which I found greatly amusing was the idea that the sun makes one stupid. I was on an upper balcony of her house one day, looking out to sea, facing the East, when the sun came up high enough to give me some warmth. I leaned back to enjoy the sun, rare at any time in England. My mother-in-law came out after a while and said, "You know, you mustn't get sunburned or stay in the sun too long. It makes people stupid." I looked at her in surprise. "Why, of course," she said, "people who live in hot countries have thickened skulls and can't think as well."

I couldn't resist the temptation to reply, "Not as well as people who live in a fog?" She was taken aback, not so much by my remark but by the very fact that I would question her statement. So I added, "Perhaps the first sign of intelligence was brought there, to Stonehenge, by the Phoenicians or Assyrians or Egyptians or wandering Arabs who came in prehistoric times with an advanced knowledge of mathematics and astronomy that the British are just now beginning to understand."

Not one easily daunted, she retorted with a long discourse on the Druids, to which I threw in remarks on Greece, Rome, Babylonia, Assyria and Egypt. I suggested that perhaps she thought the sun had been less strong in the Mediterranean in the early days and had been very strong in England at the time. Eventually, she saw the point and said in a most civilized way, "Well, I'm so glad you argue the point. It just shows how easily one can come to conclusions without having thought about them very clearly." Despite these kind of crazy conflicts going on, the English and I got along very well. They learned to accept my idiosyncrasies and I learned to accept theirs. Eventually, within a few months, I learned to speak English. I had even stopped "mumbling."

13

Considering the constrained area of the tight little island, I must say that the British made a terrific racket. I remember eating dinner in the restaurant at Stratford-on-Avon. Just before entering, I heard the most God-awful noise. I turned to Charles and said, "What's going on in there? Is it an aviary?" It was only a large collection of British women talking in their high, birdlike voices and sing-song tones. But soon I was chirping too.

Even though I was quickly Anglicized, I was not completely isolated from the doings of the American Negro community. I was amazed and delighted, for instance, when I ran into Emma Layton, one half of the Layton-Johnson musical team (she sang, he played piano). I had known her in New York and was pleased to run into her again in London. But I was struck by her semi-southern accent, adopted by many educated Negro women, which she clung to even though she had been in England for ten years. This habit seemed to be quite affected as did her blanket criticism of the English.

An even worse offender in that area was Mrs. Paul Robeson.[1] I met her at a bridge party in the home of an English friend. She and I were the only two Americans, and you could hear her constant criticism of the English, loudly and clearly across the room. She kept intimating that the British had the same color prejudice that the Americans had. I was quite embarrassed and wanted to tell her to take a look around her. She surely would never have been invited to an American bridge party with women of that class, yet she was completely accepted by the English.

Stories about Paul and her were making the rounds at that time, which might account for her obvious discomfort with the English. Paul was rumored to be having an affair with a woman who was very close to the royal family. His Rolls-Royce could be seen parked within walking distance of her home. Mrs. Robeson chased all over London looking for the car and trying to catch him, but she didn't succeed. This so-called affair was widely believed, though no one thought it any more scandalous than if the woman had been having an affair with a white man of the theater.

The English seemed to be always making the most extraordinary remarks. One evening, the men in our house were talking about the Turks. Someone said that Turkish officers had been gentlemen during the Crimean War, a good half century earlier. As usual, I stuck in my two cents' worth and asked if the Turks were not extremely cruel, as for instance in their treatment of the Armenians. Colonel Hardy, who was among the group, merely remarked, "Did you ever see an Armenian?"

In a similar vein, a friend I had known in Paris, Nancy Cunard, was planning a party to introduce a black musician, Henry Crowder. Her mother, Lady Cunard, was to throw the party. It was to be a ritzy affair to which Sir Thomas Beecham was to be a guest. When Nancy explained her intention of introducing

Crowder at the party, her mother said, "But does anyone *know* any Negroes?"

Ah, well, the season changed, and with it came our travel plans. Paris in the spring. We rented a house at Rue Hamlin, and spent a lot of time visiting friends. Charles was a little uncomfortable with some of them. He found Nancy Cunard "a little odd" and would have nothing to do with some of the others. I took him to visit Mirod Guiness and her husband, "Chile" Guevara, a former boxer who was now an excellent painter. Their home on the Left Bank was most pleasant. Their collection of art objects included a hobby horse, a wooden cigar-store Indian, a juke box and a few other things that had been gathered in the vein of surrealism and scattered about an otherwise conventionally elegant home. The effect was quite witty, and I was happy that Charles and Mirod got along.

"Chile" sat silently until Mirod and I left the room awhile. Then he tried to make conversation with Charles, which Charles reported to me afterwards with great indignation. It seems "Chile" had said the wrong thing to Charles: "Do you have a job in France?" Well, with that, Charles clammed up and wouldn't say another word. The Guevaras were having a party the following week, but when I mentioned it to Charles, he spat, "Certainly not," adding he never wanted to see them again. "A job, indeed!"

We also spent some time with Nancy Perry and Vichi Seroff. Nancy had studied voice and had wanted to be an opera singer. Her husband had been a good friend and accompanist of Isadora Duncan. Nancy had a lovely home, a great deal of money, a piano and an accompanist at her disposal, so she would often pay the male singers of the Paris Opera to come to her home and sing parts opposite her. Her voice was delicate and exquisite, but not strong enough for opera. But she certainly enjoyed herself trying. Charles and Vichi got along quite well, but he looked at Nancy with suspicion. She was extremely pretty, a blue-eyed, blonde, doll-like American with whom Charles was constantly finding fault, largely because she was an American.

After Paris, we decided to go to Italy, by way of Marseilles, hoping to find a cottage by the sea. In the '30s, it seemed that everyone we knew who went to Marseilles stayed at the Nautique Hotel on the Old Port, where they often left paintings instead of rent. Besides the paintings, there were obscenities scribbled here and there on the wall. In the men's room, the proprietor had put a sign: "Don't pee on the floor." Under that was a handwritten answer, "No, pee on the ceiling—Pissez au plafond." Since Charles wanted to know the writers and painters, we took rooms there.

One morning, while Charles was sitting with his Scotch and soda, he became upset over a report in the paper that some English engineers had been arrested in Russia on charges of sabotage. He could not contain his anger and he whirled on me. "Those dirty Bolsheviks have no law that compares to English law," he stormed. "English law is the foundation of all the civilized codes of law. Englishmen anywhere in the world should be sent home for trial and not be subjected to the barbarous so-called laws of countries like Russia!"

As usual, I couldn't just let it pass. "Well, if they don't want to take a chance on being accused or arrested in other countries, or if they don't want to live under the laws of another country, they should stay home." At that point, Charles' glass came flying towards me so fast, I barely had time to duck. It hit the side of my face, very close to my eye, leaving me with a black eye and him with a heavy conscience. Suddenly he realized what he had done. He had never before struck me or thrown anything, even though he had never taken my "Bolshevik" remarks with good humor. Now he was frightened and came dashing over to see if he had really hurt me. It was Good Friday, and on Easter Sunday I wore a white serge suit with a white straw hat and a black patch over my eye, thus augmenting his guilt.

I believe this was the turning point in his social attitude. Apparently my battle scar had brought about a change of heart. (I should have gotten a purple heart.) He began to see the other side, but it was not as I saw it, balancing one thing against the other to come up with an idea that embraced the best of all viewpoints. When he changed his mind, he changed it all the way. He decided he was completely opposed to all forms of colonialism and had, in fact, felt that way ever since India. He became an anti-imperialist to the point of agreeing with the communists. He became a sworn enemy of the exploitation of the underdeveloped nations.

Now it was my turn to be confused. I had always thought that however evil the colonialists might be, they had something to offer. The French, for instance, could give the Arabs all the help they could spare in medicine; it had been practically impossible for me to get my Arab neighbors to go to the Institut Pasteur or French-run hospital. And plumbing would have been nice, for that matter. I assumed this must have been true in India as well. There simply weren't enough Albert Schweitzers around to fill every corner of the underdeveloped world.

Charles, however, could see none of this, any more than he had been able to see the other side. Apparently he needed some authority to tell him what to do; if not a superior officer, some-one. So, he left the authority of the British Empire and got ready to plunge headlong into the Communist Party. I had never had anything to do with the Party. I had jumped out of the way when the communists approached me in New York in the '20s, with offers of an education in Europe and Russia. I think Paul Robeson, Langston Hughes and others took advantage of the offer, but I found communism distasteful. It reminded me of a furniture company which advertised: "We stand behind every bed we sell." I didn't want them standing behind my bed.

Charles, however, slipped more and more from the empire into the communist religion. Of course, he argued that the notion was a conflict in terms, that "religion is the opiate of the people." I snarled back that "work is the opiate of the people; the more people work, the less time they have to think." Marveling that my skepticism had wrought such a changeabout in Charles, I tagged along, raising my eyebrows at all the dogma of his new religion. I'd heard it all before, the dialectical materialism, the notion of the people holding the means of production. But it did sound most strange in his clipped accent.

Anyway, Italy beckoned, and we went from the communists to the Fascisti. Spending a few days in Genoa before taking the train to Rapallo, Charles caught the flu (which eventually turned into tuberculosis.) While he was recuperating, I rented an apartment in Rapallo. The trip was my first contact with the Fascisti in Italy. We had taken only a small trunk in which we put a few summer things, buying needed clothing as we went along. But getting even that one trunk onto the train for Rapallo turned out to be quite an ordeal. The porter said he couldn't put the trunk into the compartment because it wasn't "properly sealed." So, I paid the liras to get it sealed, which meant a wire was put around it with a seal clamped on. Then the porter decided he needed more money to carry the trunk onto the train.

Finally, I found a Fascisti guard who could speak French. He was a rather small man in a sharp uniform with shiny boots and a shiny hat with cock feathers over one shoulder. As soon as I explained my story to him, he took two guards and had the porter placed under arrest. I finally got the trunk aboard, but the three guards stayed with me, openly flirting and suggesting that I not go to Rapallo after all. Their "courtesy" was fast approaching seduction when the whistle blew for the train to pull out. Helpful Fascisti—they jumped off!

I knew that Ezra Pound was in Rapallo. I had met him once in Paris, but I was not one to ring the doorbells of the great with the excuse of a conversation about a mutual friend. Anyway, I didn't care much for his admiration and support of the fascists, so I did not look him up.

In any event, I found a nice small apartment on the water. We felt a little closer to the sun, though not quite close enough, and we planned to move down the coast until we found a village where we could buy a house we could go to every spring or summer.

Our search for the sun took us in 1935 to Tunis, where we ventured in the hopes of finding it to be like Morocco. We visited the American consul and asked if there were a small village, perhaps a fishing village, down the coast where we could buy a small house. He suggested we look at Hammamet, which he described as a community of British and American artists. Charles shied away from that notion, so we took a train to Sfax and craned our necks looking all along the coast. On our way back to Tunis, the train was put onto a side track, and we found ourselves in Hammamet after all. My curiosity got the better of my distaste for colonies of British and American "artists," whom I pictured wandering around in sandals and smocks. I went off, leaving Charles in a café in town.

The whole town was built up around a great fort on a promontory on the Bay of Hammamet. I remembered that a friend in Paris had told me there were a number of homosexuals who were attracted to the town because of the handsome Arab boys who were having their military training at the fort. I went into the street and found a little boy who knew enough French to guide me to "where the British and American people" might be living. We followed the sand from the little village of Hammamet down the coast for almost three miles. It took a long time, practically the entire afternoon, and I was getting a little afraid of where I was being led.

Finally, I noticed we were approaching a place where there were rose bushes planted in the sand. Intrigued, we went toward a large house, some distance up the sand, part of an extraordinary estate. We found not a house but an Arab palace, one of the most beautiful I had ever seen. Leaving my young guide to wait for me, I walked toward a sunny marble terrace facing the sea, and when I arrived, an Arab servant told me that "Monsieur Sebastian" was in the garage, pointing toward the building.

In the garage, George Sebastian, the photographer Hoyningen-Huene, and an American stockbroker named Plumb were busily arranging lunch baskets and wine in a Rolls-Royce.[2] They were effusive in their welcome and invited me in for a drink. I explained that my husband was in town and I had to go back to the café, but said we were looking for a house somewhere in the area. They suggested that I go next door to ask the Hensons if they might know of a place.

From the road, I walked into the garden of another elegant villa, past a striking collection of antique statues, toward what seemed to be a living statue, a blond Greek god approaching me from the sea. I had rarely seen such a gorgeous physique. He approached in a beach coat of hand-woven wool in its natural shade of off-white. The cord more-or-less held it together but still managed to expose most of his body. He was extraordinarily good looking, and he came affably in my direction with his hand held out. I could hardly believe my ears when he spoke: "Well, hell, honey chile. How're you-all?" in the sweet honey tones of a Southern American gentleman. I kept my composure and told him my house-hunting story in my now clipped British manner of speech.

He responded not in answer but by asking, "Where'd you-all get that beautiful tan?" I replied as I had many times before: "It took me over a hundred years to get this color." He laughed, apparently thinking there must be some great joke going on but not understanding it a bit. He took me into his house and introduced me to his wife, Violet, a very charming, hospitable English woman. Then he went to get dressed to take me into town and bring Charles back out to the house. We took our little Arab boy with us and paid him off handsomely for his service. Charles came out, rather reluctantly, to be introduced to the "artists of Hammamet." Violet, however, persuaded him to take a small house across the road from their palace. Being British, she spoke a language he could understand. George Henson and I also had great fun being very American and speaking in counterpoint to their accents, although now I spoke more like Violet and couldn't really imitate George's Georgian accent.

As we came to know all the members of the small colony, I liked more and more the cosmopolitan nature of the group. Each couple was different, and every husband and wife was of a different nationality. Sebastian was a cousin of King Carol of Rumania, and his wife was from California. The Hensons were British and American. Hoyningen-Huene was Russian, and although he did not have a wife at the time he had been married to Ilka Chase.[3] Mr. LeFèvre of Lulu Biscuits was French and his wife was Belgian. Before we moved into our house, it had been occupied by the Belgian consul to Tokyo, who was married to a Japanese woman, and Mr. Plumb, the stockbroker, was an American. The members of the colony were certain the next world war would go through the South of France, so they were getting out of the way by living in North Africa. They were not able to foresee that Rommel would soon be rumbling through there, followed by Montgomery, followed by American troops, all leaving their dirty boot-prints in their lovely homes.

Each house was a palace, and each was all white. Only minor differences distinguished them. Mr. Plumb's house had mirrors and white and blue satin. Hoyningen-Huene's home was white and terra cotta, and the Hensons had a great deal of statuary in their home. Early in the morning, everyone went to the beach and sat around. The men wore only a G-string, the least excuse for a swim suit that anyone ever saw, but at least all of them were good looking. After the beach, the couples would visit each other for lunch, after which it would be siesta time. Later we would return to the beach or visit or just loaf around before getting dressed for dinner, either at home or at one of the frequent dinner parties.

The group held together beautifully. They were the most civilized people I had ever known, quite possibly because no one ever mentioned politics or policies, ideologies, nationalities, religions or any other subject that might be considered in the least controversial.

After a while, Charles said all they ever talked about was "jasmine and camel dung." I must confess, these two subjects did seem to come up in the conversation more often than almost anything else. In any event, the conversations were always superficial, light and airy. And I loved every minute of it. Charles, who was more tense, more interested in talking about what was going on in the world, was sometimes quite annoyed. He got enough contention from me, but he missed it in the group and didn't care much for the light and gay conversation that went on in the homes of Hammamet.

I fell into the superficial social life like falling into a feather bed that I had always looked for. There was always a tendency on my part to fall into luscious pleasures of wealthy loafers when I had the opportunity. Certainly, I never felt hurt by the so-called "easy arrogance of wealth." The arrogance never touched me, perhaps because my own matched it. I was certainly more at home with inherited wealth than in the presence of the uneasy arrogance of persons struck with their racial superiority or of the newly rich. An example occurred one evening on the terrace of George Sebastian's home. George Henson was sitting with his shoulder against my knee while I strummed a guitar and started to sing "St. James Infirmary." The Georgian looked at me in surprise and started to laugh. "My God, chile, I just realized what you meant about all those generations giving you your color!" And he laughed very heartily and found it a great joke as he realized I was not an East Indian, I was an American black. The others, I am sure, paid no attention whatsoever.

I believe that George and I were the only ones who appreciated thoroughly the great joke surrounding the arrival of one of the very first American Negro Moslems. I had known in New York when I was there in the '20s a brilliant young woman whom I'll call Mimi. We had had jolly times together, and I sometimes went to her home in Newark where her family lived. She was a slender, blond girl with gray eyes, slightly crossed. She had a tendency to drop her head and look in the direction of her good eye. Her weakness seemed attractive to men, but I found her erratic and I avoided her company many times because she drank and did stupid things. I certainly never expected nor hoped to see her again. How she discovered that I was in Tunis, I'll never know. Perhaps by then I had forgiven her and had written to her. Anyway, she wrote to say she was coming to visit us with her "Arab" husband.

I was rather intrigued, and George Henson and I went to the boat to meet them. Well, we almost fell over with surprise. At a glance, we could see her husband was an American Negro, and from the way he was dressed, obviously a Harlemite. He was, however, wearing a fez, and he had the effrontery to come toward us with some words he must have thought were Arabic. I didn't recognize them, though he had learned the Moslem salute, touching his head, his lips and his heart. But then he went on talking in Harlem English. It was hilariously surprising, and George and I had a hard time not laughing. Mimi was beautifully dressed in a gray tailored suit. She had always made good money in the New

York City school system, where she was a supervisor. Now she was wearing a pale yellow shirtwaist and a yellow turban, with fashionable jewelry.

When we took them to our home, Charles was quite overwhelmed. He saw the contradiction in a man pretending to be what he most obviously was not, and he was quite bewildered. He wanted to tell the chap to drop his pretenses, that he didn't have to pass for an Arab among us, but "Abdul" was set on persuading himself that he was an Arab. He pushed a bit too much, as far as I was concerned, by saying that I was either prejudiced or a thorough bitch not to acknowledge his being an Arab, "originally from Africa, by way of Florida." He also tried to make the Arab postman and others who came around understand his "language." Of course, they couldn't understand him. We thought he was quite ridiculous.

I don't know exactly how Mimi regarded her "Arab," but she did seem to be very happy with him and showed almost no reaction to his behavior. Finally, I told her I really had had enough and perhaps it was time they moved on to France. She left with the same dignity with which she had come, and she took her "Abdul," the first of a long line of American black Moslems, away from Tunis and out of my life. I often have wondered what happened to Mimi. I am sure "Abdul" got along fine and may have even become an officer in one of the black Muslim organizations that expanded since the middle '30s.

Anyway, there was always more company. I was delighted to learn that E. E. Cummings was coming to visit us. He had a fellowship that year, and he arrived with a lovely woman, a model. Hoyningen-Huene was quite pleased with the young lady, and he often came over to take pictures of her or the two of us together.

I was surprised that my enthusiasm for Cummings was not shared by many of the others. Violet Henson said, "Just who is this E. E. Cummings?" I turned to look in her own living room bookcase, where a first edition of his book, *The Enormous Room,* was conspicuous. "He is the author of that book," I said.

"Well, I suppose so," Violet said.

Then I looked over my shoulder, with a suspicion of know-nothing snobbery, and remarked, "By the way, I didn't know you owned that Picasso."

Violet said, "By Jove, it *is* a Picasso, isn't it?" Well, that was the limit! But I tried to slow down my enthusiasm for the arts from then on, trying to be blasé like the others. I didn't quite succeed, but I put on the best façade I could.

E. E. Cummings and Charles got along beautifully. They went for long walks and talked about things they both understood and liked. They were in accord in their suspicion that most of the men in the community were not very masculine, and that perhaps they had come to Hammamet to be near the handsome boys at the barracks. The men, for instance, often organized trips at night to go out to look for artifacts. They combed the countryside for statues and relics of the earlier days in Tunis and often came back with fine things. They were usually guided by some of the most handsome boys in the community. The young men in Tunis in those days were made even more striking and seductive in their white djalabas and red fezzes. Each wore a decoration of jasmine stuck on a feather over an ear. The white jasmine against the often quite dark skin, red fez and white djalaba made a fine picture.

The women seemed not to notice their husbands' taste in companions. Only Charles and Cummings were upset by it, saying that it looked as though they were the only "men" in the community. Well, I'm sure that was an exaggeration, but Cummings's attitude increased Charles's slow but surely growing discontent with the group. When Cummings left, Charles began to long again for the white cliffs of Dover.

We had a long lease on our house, but we left Jane, our Scottie, with George Sebastian, who had a well-bred male Scottie, and we returned to England. Later we heard that Jane, though long in the tooth, had become the mother of the first Aberdeen Terriers born in Tunis. She remained with the Sebastians. We never returned to Tunis.

14

The years between 1932 and 1935 are jumbled in my mind, but I can remember in 1935 the invasion of the Italians into Abyssinia.[1] By that time, Charles was violently anti-colonialist and antifascist. Of course, we all were but he was ready and eager to go into Abyssinia to train the people in old North West frontier fashion.[2] He thought of making an Abyssinian army that would defeat the Italians.

So, we chased all over Paris looking for someone to send him to Abyssinia. We found the Abyssinian legation, but they just referred us to the British Embassy. We went there, and they told Charles to stay the hell out of Abyssinia as it wasn't any of his business. But Charles wouldn't take no for an answer. He hightailed off to Egypt to try to get through from there to save Abyssinia, the last non-colonized corner of the Dark Continent. As it turned out, he never did make it there. Instead, he became involved with some Egyptian radicals for whom he financed a newspaper. It took a lot of his capital, but he enjoyed working there. Meanwhile, I was doing my bit for the Abyssinians, collecting money for them in Paris. Everyone I knew was willing to give, each according to his means.

While living alone in Paris, I stayed in the apartment of Leonor Fini, a beautiful woman who claimed to be the daughter of d'Annunzio.[3] Her studio was most unusual. It consisted of a large atelier, the most unusual feature of which was the bedroom salon. The bed was a huge velvet square as large as a small room, with red velvet drapes closing the entrance. It was lined in gold, with pale blue satin tufted and embroidered with stars. When the curtains of the bed were closed, it became a "temple to Venus," guarded by two enormous carved and painted blackamoors who stood with spears at the entrance. She let me use her apartment so I would take care of her fancy Persian cat, very fuzzy, selfish and quite unloveable.

By the time Leonor returned from Italy, I had collected quite a bit of money for Abyssinia, and I had called Abyssinians from their Paris legation to receive it. When they arrived they were so taken with Leonor, they could hardly see the money, and when they wrote to thank me, they asked in the most old-fashioned English imaginable if they could take us to dinner at Maxim's. They were utterly overcome by Leonor, and it was fortunate she was not interested in the war or Italian politics or she could have done some rather serious damage to the Abyssinian cause in Paris. It was quite clear to me that men's ideologies, their love and their common sense rarely coincide.

Eventually, I left Leonor's home and moved into the Hotel San Benoit, waiting for Charles to decide whether or not he was going to return from Egypt. At the hotel, I was home again with my dear unconventional comrades of the Left Bank. I still saw Tonny occasionally. He was married to a young woman named

Marie Claire, and they seemed to be quite happy. I also saw Man Ray, who was recovering from a bad love affair with Lee Miller. I saw again Mirod Guiness and Chile, whom I could visit without Charles, and Mirette Oppenheimer and Djuna Barnes, Kay Boyle and my dear friend Louise Bryant.[4]

But Louise was not the same as I had known her before. In the '20s she had been fashionable and fastidious, slender, beautifully groomed and strikingly good looking. When I met her again in 1935, she had become bloated and distracted. This was long after the five years she had been told she had to live, and, no doubt in discouragement and bewilderment, she had begun to drink too much. I've never forgotten our last meeting. I was standing on the Avenue de l'Opéra looking in a florist's window. There was a mirror that made it possible for me to see back into the street. I noticed a woman standing looking at me. When I turned, I barely recognized Louise. She was puffy, more than fat, dressed in a long, military-like cape of navy blue with a red lining. It was thrown over her shoulder in a way that exposed the lining, and she had an enormous fur sheshia on her head.[5] She looked rather like a Russian soldier that one would see on the stage. I was astonished and upset to find her so changed, but I loved her still and was so indebted to her and so happy to see her in any shape, I took her arm and asked her to come to lunch with me, recalling the many lunches she had bought for me and all our friends in the '20s when she was rich and none of us had any money.

Prunier's was my favorite restaurant for celebrating, so arm in arm, Louise and I walked to the corner where I hoped to hail a taxi to take us there. She talked most pleasantly as we walked, but just as we approached the curb and I was about to signal for a cab, she turned to me abruptly, jerking her arm away, and said, "I

can't waste my time with you. I have to get back to my apartment. Liam O'Flaherty is waiting for me. He cannot write or do
anything without my guidance, and here I am wasting my time
with you." Without a goodbye or handshake, she almost ran in
the direction from which we had come and disappeared in the
crowd. That was the last time I ever saw her.

I understand that later, although there were so many conflicting reports, when her husband was named ambassador to France,
the sureté had the job of finding her in Paris and sending her back
to the United States, perhaps to a hospital. Then I heard that she
had died before Bullitt arrived in France. I didn't know the details, only that I had lost a very dear friend and the world had lost
a clear-thinking wife of an American ambassador who very well
might have helped to change the course of history had not that
idiot specialist told her in 1929 that she only had five years to live.

In the mid-thirties, the western world was in confusion, and
we were all headed for more confusion and deeper darkness in
relationship to fascism and the coming war. But Paris in 1935 was
still most pleasant for me, and I went to dance again at the Boeuf
sur le Toit.[6] I remember one afternoon dancing there with Man
Ray and mentioning, without thinking, that I had posed for
Hoyningen-Huene while in Hammamet. When I told him that
Huene had said Man Ray was the greatest photographic inventor
of the century, Man became furious. He stopped dancing and
said, "I am not an inventor; I'm an artist." After a little outraged
silence, he plunged into Huene in a way that was so unlike him,
it shocked me. He said Huene was hardly an artist at all but a
gigolo, that he had married Mrs. Chase's daughter and given Ilka
the title of one of the Georgian princes in such large numbers in
Paris so that Mrs. Chase would have his photographs published in

Vogue. After they were married, he said he didn't like girls, and so the marriage had been annulled. That was Man Ray's story. I never tried to verify it, but it was so unusual for him to say anything of that sort about anyone that I realized he had been very hurt by Huene's remarks.

Early in 1936, Charles came to join me in Paris. He was discouraged and disgusted with the Egyptian experiment and was not very happy about Abyssinia or anything else that was happening. His solution by this time was to completely immerse himself in the communist line. We sat on the terrace of the Deux Magots having coffee and croissants, as we did every morning as the sun rose over the church of Saint-Germain-des-Près. He was reading *L'Humanité,* and I was reading either *Figaro* or *Cahiers d'Art* or *Le Monde.*[7] I remember his looking over his paper and asking very grumpily if *L'Humanité* weren't good enough for me.

Unfortunately, he had stayed too long in Egypt, and his bronchial problems had become more serious. It was now pretty obvious he was in danger of tuberculosis, though he still did everything he could to hide it. We returned to London, where two or three incidents became deeply implanted in my memory. The first concerned the man Dell, who had been Charles' friend at Repton and later at Sandhurst. Dell, as I mentioned before, had been reported missing in France, and no one knew what had become of him. Charles mourned him deeply. One day, Stewart, the butler, answered the phone and came to tell me there was a Mr. Dell on the line who wished to speak with Charles. Charles wasn't at home, so I went to the phone and spoke with him. I recognized immediately that this indeed must be the long-lost friend, so I took his number and said I would have Charles call him.

When Charles returned and I told him about the call, he couldn't believe it. He thought I was making some macabre joke. But finally he had Stewart return the call. When Dell answered, Charles was overwhelmed with joy and surprise. He asked his friend to come over immediately, and almost immediately he arrived, in an open sports car, looking quite prosperous and healthy. We had some Scotch together, and then I left the men to their reminiscences. Later, after Dell had left, Charles told me he was well and had been living in England all the time since the war, fourteen or fifteen years. He had not gotten in touch with anyone during all that time because of some romantic secret. I also found out that Charles had loaned Dell fifty pounds. He was to return it when he came to dinner the next week.

Well, a week went by with no more being heard from Dell. The telephone number he had given us was that of a pub, and there was no way to reach him. Charles could hardly contain his grief at this second loss of his friend, nor could he face me when I suggested that he was really much too sentimental about all those chaps who were "lost" in France in the First World War. An emotional argument followed, the strain of which did not end, even when the Repton News published an item that "members of the Class of 1917 are advised that lending money to D.D. may prove unwise, loans not repaid." This just added to the growing list of adversities in our relationship, which was worsening and was about to fold altogether.

One afternoon, I discovered on coming into my own little salon, bright with *my* garden furniture, *my* yellow chintz drapes, *my* many plants and *my* own paintings, a woman who looked at me in horror and exclaimed: "Why she's a nigger!"[8] It was Sally, the Irish girl whom Charles had married in India. He thought he had gotten rid of her in a Reno divorce, but Sally had a different idea. She considered herself still married to Charles, and she had come to argue about the allowance she was getting through his solicitor. She wanted more. The cost of living was going up, and she had come to claim her pound of flesh.

I bowed out and left it up to them to hash it out. But it made me think more about the relationship in which I called him "husband" and he called me "wife." I wondered whether our marriage was a marriage at all, a ceremony in the presence of someone who had called himself a priest in Morocco. I had thought so little of it that I had written to my mother to say that perhaps we might get together and have a wedding she could attend. I had a ring with two lovely diamonds, and a wedding ring that had been part of the Tangier ceremony, but underlying it all, I had a deep suspicion that there was a hint of phoniness in the so-called clergyman who had married us. I didn't care all that much. I rather relished the idea, in fact, because as Man Ray had pointed out, the only reasons for marrying were for property and protection of children. I had no children, and my property was in California. I had also seen to it that the stock Charles had given me, from which I drew a small allowance, was put in my maiden name. Charles' instability increased as I began to comprehend more and more that our marriage had not been made in heaven. I became progressively happier as I realized that the exit door may have been left open.

While planning to return to the sunny Mediterranean for Charles' cough, we were fortunate to count among our friends the Baron and Baroness von Munchausen. Baron Munchausen had been a friend of Charles at Sandhurst. He was a German officer whose mother was a wealthy New York Jewish woman. At the time Hitler came to power and said all those with Jewish relatives should leave the country, the Munchausens knew they might be persecuted if they stayed in Germany. He wanted to resign from the Army, but the authorities asked him to stay as he was an excellent officer. He had enough sense to leave anyway, and he took his Viennese wife and settled in London. They liked London, and when we were ready to return to the Mediterranean, they consented to stay in our house and take care of the household, the business and the servants while we were away. We were most fortunate in being able to leave it all with them. I was especially relieved that there would be someone to take care of Charles when he returned to London. After all the Catholic confusion, the communist confusion and all the elements of confusion in Charles' relationship with Sally, the tragedy of Dell and the war and the rest of it, I was determined to leave London and Charles as soon as possible, and forever.

15

It was Charles' illness that finally provided an out for me. We returned for a while to Monte Carlo. Charles sat on the terrace of the casino in the morning, playing the "system" he had worked out for roulette, while I sat in the sunshine. And when he went into the playing rooms in the evenings, I would go to the performances of the Ballet Russe de Monte Carlo. Occasionally, I would go over to the casino and watch the people who sat there day after day with their pads of paper, struggling along, losing their small incomes trying to best the game. Charles enjoyed it, though. At the end of one of our visits years earlier, he told me we came out thirty-seven francs to the good; he had it all balanced in such a way he felt it was not costing him any money. I managed to take some pleasure from the "far niente" of the life until I found Charles was becoming too ill for me to handle. I insisted that he see a doctor, and when he finally did so, the doctor suggested that Charles go up to Grasse to a sanitorium to get some rest for a while. I went with him to get him installed, then I went back to Paris, feeling an urgency to get a job to be independent.

There was work I could do there, though it was not really a regular job. I had been told by Djuna Barnes or Kay Boyle that I would be able to make some money translating into French stories from Hearst's sensationalist *American Magazine,* which appeared as a supplement in the Sunday paper. It featured gossip and every bit of scandal that the reporters could dig up. My friend Bill Seabrook confirmed that I would be paid well to translate these features into French for an agency called Opera Mundi. Another friend, Jacques Baron, offered to turn my petit Nègre into proper French so we could both make some money.[1]

I dared not write my mother that I was leaving Charles for Hearst. She had already been convinced that I was going posthaste to hell when my name had appeared in a feature in *American Magazine.* I had been with friends at the Coupole when a news photographer came to take the picture of Man Ray's mistress, Kiki, whom I was friendly with and liked very much. Her life story was being featured by the publication, and when they took her pictures, some of us were also included. The story appeared across the United States. The life story of the notorious Kiki unnerved my mother. Her friends started writing to her from all over the country asking what I was doing in Paris with a bunch of models. The caption of the picture didn't help. It said that "These models are getting their first meal in a long time because one of them has been paid for a job and all the rest of them are hungry."

Perhaps the only one who could have persuaded Mother of the respectability of my life at the time was Mercer Cook, the son of a friend of my father, who was in Paris with his wife Vashti. I took them to the Deux Magots and the Café de Flore and into some of the studios and homes of my friends.[2] The Cooks seemed delighted with all they saw, and this helped calm my mother's fears for me. She knew most of the names of the artists, and she sent me a subscription to *Vanity Fair* in which they were sometimes mentioned. She knew of my friendship with Dora Maar, and I sent her photographs that Dora had taken of me.[3] I also told her about Picasso's studio and sent her a little sketch of me made by Matisse as we sat in the Deux Magots.

Mother knew of Léger's work, too, and I wrote her about a dinner that I gave for him and his wife and young friend who had just published a book in which I showed up as a character. I showed up in other books as well. Eric d'Haulleville had me in something in the Galapagos, and Jacques Baron had several poems about me.[4] The one I liked most said that my feet never touched the ground. With my old flighty feelings, that pleased me. I think I sent copies of all these books to Mother. Sometimes I was called by name in the books and sometimes I wasn't. My friendship with these persons had not involved any scandal. Everyone had his own partner, and there really was very little jumping around with secrets and hiding. My own life was really scandal free and pretty dull, but Mother, of course, was influenced by what she saw in the newspaper, and I am afraid that the *American Magazine* story about me with Kiki disturbed her.

A friend of Jacques Baron I most admired was Antoine de St. Exupéry. He was certainly the most beautiful ugly man I had ever seen.[5] He was big and had a large nose. He was certainly not good to look at, with his heavy lower face, but he had a personality and a presence and a consideration for his silly little wife that touched everyone's heart and made me admire him. His wife was perhaps the only really silly woman I knew at the time. She had been the wife of a Brazilian, I believe, a poet whom St. Exupéry had known in his flights to South America where he had met her. It was rumored that he had always been in love with his cousin, Louise de Vilmorin, whom he could not marry. He certainly had married Louise's opposite in Consuela. She pretended to suffer each time he flew away into the wild blue yonder because she was "sure he was off suffering." I remember one afternoon at the Brasserie her hacking away at her wrist with a razor blade and how we were all disgusted by her histrionics. She always seemed to be playing around with one gigolo after another, all part of her "suffering" no doubt. But when St. Exupéry showed up, she would throw a fit of hysterics. He would pick her up and carry her, like a child, to put her into a taxi and take her away. We, liking him so much, disliked her in proportion.

Well, I probably didn't tell my mother about Consuela. But she wasn't typical anyway. I might not have told her about Cecile's experience, either, though I found it most amusing. Cecile was engaged to a most delightful young man in Nice, and we used to go to Villefranche, next to Nice, to sail on the star boats there each summer.[6] She had an apartment in Villefranche. Some young men who had star boats took us to participate in regattas every Sunday. I learned to handle the jib as we sailed along the Mediterranean coast from Genoa to Marseilles. They were all handsome, charming and nicely brought up products of "Les Sacrés Jésuites."

Cecile, however, had become fascinated in Paris by a poet, a wild man named Antonin Artaud, and she took great pride in helping him arrange his papers.[7] He was on drugs most of the time, with the "help" of some friends who believed he couldn't live without them. Yet despite this, he always seemed to have the money he needed. He produced a play called *Les Cenci,* in which

Lady Abdy played beautifully the part of the daughter of a sadistic Renaissance Italian father who tied her to a large wheel. It was an interesting play and probably the only constructive thing Artaud ever did.[8]

I had given Artaud an old walking stick from my days in California. It was made of Manzanita wood with twists and turns, and it had Mexican Indian carving and a metal tip. Artaud said it was a magic wand and used to go about Paris throwing this thing in the air and pointing it at people and telling them what he thought of them.[9] When he walked along the pavement, he would hit the cement with the metal tip so that sparks flew. He tried to persuade everyone that it certainly proved it was a magic stick.

Well, he had lots of magic ideas. He convinced Cecile she was the only one who could handle his papers properly, and she was very involved in finding scraps of things he had written and getting them together for publication. Her parents were of the bourgeois type in Brussels. Her father was an officer in the tram company and her mother was at the Belgian court. They were certainly not people who could have appreciated Artaud. When her mother came to Paris and saw Cecile with him, she made a surprisingly non-bourgeois statement, suggesting that "One doesn't have to marry the man one loves." But Cecile disagreed and insisted on taking her "fiancé" to Brussels to meet her mother's friends. So her mother set up the salon with tiny gold chairs, and Artaud was presented to the family and friends as a French poet.

He spoke and acted in such a deviously unconstructed and uncontrolled manner that the women assembled didn't know what he was talking about, while Cecile, in the library with her father, was very much amused. After a while, her mother flew into the

library and said Artaud was being disgraceful, lecturing on "pederasty chez les Jésuites" until the ladies, one after the other, awakened from their dozing, caught on to what was being said and left
indignant and furious. But Cecile was amused, and Artaud was
proud of himself. He went off in great dignity with her the next
day, at the urging of her parents, of course, and returned to Paris.
After they got there, the story made the rounds of all our friends
in a short time and everyone enjoyed repeating it.

Artaud did not remain in any way consistently friendly with
Cecile. In fact, he threw a bar stool at her once and bruised her
face rather badly. But she stuck with him for art's sake and helped
him as long as she could. She was lovely, so self-confident and
proud, and his eccentricities only added a sparkle to a shining collection of inherited jewels. Aside from the early morning occasion when she arrived *chez moi,* black and blue after the bar stool
incident, I always saw her erect and unaffected by her fiancé's
obvious insanity.

He eventually went off to Ireland to look up some fairies at
someone's expense (perhaps Cecile's father, which wouldn't have
been a bad idea). When he tried to return to France, the British
held him in England long enough to have him confined for mental examination. Finally, it was decided he should enter a mental
hospital when he returned to France. His best friends were indignant, but he was safe, and I suppose more comfortable in a mental
hospital than he would have been on the streets again. Cecile's
return to Villefranche, if not romantic, at least made my friendship with her more agreeable.

Remembering my exquisite friend and the conflict in mores
with those of our families, I must describe the evening her father

came to Paris to visit her. Her father, a gentleman of the old school, took us to an excellent restaurant for dinner and was taking us to the theater in a taxi. Driving through the Grand Boulevard, we passed an enormous billboard on which Cecile was displayed, looking as though she were nude. She stood in the photo, exposed from the waist up, with her right hand over her right breast and her left hand holding a bath glove and a bar of Mon Savon, a soap that was popular in France. In one of the magazine jobs, she had consented to this advertisement, not knowing it would be enlarged and displayed over the Grand Boulevard. Cecile and I both realized we would be passing right by the brightly lit billboard, so we started talking to her father, one of us on either side of him in the taxi, each of us jabbering as fast as we could to keep him from looking out. He certainly must have thought we were crazy, but we got him past the sign without seeing it.

The advertisement also appeared in a newspaper in Nice, and her fiancé there rushed out to buy every copy of the edition to keep it from going into his family's house. A very expensive ad; we had never earned as much as models. Fortunately, that was the only photo in which either of us had posed in anything like the nude. Jolly fortunate for me, certainly, because I knew no one rich enough to buy up a whole edition of my indiscretions. From this riotous bohemian life, Jacques Baron and I, the two journalists, took off to go to Spain. It was just before the outbreak of the Spanish Civil War, though we were not going there to look for it.

Many of our friends were deeply involved in politics. We had a good companion named Boris Souvarine who had been secretary to Trotsky, and there was a great deal of talk about Russia.[10] Aragon and Breton nearly broke off a friendship of years in surrealism because Aragon was a Stalinist and Breton was a Troskyite.

While politics and psychology were the big topics of the time, there was much more involvement in the political. Most of us agreed that those we knew who had gone to Vienna to be psychoanalyzed came back crazier than they had left. It seemed to us that the fantasies of lunacy made much more sense than the ghastly counterpoint we got from Germany, with Hitler raving on the radio like a mad, hysterical bitch on the other side of the frontier.

There had been other political confusions. In 1933, when Tonny, André de la Rivière, Robert Desnos and some others who were willing to fight for their ideals had "descended with the people into the street" in the Stavisky scandal, they found everyone ready to bounce a brick off someone's head or get a brick bounced off his own for some political concept.[11] But Jacques Baron and I were not among the fighting adherents of any political philosophy. In fact, neither of us belonged to a political party at all. We were translating for Opera Mundi and had actually been planning to go to Greece. But at the last minute, our plans were changed and we accepted the invitation of André and Rose Masson to spend the summer with them in Costa del Mar in Spain.[12] It was only to have been a pleasure trip, but it threw us into the midst of the war.

I might have argued half the night about politics. I might even have taken a pot shot at Hitler had I either been Jewish or seriously enough involved in the German situation to risk my life. But I had no intention of giving my life for the government of Spain, whichever one it turned out to be. So we went into Spain in a light-hearted mood; that is, Jacques went into Barcelona immediately. I was held up at the frontier, and most unintentionally I became a *cause célèbre* for the government of Catalonia.

When I asked the guard at the railroad station in Paris if I needed a passport to go into Spain, he told me I did not. As it turned out, the French didn't need one, but the Americans did. When we arrived at Portbou I was stopped at the frontier. The frontier guards on the day I arrived were three smallish Spaniards, wearing cocked hats, boots and guns. They impressed me as being pushy and military. They took away my passport and said I would have to get a visa.

Well, getting a visa was a problem without an embassy or consul, so I chased back into France by taxi and tried to find a Spanish consul. The taxi ride itself was quite an adventure, since the driver seemed to know nothing but the accelerator and the horn. We went sailing around mountains that I never would have guessed had roads. Around a corner, we suddenly faced a poorly dressed statue of the Madonna with her laces in shreds, with clothing and other things of value to the poor people, hanging around her as jewelry and piled up next to her in supplication for the peasants' modest needs. My need was not for a virgin or saint, though. All I wanted was to get out of the mountains, out of the taxi and onto solid ground.

After the hysterical ride, needless to say, I did not find a consul. So, I finally went back and telephoned to Barcelona, to Casanova, the president of the parliament in Catalonia. We had known him in Paris when his government was not in power. When I called him, he said he would call back. But when he did, the guards refused to believe it was he who had telephoned. They held my passport and me for two days in a small hotel, attended to by those clowns whose behavior became more and more seductive.

I telephoned to the American representative in Barcelona, and he said there was trouble in Spain and suggested I go to Greece or Villefranche or wherever it was I was in the habit of spending the summer, because Spain was no place for an American to be at that time. Well, I couldn't take that. I called Casanova again, and this time he sent down two guards who really were in the military. They came to the frontier to escort me to Barcelona and arrested the three immigration officers who had held me. I don't know what became of the guards, but when I went to the palace to thank Casanova, he said he had to thank me because my encounter with the guards had permitted him to take control of the border frontier between Catalonia and France. This was proof of the Madrid guards' inefficiency. And so, I became an "international incident," and the guarding of the frontier was taken out of the hands of Madrid and given over to Catalonia.

In Spain, the summer was beautiful. Our visit with the Massons was very pleasant. Their children were growing and lovely. Often we went to Barcelona and sat on the Ramblas, watching the people and going back out to toast ourselves on the beach. We danced and dined in a country house decorated in art nouveau by an elegant German couple who were refugees from Hitler. We were having a pleasant vacation when, on the 17th of July, a general strike introduced the Spanish Civil War.

On that day, a Sunday I believe, some striking truck drivers refused to deliver soda bottles, the kind used to siphon soda water. The bottles were delivered on pushcarts by strikebreakers, and a fight broke out in the street. We sat on the terrace of a café in the Ramblas, dodging flying bottles. This was my first encounter with the war. While the siphon bottles were being thrown, we got under the table until things quieted down. In the following week, it was understood that Franco was arriving in the south of Spain, and all our part of the world became mobilized.

The mobilization started with the takeover of Navy craft in the harbor of Barcelona. The sailors evidently mutinied and took command of the ships while the officers were in Barcelona on a leave. The officers hid themselves in the Colon Hotel after the sailors took over the ships.

Rose and André and Jacques and I were in the Ramblas looking at what was going on one day. The streets were quiet, the shops were closed and men in their rope-soled shoes ran through the streets with rifles held over their chests with pieces of cloth or string. They ran very quickly, and one of my impressions is that of the sound of the rope-soled shoes on the pavement. There was some distant shooting, though we didn't see any. The prostitutes were busy, too. They had gotten hold of guns somewhere and were having a jolly time in the streets. They would point their guns at men and make them empty their pockets onto the sidewalk. They would kick around the keys and money, then, using the gun as a stick, would tell the men to pick them up again and get going.

Eventually, the fighting became very heavy in the Place de Catalonia, the end of the Ramblas. This was a large square, on which the Colon Hotel was located, facing the sea. The engagement there is perfectly described in Malraux's book, *Man's Hope*. Malraux and a journalist named Jean Oberle, a friend of ours, had shown up at the first sign of war. They were in the hotel, in back of the mattresses protecting the naval officers holed up there. I myself am incapable now of telling any more about the beginning of the Spanish Civil War except for the little that I experienced.

In Barcelona, Jacques and I were sitting on a terrace of a café sending beer up to the men behind sacks piled in the street around Catalonia Square. There were dead horses in the square that we could see from that distance. There was some exchange of fire between the hotel and snipers on the roofs surrounding the park. Suddenly, from around the corner of the street on the right-hand side of the square came a small troop of uniformed men of the home guard, the Guardia Civil, in very dark blue with black patent leather hats, like Napoleon's melon-shaped hat. There were about fifty of them behind an officer, a short, elderly man who walked with a limp. He and the Guardia Civil represented the government of Catalonia, the Republic of Spain, fighting against the officers in the Colon Hotel, who were representing Franco and the rebellion. It was the Fascists against the government. The elderly officer, going ahead of his men, crossed half the square to the center column and then turned right towards the hotel, from the middle of the column, right straight up to the door, limping as he went and holding the flag. I was reminded of Sarah Bernhardt the time I had seen her carrying the tricolor in a vaudeville show, walking on a wooden leg. The soldiers shot at the hotel and then used a ramrod to break in the door, entered and captured the naval officers who were there.

During my two-month stay, the only part I played in helping the cause was to select works of art that might be harmed in small churches and other places taken over by the local anarchists. The anarchists, with all of the left, were loyal to the government and carefully disciplined by, as a matter of fact, the communists in the area. They were an active group of very angry young men. They wore red bands on their arms with black lettering. I was asked to go with these young men to pick out the works of art when they cleaned out the small churches in the villages around the countryside that they intended to turn into schools.

This was not a difficult nor very dangerous job. I sat in the car, and the young men who would not dream of sitting, stood on the running board with their flags flying and their red armbands conspicuously displayed as we went into the villages. First they went into the churches and took out the furniture. I picked out those things I thought were of lasting value, and we put them in the car. All else was put in front of the church for the local people to pick up and take home if they cared to. I don't know how many of them did so. I imagine from the look on their faces they were too frightened to take anything. There were mostly old women saying their rosaries very fast, the children clinging to their black skirts as though the devil himself had come. None would touch even a candle that had been put out, and I wouldn't be surprised if they dashed right behind us and replaced all the furniture in the church. We also took many crates that had not been unpacked and a great store of church materials just over from St. Sulpice in Paris. Much money had been spent on altar pieces and other materials, and we took these back to Barcelona to sell.

The only danger I ever faced was the possibility of being shot by one of our own men. Leaving the Massons' home, I walked one evening to the top of the hill. There was an old building there, and I stood near it looking out to sea where the fishermen were using lights to attract fish. I was accosted by two red-armbanded young men with guns who asked what I was doing there. They were certain I was at the very least a spy. One held a gun at my head while the other questioned me. In my foreign-accented Spanish, I told them I was just looking at the lights of the fishermen. They told me to go back to town to the house where I was living. So I walked back to the Massons' house, while they went along the road ahead of me. Suddenly there was the sound of a shot being fired. André and Rose went out to find that one of the men had shot himself through the foot, quite accidentally, just fooling around with the gun. I felt lucky that the shot had gone through his foot and not my head.

16

We stayed in Spain until the food became scarce and it seemed as though there would soon be nothing left to eat but anchovies and honey. By October, Franco was appointed by the invaders as Chief of Spanish States. But by then we were back in Paris, at the Café de Flore, telling a much-interested Picasso the little we had seen. Picasso was no longer the nonchalant artist we had known before. His concern over the fate of Spain was very genuine, and he asked us to explain all we knew. This was the longest conversation I had ever had with him in the many years I'd seen him, almost daily, getting out of his old Hispano-Suiza that always looked a bit dilapidated.

Although we were glad to share our experience, Spain was not our prime interest. We did, however, begin to look a little more closely to what was going on in France. Since 1928, when the franc was devalued and many people suffered as a consequence, there had been a National Workmen's Insurance law giving some protection in sickness and old age to workers. There, too, had been the evacuation of the Rhineland and the short presidency of

Doumergue, who had been assassinated when I was in Tangier.[1] The elections began to turn more and more toward the left. The Stavisky case in 1933 had centered on some wild money scheme that was never really cleared up, but the right wing politicians and the young rightist clubs like the Camelots du Roi were constantly fighting the leftists, until the latter finally became a strong political party.[2]

In the summer of 1936, we were sure that the French government, now under Léon Blum, would help the Spanish government. We were disappointed, though rather later than many of our friends, who had been wondering why France had been finagling around with the Italians during the Ethiopian crisis. We began to look more carefully to see what had happened, why we had been disappointed. Then the French KKK, the "cagoulards," were discovered. They were a rightist/fascist group that had all sorts of fortified dugouts and ammunition, a real revolutionary movement intending to overthrow Blum. All of their munitions were taken away when they were found, but Blum was having an almost impossible time trying to hold the government together. The ordinary people were not only withholding their taxes, as usual, but the bankers, industrialists and merchants were trying to undermine the government, so the treasury was just about empty. All the have-gots were saying they would rather have Hitler in the Élysée than Léon Blum.

Still, I danced as usual in the afternoon at the Boeuf. Sometimes in the evening, Jacques and I would go to the Bateau Ivre upstairs, where I knew the pianist, an American, Val Garman, a cowboy type from Colorado who was very popular at the time. Val and I spent many a delightful afternoon together singing duets. He introduced me to his friend, Antonio Castillo, who was

Chanel's first designer.[3] Through him, I was not only dressed by Chanel, I often wore her own dresses, discarded after she had worn them just once. Antonio sold them to me for as little as five dollars each.

I was wearing one of Chanel's hand-me-downs when I was taken to the Bal des Petits Lits Blancs in Cannes. My escort was Felix Rollo, who was related to Egypt's King Farouk and who often stayed at Villefranche near the summer apartment Cecile and I rented. Felix was a friend of Coco Chanel, and between dances we stopped to chat with her. Mlle. Chanel mentioned she was thinking about where to put her money. She was, "of course," taking it out of France "because of the socialists in the government." She was, however, undecided between New York and London. Indignant and haughty beyond my boots, I said, "If I were French, I would keep it in France." She laughed and changed the subject, no doubt to keep from reminding me how easy it was for me to say that since I didn't have any money to invest anywhere. Or perhaps she recognized that I was wearing one of her hand-me-downs.

Despite the social and political turmoil in France, I was not terribly concerned, certainly not that evening. I remember much more clearly walking out in the moonlight between the casino and the sea with Felix Rollo, who had hold of my arm. I'm sure he was not so nearly impressed by me as I was by him. We were talking about déjà-vu and experiences with premonitions, and as usual, I was inserting my two cents' worth while also trying to be as seductive as possible. Felix came to the Welcome Hotel in Villefranche each summer, not, alas, to be seduced by either Cecile or me, though we both had a terrific crush on him. We suspected he much preferred looking at the "pretty American sailors."

Our apartment was on the quay, from which we could see the American ships in port and hear the "Star Spangled Banner" and the "Marseillaise" played at sunrise each day, usually off-key. In back of us was a small bordello to which the sailors came in the evening. We could see into the room where they were entertained by the girls. They danced to the music of phonograph records, and I can remember only one record being played over and over again: "The leaves of brown came tumbling down in September."[4]

When Cecile and I were together in Villefranche, we complemented each other quite nicely. Her extreme blondness and my darkness went well together. I would wear a white crèpe dinner dress, and she would wear a black one. During the summer on the Côte, instead of wearing jewelry, we always wore carnations. We had them in our hair, around our necks and wrists. We used colors we thought would set off our coloring and hopefully be attractive to the young men, all of good families, of course, and mostly quite good looking. We would sail in their star boats, and go dancing in Cannes, at the Chez Victor.

One night, Cecile and I decided to go there alone. The maître d', who had seen us there before with our friends, knew us and apparently thought the men were putting up their car, so he led us to a table. We sat there very demurely until the waiter came over. He asked if we were alone, and we said yes. Well, women were not supposed to be there alone, but he decided to take our order anyway. We ordered some port or other harmless wine and enjoyed listening to the dance music.

At the table next to ours was a group of middle-aged men, all speaking French with different accents. Cecile and I were speaking English. She was trying to learn my American-accented

English since she thought she looked like a Hollywood starlet. Finally, one brave man came over to us and addressed us in English. He told us he was from the League of Nations and had been in Cannes on some commission or other. He wondered if he could invite one of us to dance. "Why, certainly," I said, knowing they were respectable men. Cecile was a little surprised, but I went off to waltz with the man, a Czech, heavyset, but a beautiful dancer. Soon I saw Cecile on the floor dancing with someone else, and we wound up dancing with men of all different nationalities.

Suddenly, however, Cecile broke away from her partner with a look of deep annoyance, returned to the table and insisted we must leave. It seems she had danced with a man who asked where she was from. Instead of telling him, she had replied, "Guess," fully expecting him to say Hollywood. Unfortunately, he answered, "Brussels," which was where she was from. He had recognized her accent because he had been the Mexican consul to Brussels. He said he loved everyone in Brussels and that she was very beautiful, but it didn't pacify Cecile. She was convinced she was speaking with my Hollywood accent and was quite disappointed. That ended our unescorted nights out on the town.

In the winter, we went to the Maritime Alps, to the cottage of one of our beaux on the Côte d'Azur. We all ran through the big old house posting signs declaring, "I've come here for peace and quiet. Leave me alone," and the like. But none of us paid any attention to them, and we made as much noise and mischief as we could. I distinguished myself by cooking what they called "an American mess." I would leave a large pot of water on the back of the coal stove into which I scraped off everything left on everyone's plate after dinner to make a grand soup. Once in a while,

I'd simply add more water. "So that's what you eat in the United States," they said. They complained and laughed and made a great fuss, but every afternoon, when we came in from skiing, they would go one by one to take the ladle and dip out a cup of the hot soup.

It was in that pleasant house with the pleasant company that we heard on the radio the reports from Munich, of "peace in our time" and all that political rot. The men in our group belonged to Les Chasseurs Alpins, the Alpine Regiment, trained to fight on skis in the mountains. We knew it would not be long before they would be on active duty. We returned to Paris with one eye and one ear tuned to every gesture of the lunatic in the East. Hitler did not disappoint us.

I remembered the afternoon years earlier that the Germans at the Berlin Olympics refused to salute Jesse Owens on his victory. I sat on the terrace of the Deux Magots at a small table beside André Derain, who, on that afternoon, lost all of his smooth sophistication. He was furious! I had never seen him like that. He had always seemed to be above all the foolishness of mankind and looked down on the politicians, chuckling over their stupidity. But this time, he was indignant, fighting mad. And the struggles of the American blacks, from which I was becoming gradually more and more detached, came home to me with a bang. Thinking of all the beautiful athletes I had loved—Charles West, Ned Gardine, Ralph Bunche—I began to boil. I dreamed of ways of shooting the world's most hellish racist.

Of course, it was only a dream. When my cousin, Langston Hughes, showed up on his way to a Geneva peace conference with Theodore Dreiser, his stories about Harlem kept me in stitches. I laughed with him and forgot all about shooting anyone.

Peace and joy and good will toward all men shined through Langston's entire personality. Even his description of the funeral of my friend A'Lelia Walker was as funny as it was sad. (Picture the four Ink Spots singing at a funeral!) As Langston said in one of his poems: "When you come to my funeral, come dressed in red / 'Cause I ain't got no business being dead." That's how I felt and still feel. When it comes my time, just lower me into the sea to the sound of a good jazz band playing "When the Saints Go Marching In."

But in 1938, Langston and I were both very much alive and kicking. I gave for him one of the funniest cocktail parties I have ever given. He invited a lot of his friends and I asked a lot of mine. What a combination! His friends included East Indians, Africans, and other colonial people who lived in Paris or were studying there. My friends were artists, intellectuals and the aristocratic Russian princes, friends of Guy de Châteaubriant, about whom I was quite mad at the time. These assorted groups tried to talk to each other, and the result was an outrageous shambles. None of them seemed to speak the same language, and no one knew what the others were talking about. Langston and I, with an ear here, there and all over, would glance at each other and break out laughing at all the confusion. Even the young women were divided. There was Cecile, always the lovely lady, who had arrived with Artaud, Mme. Léger and Kiki. There were the dates and wives of some of Langston's colonials, proudly wearing native dresses and bright exotic jewelry, most of them very radical, many of them communists. And there were Guy's friends, royalists, Camelots du Roi, with their girls. Everyone was talking at odds. It was the greatest mish-mash!

I became angry once, however, despite my efforts to remain above it all, when I heard one of the colonials saying he preferred Hitler to the "hypocrites" of France, England and the United States. I told him he didn't know what he was talking about, that he didn't even know what rights of men were, having experienced the enlightenment of the Europeans only secondhand, until they had taught him. Now he was using that enlightenment as a stick with which to beat his teachers. They had taught him the notions of fair play, equality, decency and brotherhood. Even if they couldn't always live up to their ideals, at least they tried. The Nazis didn't even pretend to employ the concepts, made no effort to do so. They were of a different race, all right, out of the human race altogether. I might have gone on all night, but I remembered my mother's recent admonition to leave social, racial, religious and political involvement to the professionals and live, as she was now trying to do, for each day's simple pleasures. So, I dropped the sermon.

During the '30s, until the time she died just before the war, my mother had been concentrating on those things that interested her most deeply and gave her more satisfaction than her involvement in philanthropies and political organizations ever had. She was reading everything she found interesting, and she would often write me about what was happening to Gertrude Stein in the United States, mostly not anything very good. She reported on ballet, opera and symphonies. She was also very interested in my brother's life and his involvement with a woman she didn't like.

One afternoon, I was preparing for a dinner party I was giving that evening when a messenger came by with a cable. It was from my father and stated simply, "Your mother died quietly in her sleep last night." I read the cable with great surprise; I hadn't even known she'd been ill. But I went on fixing dinner, as yet untouched by the realization of her death. I tried instead to understand the significance of a dream I had had the night before. In it, I was mounting the column in the Place Vendôme when a woman ahead of me, whom I was following to Napoleon's statue, turned and threw from her shoulders a burlap cape she was wearing. It was dusty and I found it very disagreeable, but I left it on and continued to follow her. Then I woke up. Somehow, I knew this related to my mother's death. She was passing on to me the burdens of her life.

When my guests arrived that evening, I remarked that my mother had died. Everyone was most sympathetic and suggested that perhaps I didn't feel up to entertaining. Well, that had never occurred to me, but all of a sudden, I realized I didn't have my mother. And with that, I started to cry like a baby. It had taken someone else's expression of my loss for me to understand it myself. I have no recollection who was at that dinner or what we had to eat, but I went through it, "chin up," as Mother would have wanted me to do.

As far as cooking for company went, I had two specialities. One was an American meal, and the other was "stockfish," a complicated meal that I learned to make in the south of France. It consisted of dried codfish that had to be soaked in the bathtub for two or three days to loosen it up, stinking up the apartment abominably, then cooked with many long-forgotten ingredients.

Stockfish was first suggested to me by an elderly poet named Davout, who liked me, he said, because I looked like Jane Avril, the mistress of Toulouse-Lautrec, a long-gone friend of his from the turn of the century. Somehow he related me to that period.

He wrote a few poems to and about me. He was old and a little lonely, so sometimes I asked him up to a meal, and I always made stockfish for him.

One night, when I was making mashed potatoes for Wendy Braithwaite, an Australian friend, and her American boyfriend, Antonin Artaud came in and asked me what that "American garbage" was that I was beating up with butter and heavy cream. "Let me taste that garbage," he said, and he took the pot away from me. With a large serving spoon, he sat on the stool in the kitchen and finished the whole thing before I noticed what he had done. Then he said, "Alors, ce n'est pas mal, ma petite Américaine," and walked out, slamming the door. I had to cook more potatoes and do the whole thing over again, but with the tolerant attitude everyone had toward genius, I went along, happy to have had Artaud in for "a meal," so to speak.

While I was preparing the salad dressing the young American came into the kitchen and saw a garlic for the very first time. He asked to taste it, so I cut a piece of French bread and put on it some olive oil, salt and pressed garlic. That was a dish popular in the south of France, and I told him it was a school boy's lunch he might enjoy. He thought it was great.

The sequel happened in quite an amusing way. One time, after eating a meal of bread, olive oil and garlic, he went to a cinema. The movie houses for avant-garde films were very small, more like a club than a theater. During the intermission, everyone looked all around to see who in the world was stinking up the place with garlic. They fixed their eyes on a dark Frenchman in the back of the room who had heavy eyebrows and a big, black moustache. They took it for granted that he was the "Marius from Marseilles" who was ruining the atmosphere of the place. The young

American, in his blond innocence, was never suspected. When the lights went out, he breathed even more heavily, he said, and had a great time shifting the guilt to the poor man in the back of the room.

He and Wendy were very interested in the Wally Simpson affair that had ended in the King of England's abdication. At this time, the now-Duke and duchess of Windsor were in Paris. Many persons conjectured on their situation. My own theory was that the king was not very clearly sexually oriented. There was his devotion to Georges Carpentier, his rumored attachment to an aggressive woman and his friendship with the Big Boys in Berlin. Pictures of the apartment of the Duke and Duchess in Paris, illustrated in fashion magazines at the time, showed on their grand piano huge framed portraits of the Duke shaking hands with Hitler and Goering. He seemed very proud of his friendship with them. All this was at odds with his remarks about having given up the kingdom "for the woman I love."

The English and the French treated royalty quite differently from each other. The upper middle class in England felt distinctly separated from royalty. Charles, for instance, had objected to my wearing any of my three modest little fur coats. He said only royalty and kept women wore fur. The nobility in Paris, on the other hand, were so supported by bourgeois money, largely through marriage, that many of the haute bourgeoisie were related to nobility. It was the aim of the nobility to get money to keep up their chateaus; it was the aim of the bourgeoisie to add a "de" to their name.

Leftists, rightists, bourgeoisie, nobility—I went shining through it all with an inner light, for I had a deep, secret love, one which I knew was reciprocated. It kept me flying through the banality of my daily activities with the joy of an angel. After Charles returned from Egypt, discouraged, disheartened and sick, he made my own life very difficult. He was angry with me because I wouldn't accept the dialectical materialism and all that claptrap that he thought was Marxism. He was lost, sick, and often drunk. One evening, we were having dinner at the Saint Benoit when in sailed "Sir Galahad," which is as good a way as any to describe the handsome man who came into the restaurant and into my life. He was well over six feet tall, beautifully made. He walked past our table, looked at me rather fixedly and sat not far from us, facing, however, in the opposite direction so that I saw only the back of his head.

It was a blondish head with soft, straight, light brown hair, sort of a square neck, on the shoulders and rib cage of a hero. I thought he was a beautiful man, the most unusually attractive I had ever seen. I was fascinated by his neck, his shoulders, his back, and I wanted to touch them. He did not turn around, but when he finished his rather hurried meal, he walked past our table again, and in passing, he smiled at me. I dropped my head in confusion. The smile had completely bowled me over. He had deep blue eyes and a long straight nose like on a Greek statue. But what attracted me most on that occasion was the soft warmth of his smiling lips, full lips that seemed to roll away from his teeth in sensuous pleasure. (What a trite description that seems to me!) Well, his teeth seemed to be pearly. At least they were shining in the light, or perhaps it was the light of our communication that made him seem to me to be all pearl. He was obviously an educated man, perhaps an officer, elegant in a casual sort of way. He walked with dignity, with ease, without haste and with a self-assurance that was just short of arrogance. It seemed to say: "I like you, and I'm going to get you."

After dinner, when Charles and I returned to the hotel, I saw the man sitting in the lobby, reading. His back was to the door. I went up to our room with Charles, who was then quite drunk. He became disagreeable, accusing me of betraying him politically. In that moment, I became quite hysterical. I went to the window (we were on the third or fourth floor), and perhaps without the recollection of the smile in the restaurant, I might have jumped. I was far from stable. I caught myself, however, and found an excuse to go downstairs, to check the mail.

He came out of the lobby toward me as if he had known me forever. He held out his hand and said, "Good evening, Madame," and told me his name, Guy de Châteaubriant. He held my hand and looked at me firmly, as a doctor might, with a reassuring smile, and asked me to join some friends for bridge. I told him I didn't play and that my husband was ill and I had to return to him. Then I turned on my heel and flew upstairs, but I was no longer interested in jumping out of any window.

I don't know how I contrived to meet him again and again, but meet him I certainly did, and our lovemaking became the most exquisite experience of my varied love life. He was a tender, protective and all-satisfying lover, difficult to describe, except to say that for me he was perfect. So even before Charles went to the sanatorium in Grasse, I had acquired the strength to live again. As Vincenzo used to sing: "The heart of a woman soon forgets, soon loves again."

I stayed in Paris and lived the life I have described, the casual life of Saint-Germain-des-Prés. The war in Spain, the jaunts to Villefranche, the pleasures of Cannes or skiing in Bereuil were the everyday things I was involved in. But it was the clandestine relationship with Guy de Châteaubriant that kept me happy, that would remain good, light and wonderful through whatever other experiences I might be having. To my other friends, it seemed just a friendship of no importance. They considered him to be a *sacré Jésuite,* certainly not someone to be in love with.

There was never any question of marriage. I didn't even know where he lived; I never asked. I took the beauty of the relationship as it came. He would show up at ten or eleven in the morning, after my masseuse had come and gone. I would be relaxed and feeling quite refreshed, and our lovemaking was in tune with my mood. Then we would go out for lunch. After that, he went off (I thought) to sell insurance, and I spent the afternoon with Cecile or at work with Jacques Baron.

I knew who his father was, quite a famous writer, one we would call a typical old *sacré Jésuite.* He had translated Protestant works into French, among them Mary Baker Eddy's *Science and Health with Key to the Scriptures,* the Christian Science textbook. That was a great joke because the Jesuits were not supposed to be making money doing anything like that. Guy told me lots of stories about his father that made him seem just about what we on the Left Bank thought the extreme right were like. And I took it for granted (as did anyone else who happened to be with us) that he was in accord with us and certainly in horror of his father and those others who were collaborating with de Brinon and Abets of the Hitler group.[5]

He sometimes told me of the things they were doing just to get me to protest. I was deeply hurt, annoyed to think that he even knew anyone who was involved in such things. They had, for instance, arranged for French youngsters to go on hikes into Germany and brought German youths into France. The French rarely involved themselves in Boy Scouts and such group activities, and so few French youngsters participated. But in came mobs of German youths who, in a few years, would become members of the Panzer Division. That was the idea of the Jesuits, Abets and de Brinon and the rest of the reactionaries. All of this annoyed me, but Guy thought it was a jolly good joke.

Actually, most of the religious, financial, big business, military and even the political greats of the time were willing to collaborate with the Nazis. They were so afraid that Léon Blum and the socialists would bring Russia into Paris, they were perfectly willing to sell the country, turn over the keys to the factories, turn the government over to the Nazis. Guy's father was not unusual. He was not a freak of the culture; he was just doing what was expected of him as a member of a rich and noble family, and one very high in the church.

His family's money came out of the Companie Trans-Atlantique, the French line. They were from Brittany, and Guy spent a great deal of his youth sailing. He loved the sea and the Antilles and all the far-away places. He often told me I was his dream of the island child come true, the creole, the exotic girl of the islands who could live with him in France in a civilized world and yet retain all the charm of the jungle.

I didn't care how he fantasized about me. Every word, every gesture of his love, every moment spent with him was one in which I was enveloped in all the romance I had ever imagined in the presence of a man. And like a psychotic, a schizophrenic, I lived a life of waking and dreaming. When I was with Guy I was in the dream world, and when I was with Charles or Cecile or Jacques, my dream world lay just beneath the surface, coming to me any morning or evening. Always there was a hidden beauty, something shining within me that made me feel comfortable. I hardly knew the difference between the great joys and the less joyful moments, the "real" moments of everyday life.

Tonny, whom I still saw occasionally, was perhaps the only one of my friends who suspected something was going on. Making fun of me, he said: "When a count encounters a count, what does he recount? Always stories of counts!" That was his way of letting me know that I was fooling myself if I thought I was in any real communication with Guy de Châteaubriant and that I had better stick to my own associates, those who appreciated me and who were not so far removed socially.

But I had that fixation, my idea of a gentleman, like my father, my brother, my uncle and Charles. I demanded gentleness and all the things that went with it, well-washed hair, delicate and fresh linen and all of the personal habits I associated with a gentle up-bringing that I found lacking in strong, direct, dashing men. Guy teased me sometimes, saying I liked only royalty.

Perhaps he was right. Cecile was a princess, in her own way. Mirette Oppenheimer would stand for no *lèse majesté;* she once slapped Max Ernst quite hard across the face at the Coupole when he called her a "bonne fille," a good gal. I was also friendly with a Hungarian countess named Margot von Huszár. She had been for some time at the Hungarian legation in Berlin. She was sympathetic to the Nazis and rather liked some of them personally. She and Châteaubriant teased me about my abhorrence of "the beasts," i.e., the Germans.

We sometimes visited my friend Nancy Perry, whose husband, Vichy Seroff, had been an accompanist to Isadora Duncan. He was able to confirm for us stories we'd heard about Isadora. One told of a cocktail party where she was asked if she knew a male guest there. "Why, of course I know him," she had said. "He's the father of my second child." Nancy was a pretty, blonde American, and knowing that she was attractive to Frenchmen, she tried often to flirt with Châteaubriant. For his part, Guy liked to tease her. He told her one time that no one who had lived in France for a long time and really knew anything about eating would dream of scraping off the outer coating of a cheese before eating it. A real gourmet, he insisted, should eat the rind. Poor Nancy went on chewing rinds for the longest time until I finally tipped her off.

She had been teased before. Vichy had told her, while visiting some friends in Berlin, that it was proper for her to wipe her feet on the doormat until their hostess wondered what Nancy had stepped in that was taking so long to get off her shoes. That sort of thing happened because Nancy was so anxious not to be mistaken for a "barbarous American." I sympathized with her; I, too, was trying not to be too American. But I was a "noble savage" and not a rich, beautiful blonde, so I attracted more sympathy than she did. Like the attraction of opposites which had brought Châteaubriant and me together, Nancy and I were very attached to each other. We referred to ourselves as "Topsy" and "Eva" and we spent days together in her luxurious apartment, singing duets.[6] She said it would be good if she had my voice and her training, a great compliment!

As Americans, we were both deeply ashamed of the treatment that Marian Anderson received from the Daughters of the American Revolution in Washington, where she was denied permission to perform in the DAR hall because she was black.[7] We were also quite outraged by the behavior of the Gold Star Mothers who came to France to put wreaths on their sons' graves.[8]

Arriving in Paris, the black women segregated from the whites, they marched up the Champs Élysées like the hordes of Berbers who used to come up from the desert in North Africa, stamping and making frightful noises and causing all the Europeans to run off the streets. Well, the Gold Star Mothers stomping up the Champs Élysées were almost as aggressive and frightening. To top it all, when they got to the Arc de Triomphe, instead of observing the customary one minute of silence, one overzealous, vociferous mama made a speech in a loud, booming voice.

All the taxis, all the traffic had stopped in respect, and there was such a silence in the Champs Élysées, you could have heard the birds. The voice that came through the silence sounded like a parrot squawking. In astonishment and indignation, the taxis all sounded their klaxons, and everyone beat on glasses all around the Arc de Triomphe to protest the woman's ignorance. Fortunately, the black Gold Star Mothers were trailing behind, as usual, and were far from the bleating voice at the Arc. They were applauded the length of the Champs Élysées.

17

One evening, I was surprised to find Man Ray in a restaurant in a little town high above Nice, where Cecile and our friends went often to dine and dance. Man came from a corner of the restaurant and asked me to dance with him. When we were on the dance floor, he asked me why I had passed the table without speaking to Lee Miller. Lee was a friend of his, with whom he had been deeply in love at one time. But she had run off and married someone else, a wealthy Egyptian. This all had happened several years before, and I didn't know Lee was back in Europe. At the end of the dance, I went over to the table. I found Lee transformed from a slender, long-legged beautiful American girl from the Middle West into a big fat babe. When she spoke, I saw that she had a front tooth missing. I took it for granted that Man was over his deep hurt.

Later, he confided to me that he was, indeed, cured. He had invited Lee to lunch earlier, he said, and she had eaten, before his very eyes, three dozen oysters. The sight of all those oysters being gobbled up had completed his cure. He was tolerant to the point of detachment most of the time, but above all, he was fastidious. The war changed many of the spoiled brats, however, and later Lee distinguished herself by becoming one of the most courageous and successful photographers of the London Blitz. Felix Rollo, the most delicate of the Don Juans on the Côte d'Azur before the war, became a heroic RAF pilot.

I leave it to the historians to record the exterior events of the time. We were busy attending the vernissages of the Berman brothers and Dalí, Miró, Max Ernst, Bracque, Man Ray, Giacometti, Tchelitchew, Tzara, Amillot, Brancusi, Léger, Derain and Picasso. These shows were going on constantly. And, of course, there were the literary productions, the *Révolution Surréaliste* and the *Cahiers d'Art*. Oh, there were so many things to do and read and attend to each month, each more amusing and delightful than the other.

I also had great fun dancing. When I wasn't looking at the ballet, I was taking lessons, at one time from a Chilean protégé of "Chile," Mirod Guiness' husband Guevara, who taught me South American dances. I hoped, for a time, to become a professional dancer, but I was never a professional anything in France. I prefer to think it was because foreigners were not allowed to have a work card and that the only job I might have gotten would have been modeling clothes for Chanel, since they always needed models with a "good sunburn." Photographic modeling was never checked on by the powers that be, fortunately, and so I was never thrown into jail for having those dinky little paydays, nor for my Opera Mundi translations.

Thus, with the pittance the Westminster Bank gave me from the stocks from Charles and from my father's contributions, I lived as well as anyone could in those "broke days." They were cheap days, at least. The apartment cost forty dollars a month, and one lived well on about one hundred fifty dollars a month. That is, I could because I was a woman. But there were among our friends people with a great deal of money who entertained lavishly. There was the Bal of the Comte de Beaumont, a great event to which many of us were invited, and the hospitality of Madame Cutally, Caresse Crosby and Mirod Guiness-Guevara.

I had an especially happy encounter with Buffie Johnson, who was a delightful companion and who had enough money to rent a large apartment in the Rue du Bac. She had come to Paris to meet the "greats," she said, and someone told her that Man Ray and I were the only Americans who knew the surrealists. And so, not daring to ask Man, she asked me to introduce her around. She was a gifted painter herself, I soon discovered, and I told her nothing would be easier than to arrange a cocktail party to which I would ask almost everyone she wanted to meet. She put out a great buffet, and I went to the terrace of the Deux Magots and the Café de Flore around the corner and said there was a rich American who was having a party. Almost everyone got up as one and walked around the corner to accept her hospitality.

She was delighted, as were all of us. Except for Tristan Tzara, who was mad at me and took that occasion to tell me he had a bone to pick with me ("a tooth against you" was the way he put it). He said he had heard that I had told a story about him he didn't care for. The story was that he had gone into the Viking one night and seen a beautiful woman sitting in a corner, obviously a stranger. He asked her why she had come to Paris, and she replied, "to find the greatest poet in the world." He said, "You don't have to look any further; it is I." He later married the woman, a wealthy Swedish heiress, and they lived happily ever after. Having married her years before he had become so respectable and bourgeois, I guess he found the story distasteful, and he told me to stop repeating such slander. I wiped the smile off my face and apologized.

On the 14th of July, 1939, Bastille Day, Buffie Johnson and I went out to dance all night with two young Frenchmen she knew who were from fine families and were very conscious of the fact. She had met them through friends of her family. We went from one end of Paris to the other and found at each corner, at each square, dancing going on, everyone celebrating. Marlene Dietrich was singing on the steps of the Opera, and Charles Trenet was at the Trocadero. It was the most frolicsome 14th of July that anyone there had ever remembered. I think we were all very conscious that it might be the last Bastille Day before the war. It was.

The long night's jubilation ended for our foursome in Buffie's apartment, where she and I pretended to be more interested in each other than in the two young men, whom we had asked up only for a nightcap. We thought it was a great joke, but they didn't think it was funny. They walked out and slammed the door.

For my birthday, March 28, Châteaubriant had taken me to the Boeuf sur le Toit to dance in the afternoon. I loved to dance with him because he moved with such dignity, grace and a lightness which reminded me of Charlie West. Guy also had a good sense of humor, and I loved all his manners and the way in which he guided me so thoughtfully. Being only five feet three myself, I had to wear high heels to adapt to his well over six foot height. We couldn't have danced cheek to cheek, but I was well aware that we looked good together because of all the admiring glances of the other couples and sometimes even of the men in the band.

The charm of the Boeuf was a nice change from Saint-Germain-des-Près. The Duchess of Kent, who was quite lovely, and many other members of the fashionable world often could be seen there. It was there that Jean Patou had asked me to be a model for his summer collection.[1]

Michael, the bartender, made a "Michael cocktail," a mixture of champagne, gin and Cointreau. It was a good afternoon drink. The ubiquitous and sophisticated Moysés was a gracious host.[2] He was a friend of Cocteau and one of the sparkling wits of the '30s.

On afternoons like this, when Guy wanted to please me, he talked about music. He was not interested in "Les Six," Satie, Poulenc and that group I had known with Pleyel, Marthe Martine, Tonny and Virgil Thomson.[3] We both, however, liked piano music, I through my senses, he through his knowledge of the structure of the music. In talking about it, he taught me, and I was a willing and loving pupil. He appreciated Beethoven, but I preferred Mozart. There was less to understand, perhaps, and much more to feel in the simple music of the eighteenth century.

The wife of Guy's best friend studied piano with Nadia Boulanger, so that I had the pleasure of getting secondhand a great deal of gossip. I got the impression there was a clandestine affair between Guy and his friend's wife. I was not jealous. I felt his world was so different from mine. I might have been La Dame aux Camélias, except that I was a healthy American and not likely to die of TB or love or anything else if I could help it.[4] I was an American edition of Back Street Love who could laugh at herself and the whole situation. Had I felt otherwise, I would have been like a salmon trying to swim upstream, quite ridiculous.

The only way I might have thought of gaining his interest in marriage would have been through my uncle, who was a member of the Légion d'Honneur and very important in Châteaubriant's social circle. But I wouldn't have dreamed of mentioning my affair to my uncle for fear of embarrassing him. My uncle would have been most upset had anyone mentioned Negroes or Indians in his family. I didn't want to enter his bourgeois world with Châteaubriant any more than I had with the German encountered at my uncle's home ten years earlier, or, for that matter, to have married any bourgeois in the United States. I was a bird in dizzy flight, going from flower to flower, with never a full meal, but enjoying every sip.

One day, Guy and I were shopping in old England. He was looking at a tweed jacket, and the salesman, trying to encourage him to buy it, took the jacket and ran a pencil right through the tweed. Then he pulled out the pencil and showed that the tweed could be pushed and pulled until there was no sign of the hole. He said that was the mark of the best tweed. "We must tell the French army about this," said Guy. "If they start making uniforms in tweed, the bullets can go through and we can use the uniforms for the next wars, from generation to generation." The Englishman thought our laughter inappropriate but we went on laughing, right into the Second World War.

My light-hearted detachment followed through into my relationship with Châteaubriant. After an involvement he had with my dressmaker that I "ignored," he went after my masseuse, a nice husky young woman. I left the house early one day, about eight in the morning. When I returned about three hours later, Guy's big old calling card was waiting for me, inscribed with the message: "I have taken Maria to my hotel."

I was surprised, not at his behavior particularly, but at the cheeky way in which he announced it. But I went to lunch with him as usual. I teased him a bit, but I really didn't feel terribly hurt. I was acquiring a "seraglio" feeling, no doubt from the French insistence that there were five women for every man in France between the wars. I was beginning to take it for granted that each man had a wife, a mistress and a maid, and perhaps a "poule deluxe," a secretary and a casual gal! I had resigned myself to falling into the one-in-five pattern without diminishing my devotion to Châteaubriant.

Although I had lots of beaux during that period, I would have left any one of them if Guy called. I would have given up a whole day with one of them for five minutes with the one man who truly possessed my heart. Now, a half century later, I suppose that Guy was important to me because he was the first serious partner who had not been a "little brother" for me to take care of. During my childhood, I thought my parents' love and approval of me depended on my taking care of my own little brother. So, I had known men who, though not younger, were of the "little brother" type. After the frantic love-making of Charles, fevered no doubt by his ill health, Guy's careful and considerate control, the mark of a grown-up love, seemed especially marvelous to me.

Cecile and I came back from our summer vacation in Villefranche in 1939 to the beginning of the Second World War. My Hungarian friend, Margot, was pro-Nazi. Her boyfriend was Jean-Marie Conti, of the French Left, as were most of my friends. He was not a communist but a Leftist, a Leon Blum-ist. He was in the Air Ministry, where my uncle was also engaged at the time. I never mentioned my uncle to Jean-Marie, but they were both working under Guy La Chambre, the war minister. We didn't know what the Germans were going to do, but Margot and Châteaubriant (who, by the way, got along beautifully together) seemed to be perfectly sure that France would be taken by the Germans without a shot being fired. And, of course, the Germans would be sweet for us to know and to get along with. The idea seemed to be that we would all live happily ever after once we got rid of the socialists.

Margot's cousin, also a Hungarian countess, had a different experience. She had been married to a Nazi officer who was close to Hitler. They had taken their son into the Young Hitlerites camp against her will. She couldn't do anything about that, but then they took her daughter and threw her into a camp, where she was sure the girl was being mistreated and probably raped. She was ready to leave Germany. She took her daughter with her and fled to Paris. Her description of the Hitler "court" fascinated me. She described Hitler as sitting at the piano, playing Wagner with one finger and looking lovingly at all the lovely ladies, there being only ladies present at his soirées. He would tell them how pretty they were and how pretty their dresses were and how their makeup was or wasn't just right for them, going from one to the other, touching and admiring them. Unlike Margot, her cousin thought Hitler was freakish.

There was a general mobilization. The young men from Nice and Villefranche went back to join the Chasseurs Alpins, and Châteaubriant went back to his parents' chateau in Brittany, where he spent August getting ready to join his group, an anti-aircraft unit headed for the Belgian frontier. Everyone went in different directions to join their military groups. I, too, had to find a place to go. At the American Embassy, I was told to go back to the United States; Paris was apt to be bombarded at any moment, and no one wanted to be responsible for Americans running around Paris. I asked where Mr. Bullitt, the ambassador, was going, and was told he would be going to Dinard. So I packed and got ready to go there, too. Leaving Paris, I willed my gas mask to Margot. She threw it aside, saying, "Do you think the Germans are barbarians?"

I said, "Yes," and fled to Brittany to be near the American Embassy.

Dinard was a pleasant little resort town on the rugged northwest corner of France. It had lots of hotels and a lovely beach or two, and, of course, the ferry to St. Malo. I registered at the Printemps Hotel, and the next morning went out to find the local chapter of the French Red Cross, La Société aux Secours de Blessés Militaires. Once there, I went to enlist as a nurse. I was accepted, and because I was not a registered nurse, I was assigned to the hotel being converted into a hospital. Courses would be given there to women who were preparing themselves for war duty.

The hospital was already staffed with male nurses, soldiers who were in medical training. It seemed evident to me very soon that we were not going to have much heavy nursing duty. Our jobs would be more like those of nuns. With no makeup and not a strand of hair showing, our first duty seemed to be that of comforting wounded soldiers, like the Sisters of Mercy. The doctors of the hospital gave the courses in whatever happened to be their area of expertise. One had been a specialist in tropical medicine, so he taught us about tropical medicine. One had been a gynecologist, which wasn't much help, but we did learn all about male and female anatomy. There was a pharmacist who taught us about pharmacy, and a surgeon who taught the nurses their duties in the operating room.

I volunteered to operate the x-ray machine, and what a great machine it was! It had wires hanging all over it. I had to wear rubber gloves and a big apron to protect myself. Heaven knows what happened to the poor patients who sat in that contraption. Thank goodness I never had to use it on a patient. I hope something better arrived before anyone had to use it. After our lessons in the morning, we went off to lunch and came back to make bandages and bedcoats and all the dressings and clothing to be worn by the patients. During the work period, the women got acquainted with each other, exchanging news and gossip. They were all well-educated, obviously haute bourgeoisie and noblesse. Some of them were attractive, distinguished by their lovely manners, their charm and grace.

Among them, Rose-Monique was the most delightful of all. She was unusually tall, with a crown of light curly hair, under which bright blue eyes sparkled, fringed with dark curling eyelashes and a really cute nose. She was so lively, so full of laughter and love, one hardly noticed her individual features until one had gone through the brilliance of the total expression. When one saw the soft ivory skin, and mouth so rosy and childlike, always without makeup, the sweetness of her spirit seemed to beam out into the world.

I couldn't understand why she chose me to be her friend, unless she knew that I was the one who needed her friendship the most. I was the stranger, and she wanted me to feel welcome. She seemed to take some mischievous glee in sending me little notes during class, as though we were youngsters in school doing something we didn't want the teacher to know about. Her notes were first addressed to "chère Anita" then to "chère" and finally to "chère amie." I always wrote back, calling her "ma petite fille." She was so much taller than I, that really tickled her.

Usually, she was simply dressed in a gray flannel skirt and a lavender cashmere sweater. She wore a little pearl necklace, one of those that has an add-a-pearl sequence collected from the time one is a year old. I think she was eighteen at the time, so it wasn't a pretentious piece of jewelry.

She rode to work on a bicycle, so that when she asked me to go out with her one afternoon, it was because her father had driven her into town and was going to take her back home. When he came for us, it was in a simple black five-seater, not expensive or showy. Her father was tall, much taller than Rose-Monique. He looked like a farmer, save for his delightful manner, his dignity and grace, and the graciousness with which he received me.

We drove out into the country, and I wouldn't have been at all surprised if we had stopped at any one of the farms we passed between Dinard and Dinan. We went through a little village called Pleurtuit, and out again toward the sea. Near the river Rance, we drove into the courtyard of a chateau, "Montmarin," the home of the family Bazin de Jessey.[5] The chateau was the first in which I was ever received as a guest.

We entered the house through the kitchen. The staff welcomed us. They were round, smiling Bretons, obviously part of the family for many years. I vaguely recall a large bosomy cook and two or three girls helping her. I believe bread was baking, and I was reminded of my aunt's kitchen in Baltimore.

I was impressed and delighted with the lovely furnishings in every room. One was a salon in the style of Louis XV, in pale blues and pinks and lavenders and gold, with a huge crystal chandelier and lovely Aubusson carpet. The busiest room was the living room, which was called the "billiards room," where we sat in the evening. The dining room was filled with heavy furniture, fairly modern. Upstairs, the master bedroom was in the center of the first floor, and there were four bedrooms on either side of it.

Rose-Monique's was in the far end, perhaps because she was the youngest. Her three sisters' rooms were occupied by the families of her married sisters and of her brother. I was invited to spend the night and given the brother's room. He was off to war, though I did get to meet him later while he was home on furlough. Following Rose-Monique down those long corridors and through the spacious rooms, I began to understand her long-legged stride.

I first met her sister Jehanne. She was one of the most charming women I have ever met. She was dark and gracious, the mother of four beautiful children. Her husband was not there at the time, and I didn't meet him until dinner. His full name was Henri Villeroy de Galhau. He might have been about thirty at the time, in an officer's uniform, composed, quiet and intelligent. He had brought his wife and children to stay in the family chateau while he was off to war. His ceramics and crystal factory was across the border in Germany, not far from Metz, and his partner was German. Their company, Villeroy and Boch, had been a partnership for generations, though he, of course, was French.[6]

The wife and daughter of Rose-Monique's brother were there, too. I don't remember them very well except that the daughter was round and pretty, blonde, I believe, with blue eyes, a vivacious girl. Her mother, Rose-Monique's sister-in-law, was handsome, of Italian nobility, I think.

I was soon to meet the four Villeroy children. After dinner, the family retired to the billiards room for coffee and to chat. The governess brought in the children. They had been with her all day, learning their lessons and good manners. There were three little boys, somewhere around four, six and eight. They looked alike and seemed to be angelic. They had such sweet expressions, delightful manners and self-assurance, I thought they might have stepped out of a Gainsborough painting. Their mother might have been an Ingres, and Rose-Monique, a Velasquez, slightly mischievous, or in idealized form, a Botticelli. The youngest child, Elizabeth, was just two years old, barely walking. She was a porcelain doll. She was put on my knee for a while during the evening, and the little boys went to talk to one person after the other, shaking hands with the men and kissing the hand of each married woman present.

When they had finished their conversation with each adult in the room, the governess said it was time to go to bed. They went without a word of protest, following her to the door. Little Elizabeth, who had been laughing gaily on my lap and seemed happy to be playing there, slid off with the dignity of someone answering a call to duty. She walked over to the governess and gave her her hand. She was brought back to kiss her parents goodnight and to hug her grandfather. Then they all left the room as they had come in, quietly, happily, secure in the center of a large, secure family.

To find a place in fine art for a portrait of Rose-Monique's father, I would have to go to El Greco. He had the fine features of the nobleman that he was, a thin skin that was freckled, weathered by the sun and the sea. He was as much a sailor, I believe, as a gentleman farmer. He was descended from a long line of St. Malo shipbuilders and owners of the ships that went to Newfoundland for cod.

My admiration for the entire family, gentle and generous, simple and grand, is still undimmed and bright. I am as pleased and flattered today as I was in 1939 to be called their friend. During my long and pleasant visits to Montmarin, I was almost persuaded that the old order should not change. I began to understand some of the qualities of the Royalists that the conservatives were trying to preserve when they fought with the Camelot du Roi or any other reactionary group against the inroad of socialism or industrialism.

Of course, their monarchy wouldn't work; no country is going to remain what it was hundreds of years before. But I understood, at least, the qualities of the traditional respect, honor, intelligence and excellence that had made France great, and the earnest desire of many of the young people to continue in that tradition. The entire family was strongly patriotic. I learned soon, though not from him, that Rose-Monique's father had been the first Frenchman, at the head of his troops, entering the newly gained Alsace-Lorraine in the First World War.

It eventually seeped through my bedazzled consciousness that I was not only being received as a "noble savage" but also as an American ally, an ally of the First World War, for whose help they were truly grateful and whom they still trusted. I learned years later that the family had thought I was a representative of the U.S. Government. Maybe that was one reason they welcomed me so warmly, but at the time, Rose-Monique and I were pals, just friends, like a couple of school girls. Since neither of us had attended a girls' school, we could play according to our own rules, giggling in class, passing notes and chasing off to lunch together.

After I was there a short time, some young men showed up, graduates of St. Cyr and Saumur, who were being trained as aviators. They went to dance in the afternoon at the hotel, and, of course, they danced with the nurses. We had little jokes and giggled about who danced with whom and the crushes that were going on, as though we were all eighteen. We could almost persuade ourselves that there was no war in the background.

I had a special role, to watch over Rose-Monique. She simply could not become involved with anyone she could not marry. There were all sorts of rules about whom this could and could not be. She would have to choose a Frenchman, more specifically a noble Frenchman, more specifically a noble Catholic Frenchman. She mustn't flirt with anyone she couldn't possibly marry. There was also the matter of a dowry. She didn't have a large one, and she must not, at any time, seem to have more money than she had, even if she found an appropriately desirable young man.

We danced some late afternoons in a tea room where all the young nurses of the Red Cross and the men in training met. If Rose-Monique wanted to dance with someone who would not be a suitable fiancé, it was up to me to see that they danced and then quickly separated. Her partner could accompany her no further than her bicycle at the curb.

Once she met a tall, handsome young man, not of her social class. He was an officer and a gentleman, but not quite up to snuff. She liked to dance with him because he was about the only man there taller than she. I received him at our table as if he were my date. Then she was free to dance with him discretely, and he could walk her to her bicycle. But that was it; he was still only the son of a local merchant, after all. In all of these shenanigans, the lambency of her smile matched the levity of my behavior, and we had good times together. I understood and appreciated, really rather liked, all of the restrictions that were placed upon her.

I was carried away by the entire family, even by their strong Catholicism, to the point of thinking about converting. When we went to vespers in the chapel on one side of the chateau, simple, austere and candle-lit, her father reading the prayers, with all of us bundled up against the bitter winter cold, I felt I was in the most divine presence I had ever known. In chapel, M. Bazin de Jessey officiated with such solemnity that one hardly realized he wasn't a priest. His leadership mirrored the integrity of his character, and the congregation reflected the harmony of the family. The walls all around were lined with peasants. Sometimes they wore the local costumes, the girls and women with their high lace coifs, like little towers on their heads, and black dresses with white lace collars. The men wore dark smocks and sometimes held large round hats in their hands. I attended chapel with pleasure when asked to join them, even in the early morning.

What a saint Rose-Monique was! She would come in shivering at five or six in the morning, after attending mass at Pleurtuit, and then go out to carry food or clothing to the poor or assist in the birth of a child or do some of her other charitable duties, as was expected of a woman of the chateau. She would tramp through the mud and the rain and then come back to the house, where I would be wearing everything I could beside the covers and a hot brick or two in the bed. Oh, I thought she was a heroine and a saint, but my common sense kept nagging me to find a way to present her with a pair of rubber boots and stop her wearing those slogging shoes.

I was in awe of the bright thread of sanctity in the fabric of the entire family. One sister, Marguerite, had entered a convent in England. Another was a missionary among the Papua in the South Pacific, and I pictured her among some wild, savage, cannibalistic heathen tribe in far-away New Guinea. This sister, Solange, worked in the "vineyards of the Lord" and seemed to be leading a fruitful life. She had a sense of sanctity and duty to mankind, noblesse oblige and self-sacrifice, saving souls and teaching sensible living.

The family was quite proud of Solange, working out there with her uncle, who was a bishop. Their task was not an easy one. Tall, as pretty as Rose-Monique, radiant, but with dark hair, Solange was also a gifted musician. A snapshot of her playing the violin for the Papui could break one's heart, so tranquil, so simple, a natural saint. Solange was dedicated to her concept of God. Her simplicity and the breadth of her love was obvious in her life in New Guinea, teacher, mother, religious guide to a primitive people.[7] The vein of sanctity that characterized the lives of the sisters who were nuns seemed also present in the daily life of M. Bazin de Jessey and the whole family. The strength and sincerity, deep below the almost jovial performance of their daily chores, their amiable conversation, struck me as being almost supernatural.

M. Bazin de Jessey paid so little attention to my observations about the state of affairs in France, I thought he hadn't heard me. I was disturbed because each day I heard an expression of sympathy, among women working at the hospital, with the fascist ideas I found most repellent in France, even accepting the possibility that Hitler would take over France to save it from the "bad Frenchmen." I couldn't help mentioning, in my *canard enchaîné* way, what I thought about it.[8] But M. Bazin de Jessey seemed so preoccupied with the concerns of the village he felt he was responsible for, he seemed not to listen to events and attitudes on the changing political scene. He just wanted to be French. He smiled in agreement only when I stopped talking about the problems. I said, finally, that they were ancient Greeks whom I had found long hidden in Brittany, and he seemed pleased at that.

So, during my pleasant visits to Montmarin, I slowly cut off my ravings, swallowing my indignation, and settled slowly into tranquility at their chateau. I felt so good to be near to the wholeness, the harmony of hearts and the family life, where, indeed, I felt surrounded by love, a feeling I had not known since I was a very small child in the home of my father's family in Chicago. I relished the concept of one closely knit family devoted to ideals that they could all understand, accept and work toward. Yet for myself, being alone, I clung to the individualistic and protesting character that had been carved for me by my mother's mother, who used to say: "God gave us our relatives, but thank God we can choose our friends."

18

Back in my room at the Hotel Printemps, I feverishly dashed off many a furious note to the *Canard Enchaîné,* the satiric newspaper, describing in sarcastic terms the behavior and conversations of the nurses and their bourgeois expressions of willingness to collaborate with the Germans.[1] It wasn't only the women, of course. Châteaubriant had written to me, with hellish glee, that his father was busily writing speeches for the Jesuits broadcasting from Stuttgart, telling the French to lay down their guns, to go home, because "the Germans are coming as friends."

My "Bolshevik" insistence that France had better prepare herself to meet the Germans must have reached the ears of the commander of the station, Le Capitaine de Jeff, because he had me invited to an expensive restaurant by one of the young society ladies of Dinard so he could sound me out. The captain was known to be a gourmet, and the dinner was very carefully prepared and quite delicious, but all through it he questioned me closely as to my feelings about what was going on. I answered all his questions with a smile and complete frankness.

Apparently he wasn't satisfied with my remarks, because some-time later he asked me to dinner again, with the same lady and a "friend" of theirs, a very rigid young officer, who, from the way they talked together, I knew was really not one of their friends at all. I guessed he was from the Deuxième Bureau, the intelligence wing of the French Army. After dinner, I asked him to come with me for a walk. We went out on the sand in the moonlight. He wanted to show off, so he told me all the things that made an intelligence officer important to France. He spoke of the evidence of disloyalty he found among the persons he investigated—treason, giving information to the enemy, homosexuality and membership in the Communist Party. I told him not to worry about me. I didn't know any Germans, I wasn't homosexual and I had never belonged to any political party. He was interested in the fact that I had written articles (never published) for the *Canard Enchaîné,* and the next day he brought me a copy of what he considered to be a satirical journal for my opinion of its content. It turned out to be a semi-pornographic joke paper with no political significance whatever. And when I told him so, that apparently ended his investigation of me. At least, there were no more set-up dinners.

I had to write to someone about how I felt, but it certainly couldn't be Guy de Châteaubriant. His letters were still full of love and affection, but they were also full of the kinds of observations calculated to irritate me. The one I remember most clearly was one in which he described with joy the "accidental" shooting down of an English plane by his anti-aircraft unit on the Belgian frontier. I suppose he knew this would heighten my blood pressure. This news, which probably wasn't even true at all, was especially hateful because I had just heard that my Australian friend

Wendy had lost her fiancé when his RAF plane was shot down. Peter had been killed in England, not Belgium, but the whole thing made me hate Châteaubriant. And yet, when I received news soon afterward that Guy would be with me at Christmas, I was overwhelmed with joy.

Without him at my side, I did have semi-serious flirtations with two young officers, though they never led anywhere. One was an abstemious and serious chap who, I believed, was fascinated by me but hardly dared express himself. The other was an articulate, gallant, direct and handsome man from Normandy, named Robert, to whom I could have responded had it not been for Châteaubriant. I was sorely tempted to betray my faithless lord and master on the occasions when I saw Robert walking in the garden looking up at my hotel window at night. With the lights out, the window closed, I looked down at him, whispering to myself, "I like you, too." Then I would jump into bed to try to sleep and forget all about him.

I announced joyfully to everyone—to Nora, vivacious and blonde, and to her sister, Tamara, quite sweet, my two Russian friends; to Madame Copinger, the superintendent of the hospital, and especially to the family Bazin de Jessey, that my beau was arriving for Christmas.

On the stage of my memory, Christmas of 1939 is all alabaster, malachite and crystal. The alabaster was the candlelight to which we danced and drank champagne. Everyone was there, and Guy was the star in my eyes. The whole setting was sad as well as joyful, though. We were glad to be alive, perhaps, and uncertain whether we would be for long.

We danced, especially at the Hot Club de France, to music that was very popular—to Louis Armstrong, whose amusing "I'll Be

Glad When You're Dead, You Rascal You" was a favorite, and to "Deep Purple" and to the Benny Goodman quartet. And, of course, we all sang sentimental French songs. "J'Attendrais" seemed to be the theme song of the war, because each of us was waiting for someone to come back. We teased Nora, because as she drank champagne and became happier, the sadder she became at the same time. We put on a pantomime in which a Russian was saying, "Oh, I'm so joyful" and then pulled out a revolver and shot himself.

On Christmas Eve, we left the dance and went out into the night, over frozen ground, in the moonlight, to a tiny Dominican chapel in which the monks were saying the midnight mass. We arrived at the courtyard of the monastery just in time to see the monks' procession, the taller ones in front and the choirboys behind them, all dressed alike and singing beautifully. The chapel, all white, was very quiet, almost like a Quaker meeting house. The sermon was direct. The priest said, "You have raised hell ever since the First World War, and now the second is on top of you because you didn't know what to do with the time between." We all solemnly agreed that he was probably perfectly right.

The boys choir rang out, and a very tall monk with a beautiful natural baritone sang, "Noël, Noël, Born is the King of Israel." He sang, unaccompanied, in such a way that it went right through us. He carried us into the spirit of hope that is in the Christmas Eve mass. We walked back to town through the amethyst night, speaking softly, toward an opal dawn. Guy stayed at my hotel, and during all of his visit I felt at home again in his arms.

One night, I noticed how nicely he and Rose-Monique looked dancing together, how much like brother and sister—his gray eyes, her blue, he taller than she. Their compatibility was a little frightening, especially since Rose-Monique liked to flirt with him and then look over her shoulder to make sure I was watching. I knew he was too well versed in the rules of their milieu to start a serious affair with her, and I knew that Rose-Monique was only playing. Even had they liked each other, I suspected that neither had enough money to marry the other. And on those terms, I was glad they liked each other. Yet, their companionship reminded me that I was indeed a stranger in their world.

Then the Christmas holiday came to an end. Guy's furlough came to an end. He and I went one night in a taxi to Dinard where he had to catch his train. The moon was still bright and the town seemed amethyst again, amethyst, I think, too, because of the popular song, "Deep Purple," which kept running through my consciousness.[2] The melody flooded my mind while Guy said that now that the war was going to change from "drôle de guerre" (phony war) to a shooting war, perhaps we should think about having a child. I was surprised, delighted, and then not surprised, but confused. However, I was made very happy by the suggestion, unaccompanied though it was by a word of marriage, and I floated off through the night's deep purple dream with Guy on his way back to the front. Our parting at the station gave me the last view I ever had of him. A warm pleasant confusion lifts me again into the night each time I hear that silly, superficial, supercilious, sentimental, sad-sack song.

Our letters continued as before, and the spring came with its violets to Montmarin. Rose-Monique and I collected the violets and other spring flowers in the park and surrounding woods so fresh in the soft Brittany sun. On May 15, the day we usually left Paris to go to Villefranche, I left Dinard to go back to Paris on leave. I wanted to clear out the few things I still had in my apartment there and to return to wait for the war to come (or the war to end). I was waiting also for Guy to come to Paris on leave the first of June. Margot, who still had an apartment in our old building, asked me to stay with her. She was still secretary at the Hungarian legation and still a friend of Jean-Marie Conti, who was a Republican, while she remained faithful to her Nazis and to the conviction that they were good guys. We still had our arguments about whether or not we should carry a gas mask and how soon the Nazis were going to bombard us. She insisted that they would never strike Paris and I was just making a big fuss over nothing.

Jean-Marie Conti was in the Air Ministry and knew my uncle Bertrand Thompson, who, with Guy De Chambre, the air minister, was trying to rebuild the air arsenal. Conti, who was in charge of the athletic program, was disheartened because he couldn't get the equipment he needed to train young recruits. He said the fellows were dying for lack of training while trying to use American dive bombers. The government was without funds because the people who controlled the money were withholding it, waiting for deliverance from the Léon Blum socialists by Hitler.

I wore my French Red Cross uniform, and I found that some friends at St.-Germain-des-Prés and Montparnasse seemed to be proud of me in a way, and happy that I was on their side. Man Ray and my closest friends thought I was doing what I should do. When Nazi planes flew over Paris or the neighboring suburbs and sometimes dropped bombs near the factories, I was glad to be in uniform because I could stay out of the air raid shelters and stay on the streets. If I was going to be hit, I would rather be hit out in the open than down in a cellar. But even with my officer's rank, lieutenant, which, by the way, netted me about five cents a day, I couldn't dissuade the "authorities" from taking a Jewish neighbor, Charlotte, to put her in "protective custodial camp" (concentration camp) when they came to the building to get her. Margot, dear, blind Margot, told Charlotte that it was really for her own good, for her protection!

On the 20th of May, the barbarians bombarded Rotterdam almost off the map, and we knew they were going to march on France. I received word from the hospital that I was not to return there. The French Red Cross couldn't be responsible for foreign nurses. I should go instead to Bordeaux and join the American Red Cross that was setting up there. So I packed. In one suitcase, I put all the books I could jam, most of them autographed, my etchings, drawings and prints. In another case I had five Chanel evening dresses, one of the black and white masterpieces that Mlle. Chanel had worn and that I was so proud of, and a burgundy lace dress put together by hand so there was no seam in it, and a lamé dress that had been worn as part of the trousseau of a princess of Albania, and a tulle dress, all dresses that I particularly liked, as I liked certain books or pictures. Three other suitcases contained what I thought would be necessary for my living in Bordeaux.

I telephoned Man Ray before I left, but when we tried to speak in English, the operator broke in saying, "Parlez français, s'il vous plaît, ou je vous coupe," telling us to knock off the English and speak French or we would be cut off. So I wound up telling Man in French that it was time to "ejaculate" the camp. But he told me he was an artist, not a politician, and the war didn't interest him. He would stay in Paris.

I withdrew all the money I had in the Westminster Bank, and Margot gave me every cent she had, which was quite a lot, and I piled the suitcases into a car that had been left to me by Marcel, an old friend whom I had taken to the Gare du Nord when he went off to join his regiment.

Marcel was tubercular, but he followed the call as an officer of his group, a cavalry unit in which he had served many years before. The sight at the station leading to the northeastern frontier made me realize we were really at war. The presence of young soldiers on open flatcars going slowly through the station, black, brown, white, all together, French, Arab and African, all comrades singing "Auprès de ma Blonde" and other war songs, loosed my throat in silent sobs.

They sang the Marseillaise, laughing, some of them tipsy with red wine. I couldn't help thinking that none of them would ever return. I stood on the platform waving to them, then went to the street and got into Marcel's old car with the tears streaming down my face. I wasn't crying for Marcel, nor for the men; I was crying for all my friends and for what I believed might be the end of our civilization.

In a few days, I'd said adieu to most of my friends in Paris, and I'd thrown my luggage into the car and headed for Bordeaux. To avoid the heavy traffic that I found on the road going south at Fontainebleau, I turned west and headed once again for Dinard. I arrived late, but I found a half dozen officers still, having a drink after dinner, at our old Dansant Hotel. I told them I had to go south to Bordeaux to join the American Red Cross, but that I would soon return with American troops. They said, in a smart-alecky way, "Come back anytime. We're delighted to have you.

But leave the Deuxième Boches on the other side of the Atlantic." Some of them so disliked Americans, they called them the "second Germans." But, as usual, they were hospitable to the "noble savage," the "American cocktail."

Early the next day, I drove down the Loire Valley, worrying and yet reassured by the presence of the chateaux all along the route. I drove leisurely and stopped to look at everything that interested me. My worries, of course, were not without foundation. I knew how little the French were prepared to meet the onslaught of the coming hordes, but I had confidence that the thread of nonpolitical Christian French civilization would somehow continue, as it had already withstood so many wars. The family Bazin de Jessey, even non-political Man Ray, who was more French than American, had reassured me. I knew that in spite of the street fights from Stavisky on the battles, the political rallies, the attacks on the left by the right and on the right by the left, no one would be less French, less loyal to France. When faced by the enemy, the French knitted the conservatives, dissenters, and the radicals, and all would do the best they could to conserve all that was truly French, including, *bien entendu,* the right to disagree. And I, distant relative of a Bonaparte bastard, would tag along as long as they'd have me.

In the villages where I stopped along the way, I noticed and admired again the intelligence of the ordinary people. Although they might be ready for an argument and were irreverent in their relationship to authority, they were respectful to me because of my uniform and always gave me what I needed in the way of lodgings and gasoline. The orderly thinking of the people was also reflected in the never-changing beauty of the landscape.

Every inch was cultivated in an orderly way, and the entire country seemed just one huge park.

After arriving in Bordeaux, I went to the home of a lady whom Mme. Copinger had felt would facilitate my transfer from the French to the American Red Cross. I have forgotten her name, but she was the head of the French Red Cross in Bordeaux, and she welcomed me into her home when she found I hadn't yet found a place to live. She gave me a room and hospitality characteristic of her gracious charm.

I learned that the American Red Cross was setting up offices in the square in the center of Bordeaux, and I set out to find them. On the way, in the street, I ran into my old friend, Fernand Léger, and we stopped for coffee on the terrace of a café and chatted, trying to be as lighthearted as was possible at the time. I asked about our mutual friends in Paris, and he told me all he knew about those I mentioned, including something he didn't quite understand about an American composer. He said someone had told him the composer was sitting on the terrace of the Café de la Paix waiting for the "Pansy" Division. What did he mean? I explained, then asked if he had found living quarters in Bordeaux, thinking that there might be room for him in the house where I was staying, since I appeared to be the only guest despite a large number of silent, anonymous servants. I thought my mistress would welcome a great French painter into her home. "Oh, no," he said. "I wouldn't go into the home of any great dame. When I arrive in a strange town, I always go to the best bordello in town, my present residence in Bordeaux." That was the last sound of gaiety and the last word from the esprit de Paris that I was to enjoy.

I went to the new Red Cross headquarters every day, moving filing cabinets and other furniture, working with some American women that I remembered vaguely having seen at the American embassy on very rare visits I had made there. We seemed to be working against time, but time caught up with us. The Italians came over and bombarded Bordeaux, dropping bombs not very far from our headquarters in the square. So we packed up again. Everyone took the papers they were responsible for and each left in her own direction. I had decided to stay in France as long as I could. The Germans were coming down the coast, so I got into the car and drove toward the Spanish frontier, thinking that if they came all the way, I'd hop over into Spain.

The day and hour of the capitulation, I was in an excellent hotel in Biarritz, having lunch. The dining room was crowded. The windows looked out to sea. At a table near mine, Moysés and his nephew and an elderly gentleman sat. The filet of sole had just been put on the table, the second course, when the Marseillaise was played on the radio, and we, of course, all stood up. Pétain announced the capitulation and the fall of France.[3] As we listened to his speech, tears filled everyone's eyes. I glanced at Moysés, who had been our so lighthearted host at the Boeuf sur le Toit for so many years, and his was the saddest face I could see. He was crying like a child. I think everyone in the dining room was crying, in rage, outrage, disappointment or hatred.

Real tragedies were being enacted all along the coast as refugees ran toward the sea and even into the sea. Many of them drowned before the crowds that came after them could pull them out. Their desperation was far beyond ours. We stood looking at them through the windows, and after the Marseillaise was played the second time, we sat down to finish our lunch.

Having decided to go directly to Spain, I went to my room and wrote a few letters, to Rose-Monique, Margot, Man Ray and other friends in Paris, to Charles through his solicitors in London, to Châteaubriant through his father's publisher. (I didn't even know his home address.) I sent a note also in the general direction I thought his home was, in care of his mother, and that was the one he eventually received.

I was getting into the car to leave the hotel when I noticed, standing on the steps, a young woman so forlorn that I couldn't help turning back to speak to her. I asked if I could give her a lift, and she replied, in French but with a slight accent that I recognized as being German or central European, that she would appreciate a ride. I asked if she had luggage, and she said no, only what was in her hand, which appeared to be only a handkerchief. She was very handsome, blonde with fine features and an elegance that shone through the simple flannel skirt and cashmere sweater she wore. I took it that she was a refugee. She got into the car with me.

As we drove toward Hendaye, she told me her story. She had left Brussels with her husband, who was attached to the Czechoslovakian embassy there. The day the Germans bombarded Rotterdam, June 22, they drove away in an open roadster, carrying all they considered important, their money, papers, silver, jewels, furs, directly into France. They had started toward the south of France when their car was strafed on the road by a German plane. The husband was killed.

The woman had stopped just long enough in a little town between Vichy and Dijon to have him buried, then she drove on by herself. Faced with the very real likelihood that she would not be able to buy gasoline after Biarritz, she had left the car and all of her possessions at the home of someone she knew there. Actually, she didn't know the "someone" very well, but she had no choice but to trust her. She had taken her papers and the money she had left. At the time I saw her, she had the money tied to her leg, just above the knee. She was actually carrying just the handkerchief. With just these things in her possession, she looked for transportation, a bus, train or anything to take her into Spain ahead of the Germans. I learned that her husband's family, his mother and father and most of their friends, all Jewish, had been involved in anti-Nazi activities, which would certainly guarantee their presence on Hitler's blacklist, so they were especially anxious not to be caught by the Nazis.

I took her with me to the Imatz Hotel in Hendaye, where I was able to find a room, I suppose because of my uniform. It was a choice place, *the* hotel, apparently, though I didn't see anything very grand about it. But Mme. Pétain was living there then, I noticed, and quite a large number of diplomats and persons who were just waiting to know how far the Germans would go before deciding whether to leave France.[4]

I drummed up a conversation with an important-looking gentleman in the lobby, who could have been mistaken for my father. He was about my color, with gray hair, a very genteel and sweet man whom I thought perhaps to be from North Africa. He turned out to be the Portuguese consul at Bayonne, and he was on his way to Portugal, but he was a little undecided about what to do. Being very religious, he had conscience problems that he was not quite able to resolve. I saw the opportunity of getting "my refugee" over the border and perhaps into Portugal with him. He had a better idea, and he produced another Portuguese, a handsome young man who was driving a small car who said he would be very happy to have the young lady go across on his diplomatic passport. So, fortunately, that story ended beautifully, and the two drove off across the bridge into Spain, to live happily ever after, I hope!

I suppose I should have gone at the same time, but my conscience had also become involved. Lisi, my refugee, had left me with the passports of her in-laws and asked me to wait there for them if they should come. Well, that chance was rather remote, but, miraculously, the father-in-law showed up. I got exit visas from the authorities in Hendaye, and the elderly Portuguese, Mr. Mendez, gave them some sort of visa which he had no right to issue, since it was necessary to have an officially stamped Portuguese visa before one could get a visa for Spain. Before we could get the Spanish visa, some of their other friends came along, and they all wanted to climb aboard the same bandwagon out of France. There must have been about thirty of them in all.

In the meantime, Mme. Pétain had asked to meet me. She was accompanied by a little priest who was very friendly and active. He came over to me and introduced himself as an authority on cathedrals, worked up a conversation and then asked if I would please come and be presented to Mme. Pétain. We had breakfast together. She asked me why I was busying myself so with what she called "the rats who were deserting the sinking ship." I said I didn't think they were the rats who were responsible for the sinking ship, but they were human beings trying to get out of the way of the beasts who were chasing them. That slight contact with what seemed to me to be anti-Semitism on her part inspired me to go to any length to try to help the refugees.

So, with Mr. Mendez in the car with me, I drove back to Bayonne with all thirty passports to try to get into the Portuguese consulate there for the all-important official stamp. But once in Bayonne, it was impossible to approach the Portuguese consulate, except by foot. So I took the car around to a side street where Mr. Mendez would not be recognized. Refugees by that time were learning that he was the Portuguese consul, and he couldn't move without being stopped for a visa. It was impossible for him to issue any without the precious stamp I was trying to get out of his office.

The crowd in the street was difficult to get through, so I called a French soldier to help me. We went into the building to the stairway leading to the consulate on the second floor, but there was no way we could move any further. Those who were on the shaky wooden steps would not let anyone through, and they were packed together so tightly I might have been killed had I tried to force my way.

Walking back through the crowd, I was horror stricken to see the window of the consulate open and piles of passports being thrown out onto the square. The crowd waiting below grabbed at passports, calling names. It was a desperate spectacle. There must have been over a thousand persons there who were almost certainly lost without passports. Their passports had either been left with the French government for an exit visa, sent from Poitiers to Vichy to God-knows-where, or lost or thrown away.

Those who had gotten as far as Bayonne and had French exit visas now needed to get Portuguese visas. But they had no chance because the Portuguese consul was around the corner in my car, and the stamp was unobtainable. It was entirely hopeless, and a very, very sad sight. I was reminded of the cattle I had seen driven in the Chicago stockyards. Only this was so much more horrible if only because the cattle had only the instinctive smell of approaching death, whereas these persons had the imagination to project torture and death a thousand times over at the hands of the brutes who were catching up with them rapidly. I left the scene with a determination to free as many as I could, at least those whose passports I held.

I started looking around the neighborhood for other consulates. The system had so locked in these refugees that they had to have a visa for some country outside of Portugal before they could get a Portuguese visa, and they had to have a Portuguese visa before they could have a Spanish visa, an exit visa from France before they could go anywhere.

It was almost hopeless. My group of thirty had no visas whatsoever. I had to start as far away as possible. It couldn't be the United States, unfortunately, because they weren't allowing refugees to enter. So I started with Central and South America and tried to find their legations or consulates somewhere in the neighborhood of Biarritz. Accompanied sometimes by the elderly Dr. Mendez, and sometimes by some of the refugees who took along money to pay off consuls if it were necessary, I went from town to town to find someone who would take the responsibility of starting these visas in the right direction.

It would not be fair now to tell which of the countries' representatives accepted a thousand dollars for each visa. It was certainly worth it to those who were trying to escape. But I do remember one consul from a Central American country who was offered the bribe and who almost cried when he took me and two of the refugees to his home and showed us his daughter. She was about fifteen years old and was playing the piano. She was a pretty girl. He said he didn't have a dowry for her and he would do almost anything in the world to get enough money to assure her a happy marriage. But he said he knew his country would not honor the visa, and the conflict brought tears to his eyes. We had no choice, then, but to take a chance on Mr. Mendez's scribbled Portuguese visas, and we took these and went to look for the Spanish consul.

In the meantime, the Panzer divisions were coming down the coast at the rate of about thirty kilometers a day. We didn't know how close they were. On the road, we met the soldiers of the allies leaving France, the English and miles of Polish soldiers going to Bordeaux. The Polish soldiers looked so much like Germans, tall with long gray coats, that the sight of them was rather frightening, but they were singing in Polish, and in their sad, retreating way, they could not be mistaken for advancing conquerors.

There were night thunderstorms all that week, and there were also bombardments at sea. One couldn't tell the difference between one and the other, but the land divisions were not yet close to Biarritz. There were miles and miles of refugees going toward the frontier. One who touched me deeply was a nicely dressed woman, or she had been before her travels. She had a little girl hanging onto each side of her dress. Their shoes were worn almost bare. She held an old fashioned radio in her arms, a model I hadn't seen in years. She seemed quite lost, and I am sure she was.

The diplomats, however, were flying across the bridge at Hendaye in great speed. They were high-tailing it out of France into Spain in unbecoming haste. I recognized many French politicians, who, to a large extent, were responsible for the plight in which France found herself. These politicians were never alone, of course. They were always accompanied by well-dressed women. Mme. Pétain didn't seem to notice them. She herself was dressed in the same way my mother had always dressed, in a tailored suit with a handmade blouse and a lorgnette on a long gold chain. Otherwise, she looked like Gertrude Stein, or a German general. She didn't make any comment on the politicians, especially the rightists who were running away, but she continued to look at me as though I were some sort of traitor, trying to help the refugees.

Eventually, we got the Spanish visas, and my group was ready to go across. Two of them asked me to exchange my car for theirs. It turned out that all the linings of their car were stuffed with money of many countries. Between my American passport and my French officer's uniform, I didn't have much fear of not getting away when I wanted to, and I was certainly willing to take the chance of exporting their only security, so I let them take my car. It was the old Renault Marcel had had for God knows how long anyway. I took their car, an old Citroen they had probably picked up cheaply somewhere, but it was certainly much more precious to them. So off we went.

Americans had been gathering in Hendaye from all directions, and I had made contacts with many of them. There were many nice people among them, especially the journalists, whom I found most amusing. They were coming from every capital of Europe. There were the diplomats, too, and representatives from companies, like the Coca-Cola agent who came from Berlin with a German wife and several children who spoke no English, and lots of interesting Americans who had intended to stay in Europe, thinking they would be able to live there despite the war. But they had changed their minds and were, like me, ready to depart.

When a convoy was made up to take the Americans out of Hendaye, I took in my car an elderly gentleman who had owned a chateau in Normandy for many years. He had been a friend of

Henry James, and during our journey he talked of good times long ago. He was especially unhappy to leave his wine cellar.

A representative from the American embassy in Madrid came to the frontier to meet us at the bridge at Hendaye. He took all of the passports. When we were being questioned by him, he suggested that I probably wasn't an American at all. He thought I was an East Indian because when I spoke, I was still using the "English" English I'd picked up in London. He simply had to go by my photo in the passport, my signature, the date of my birth and the assurance of another embassy officer that it was possible that I could have an English accent. Since my visas showed I'd lived in England, I was allowed to go through. It would certainly have been ironic to have been sent back to the Nazis by an American official, a rather unimportant one at that.

Our convoy crossed the Spanish frontier and went to Bilbao, where the hotels were set up for the arriving Americans. I took the old gentleman into one of the hotels to make sure he was comfortable. Then I went back to empty the car of my luggage, leaving the bags on the sidewalk for the porters to take care of. One porter put one suitcase under his arm and one in each hand when he entered the hotel. He came to my room and I started unpacking. About a half hour later, I called the office to find out what had happened to the other two bags. I was told there were no more on the sidewalk. Then I realized I was in the old poverty-stricken Spain that I had left a few years earlier.

I didn't like it anymore, and I certainly didn't care for France. Still, it was better to be there among them in 1940 than to be caught by the Panzer divisions. We had seen some of the German soldiers arriving in Hendaye as we were going across the bridge. From the Spanish side, we saw Spanish soldiers, little fellows compared to the Germans, run across the bridge to embrace them. They looked like a bunch of children running to greet Santa Claus. The Germans didn't look like Santa Claus to us, however, when they began to come across into Spain in their Mercedes cars, four officers and a chauffeur in each. They came to the one good restaurant we had found in town. The lobby and the restaurant dining room had pictures of France in the center, with Hitler on one side and Mussolini on the other, so the Germans felt quite at home there.

A long string of those Mercedes would come flying through the streets like motorcycle cops and stop at the curb in front of the restaurant, just about fifteen feet apart. Each car stopped at exactly the same second, it seemed. At the sound of a whistle, each man stood. At another blast of the whistle, they got out of the cars. At another signal, they marched into the restaurant. Then they relaxed, unbuttoning their uniform jackets, seeming to pop out of them. They would stuff themselves and then had to get corseted back into their stiff uniforms to leave. Then, at the sound of three or four more whistles, they got back into their cars, like automatons, turned their cars around and hightailed it back into France. It was good to be living with my compatriots.

One afternoon I went to a bullfight with Chuck Finley, a journalist, and Dwight Dickinson, an ambulance driver. I signaled to them that we should not stand when Franco's national anthem was played. So we sat through it, to the astonishment of the people around us. Some in front of us turned and beckoned us to get up, as though we didn't know any better, and some behind us prodded us in the backs to make the same suggestion. When they discovered that we did know better, because we smiled, practically smirked actually, they expressed surprise, some delight, some complicity, some fear that something might happen to us. But nothing did. I thought we had done a very brave stunt, sitting down through the anthem. I was being so cheeky, really, because I felt protected by the two men who, I was sure, would save me from the mob—a foolish and childish notion.

I told Chuck and Dwight about my money-lined car, and we had lots of fun dreaming up all sorts of adventures in which we would drive the car madly through Spain and spend all the money. I finally persuaded them to drive back to San Sebastian with me, where the refugees were supposed to wait for the car. We finally worked it out so that Chuck would drive a rented car and Dwight and I would go in the refugees' car and deliver it. Then we would all come back in the rental. But we didn't get far.

About three or four days after we arrived in Bilbao and were having these jolly times, the refugees arrived from San Sebastian. They must have heard us thinking about what fun we were going to have with their money, but missed the part about our going to San Sebastian. They roared into the hotel accompanied by Spanish police, who were going to drag me off to prison for stealing the car. They had not learned that the American convoy had driven through San Sebastian in the middle of the night when everything was closed and I could not deliver the car right away. I certainly couldn't have held up the entire convoy for such an errand. So they had taken it for granted that I was going to keep their money. It took not only Dwight and Chuck, but practically the entire American contingent to protect me from their wrath. They were given the keys to their car, and they finally stomped out and drove off, after cussing the living daylights out of me and all the Americans. After a few days with good-humored Americans, I became American again and laughed at everything, even ungrateful refugees.

Finally, we all got onto a special train and headed for Lisbon. By this time, we knew each other fairly well. There were lots of young people, many ambulance drivers, young journalists, some Ann Morgan girls.[5] Everyone had taken a little French liqueur or brandy or something, and the train ride was made gay by our exchange of samples from the bottles we had. There was singing and joking about going back to the United States and eating fried cakes and sausage, no more croissants, no more fancy omelets. Everyone sang the blues about the horrors of returning to American food.

As we crossed into Lisbon, we felt we were really on our way home. Out onto the pier the train went. We followed a brightly lighted white wall that we were advised was the side of our ship. Then suddenly into the light came the American flag, painted on the ship, a huge American flag, lighted in the dark night. When I saw it, I and some others I noticed had tears in our eyes. We were glad to be Americans. There were three Navy cruisers in the harbor. It took many years for the stars in my eyes to dry from bright on blue to dark on black. They are still dark on a red, white and black flag.

A boatload of reporters boarded the *Manhattan* before we landed. Many took photos of me as of someone of importance: Egyptian? Arab? East Indian? No one spoke to me in English or in French. I just looked so well-dressed in my Chanel suit, and carrying my latest affectation—an ivory-topped walking stick.

But the next morning the *New York Times* headed an article on the arrival of "the last ship to return with escapees of the Panzer Divisions' closing the Spanish frontier from France" with a large photo of a stout American woman emerging from her cabin weighted with many cameras—the gear of a newspaper photographer. There was no mention of the center of so many reporters' attention on me. They had learned, no doubt, that I was just an Afro-American expatriate of no importance, a common or garden variety of colored woman forced "home." Many years later, visiting Baltimore, I learned from my cousins, the Murphys, owners of the *Afro-American* newspaper there, that my *Manhattan* photo had been posted to them.

The American flag—after my living in "integrated" communities in New York, Los Angeles and the Virgin Islands as student, clinical psychologist and college instructor during the 1960s and 1970s American Negro revolts and some slow progress in the opportunities opened to blacks—the flag still looks red, white and black to me. No tears in my eyes looking at it today.

Appendixes

Notes

Index

Publications by Anita Reynolds

Review of *Tales of the Jazz Age,* by F. Scott Fitzgerald, from *The Messenger* (1922): 706, 719.

TALES OF THE JAZZ AGE.

By F. Scott Fitzgerald.

Charles Scribner's Sons.

Reviewed by Miss Anita B. Thompson.

The latest book by the author of "The Beautiful and Damned," "This Side of Paradise," etc. is indeed a highly polished bit of Jazz. Fitzgerald's style is brilliant and amusing. Modernly cynical, often he reminds one of Aldous Huxley, at other times, the human touch is suggestive of O. Henry's style. He is probably the most popular young American writer today.

The "Jazz Age" is represented by eleven short stories. I shall not describe them in the order in which they're presented but shall classify them as they impressed me.

Two are tragedies. May Day, the best story in the book, is nevertheless a bitter modern cocktail in which ex-soldiers, Socialists, college failures, flappers and alcohol are shaken together and mixed like oil and water. The Lees of Happiness, a domestic tragedy, might have been set in any age except for the interest taken now, so generally, in women's happiness. The pathos of these studies is felt keenly by author and reader.

A riotous couple are the comedies, Porcelain and Pink, of a poor peasant who lived too long. They could be produced only on a fake stage and before a child audience—although, when read, they're as genuinely amusing as they are thoroughly impossible.

Two of the Fantasies, modern fairy tales, are horribly inconsistent and nerve-racking. The Diamond as Big as the Ritz describes, in absurd detail, a mansion built on a stone actually that size and the bloody actions of the inmates. The Curious Case of Benjamin Button reveals many singular events in the career of a man, born old, who grew younger every year and finally slept too long—a baby.

Two society jokes and two on the hoi polloi are characteristic of the author's oft expressed appreciation of luxury and-at-least [sic] respect for capital. Jelly-bean, the last remaining member of an aristocratic Georgia family, has strayed from the fold. He is "bent at the waist from stooping over pool tables." When, after returning from war, he accepts an invitation, from an old friend, to attend the country club dance, he becomes a hero just long enough to slip the wealthy Southern beauty of his dreams the full contents of a "corn" flask, then set the dice to keep her from writing checks on the wrong bank to pay her bets. He returns to his room above the garage and his "bones" in the alley because she marries another Southern gentleman. Southern society. The Camel's Back is another wine, women and song farce. This time on a little higher plane up North. "O Russet Witch" a very well constructed sketch, tells the same old story of the rich vamp and the havoc she plays in the life of a poor boob. "Serio-comic" as 'twere. Jemima, the Mountain Girl, is a scream, parody on the feuds in the "wild hills" of Kentucky where the rivers run "up and down" the mountains and whiskey is the medium of exchange, the daily diet and fuel in "human alcohol lamps," lighted when the family wars are waged. Side-splitting and ridiculous.

The poetic Tarquin of Cheapside was thrown in because of the "peculiar affection" the author feels for it, having written it several years ago at Princeton. I do not appreciate its intrinsic merit—if it has any.

On the whole, this is a topping collection of impressions of the "Jazz Age." "Of" in the title means both "concerning" and "belonging to" in the sense that those not narrating words and deeds, in themselves Jazzy are written in a tone appreciated by Jazzy readers—superficial, clever, cynical.

Jazz, of this age, has nothing in common with music by Colored dance orchestras. That would be far too harmonious. Rather these ideas suggest the discord ringing through almost every thought and deed of nations and individuals existing in this transitional age. Even the comedy does not ring true; it is usually produced by impossible stage directions or liquor and the result is artificially hilarious.

The "Jazz Age" dawned upon our consciousness in 1918 at the close of the war, an aftermath of that mistake. America, another "blind moth," has accepted the flapper and the flask as the symbols of our present abnormalcy. Fitzgerald, though not by public demand, recognizes the presence of the ex-soldier, the misunderstood Socialist, the level-headed woman and a type of Negro, "living North of Georgia, who can change a dollar any time." Jazz, of course, is not the dynamic force of the day but, at least, it is symbolic of the spirit of the masses as would be any reckless, noisy, aimless, changing thing. We dance a great deal now, perhaps, to give vent to many confused emotions (it looks that way to a person not dancing, at least,) and to Jazz music because it is the newest and only surviving intoxicant. Merely the outward signs. It will be left for the next generation to fix the importance of each influence—war, prohibition, women's independence and others.

Mr. Fitzgerald has produced another splendid book, appreciable both from "muse and amuse" points of view.

Miss Thompson is a movie actress and scenario writer.

Publications in *Flash*

Flash was a short-lived African American magazine in the Los Angeles area in the late 1920s about which little information can be found. The OCLC has no record of its existence. Three pieces written by Anita Thompson (Reynolds) appeared in it in the late 1920s and are preserved in her papers at the Moorland-Spingarn Research Center. The first is a short story; the other two are gossip columns. The story is below.—*Ed.*

A Story from Paris

Paris, le 29 Juin, 1929

My dear Godchild "Flash":—

You have asked me for stories. Nothing pleases me more than giving you what you want. But your "Mumah" can tell you I am not very ingenious in narrative, having spent all my life—up to this point—in living short stories . . . however, if ingenuous re-counting of events and stories I know will satisfy your youthful curiosity, you are very welcome to my store.

There are a couple of stories current in the Latin Quarter now that I'm sure will interest you. One is fiction. The other as true as historical record in the Bibliothèque Nationale can make it. This week I shall tell you the fanciful one but, very soon, you must hear the other for it is about a famous French Queen and her African lover and their daughter. It is a very beautiful story.

But now for the tale of a chateau in the mountains above the rolling fields of the Vosges country.

It seems that a young girl named Christine, who was invited there to join a hunting party, through some mistake of her own, no doubt, arrived a day early. The chateau, an immense stone building that was unoccupied except for the short periods of time when it's owner—the Du Something or Other, was entertaining on that estate—perhaps three weeks a year—was cold now and gloomy. Its closed windows looked down on the approaching small fig-ure like the eyes of a waiting monster. Christine shuddered a little as she sounded the bell near the great barred door and heard its echo in vacancy but, I'm sure, she expected to find a blazing log fire inside.

Grinding on rusty hinges, the door swung open. The girl stepped inside. She was alone for only a second when she was greeted by a muscular, gnarled woman of uncertain age who said she was the concierge. Christine said simply, "I have come to the hunt."

"You are a day early, little one, but I shall try to make you comfortable until the master comes. You will have his own room tonight with the finest supper I can provide served at his hearth.—Now . . . go out into the country here and learn to love it," said the woman.

Christine, happy to be out of the dark, damp hall—what an air it had!—scrambled down the hillside. In the house her limbs had stiffened and she could not run as she'd have liked to. As she pushed on thru the maze, trying to reach sunlight, her feeling of uneasiness increased and certainly could not have been lessened when she realized that above those tall red-leafed trees the sky was turning black. Fright of the moment left her and she turned back to the chateau for shelter.

The concierge led her up the narrow, winding stairs to the master's chamber, set down the tray of food she had carried up, pulled back silken covers on the massive curtained bed, kicked a log or two in the fireplace, said "bon soir" and was gone.

Almost too tired to think, Christine ate her supper—a delicious one it was indeed with white wine for her salmon and red for the cold meats, and a sparkling crisp salad. Then she sat by the hearth a few minutes trying to analyse her thoughts of the place. But 'twas no use. The fire was almost out anyway. So Christine undressed quickly and got into bed taking with her and slipping under her pillow a tiny flower that she had found beside her plate. Falling asleep,

one wondered its name. 'Cryptogamia,' she thought. 'No, no . . .
impossible . . . awful word . . . cryptogamia . . . cryptogamia . . .
crypto . . .

In the middle of the night she was awakened by the loud crackle
and strong glare of her fire. Too startled to open her mouth, she
pushed herself slowly to her elbows and stared at the figure of a man
sitting in the bright light, very near the fanged flames, rocking . . .
rocking . . . rocking with something in his arms—like a baby.

As soon as she recovered strength enough, Christine slipped
from the bed, the chamber, the chateau and out thru the wooded
park down the rocky hillside into a great bare field. I do not
know how long she wandered there, but it was still very black
night when she met some men in uniform who were crossing the
field flashing pocket-lights. They took her in hand, and she told
them how she happened to be out of doors in night dress. The
officers told her that the man in her room was probably the lunatic for whom they had been searching all night.

They took her the shortest way back to the chateau. Inside,
one of the men said, "Where's the concierge? We must have
some light."

"She did not answer, tho her door was open when I went out,"
Christine told them.

"Scared out, I guess."

Then they all climbed the stairs in darkness and went noise-
lessly to the master's chamber. When they entered it, the lunatic
looked around over his hunched shoulder, uttered a hollow, sar-
donic laugh, turned back and continued rocking—toward the fascinating flames . . . away . . . towards the flames . . . rocking . . .
rocking. The something in his arms—like a baby—was the head

of the concierge from which he was pulling one hair at a time to feed the fetid fibrillous furnace.

• • •

You see that's just a story . . . but soon as I have all the names and dates just right you will have history that's stranger than fiction. The stories, however, are as different in spirit as East and West. It is purely coincidental that they are often told the same night over the fourth or fourteenth beer.

Beer is the royal refreshment this warm season. In the cafes that are the exclusive clubs of everyone with a weakness for conversation . . . much idle talk is wasted on the superiority of German beer. But, between you and me, I've never seen any other.

I hope to hear some interesting stories from the West soon.

Sincerely,

ANITA

Anita Reynolds's Correspondence with Family

1 rue Jacques Mawas

Paris XVme

My dear Mother—

It seems ages since I received a letter from you. How goes it? There are no misfortunes there I'm sure. My dreams and [*fragment of page broken off, pages missing*]

III

Who said Minnie's married? I've just received a long letter from Charlie [West] in which he says she can't keep still long enough to get married. He gave me all the news social political and athletic—& [*indecipherable*] lynched t'other day, too. God be praised—how can all you sane people rest there? I could kill barehanded all the vile whites in the world.

But I have other things to do now.

I'm going to dine this evening with a lovely French lady, the mother of one of my boy-friends. She is having another young girl (whom I met this week and with whom I went to the theatre Friday—beautiful, delicate French bourgeoisette—rich, well-loved etc.) also her brother.

One can be flattered to have French friends of this sort here because Americans are not well received except for money—which I haven't.

My French is getting good—I hope to be able to drop all the Americans soon.

Tho' Man Ray, the Bradleys, and a few others are almost too European to count. Had luncheon with Mme Bradley the other day. She says Wm Aspenwald Bradley—who is in America now—attended the N.A.A.C.P. annual ball in New York last month. He said it was beautiful. Saw "my friends" Du Bois, Spingarn, etc.

My only activity—apart from keeping house, selling Negroes, running to theatre, gallery, and parties—is sculpture. I've just finished the head of Tonny and have a command for a fountain at the home of a rich friend.

Maybe I can get something done for the Chicago Exposition in 1935. Then I go to "Amerique" . . . for a visit.

Love and kisses to you and Tada—

Yours Anita

Part of Letter to Mother—Paris 1929

> [Anita Reynolds's note in margin of a single typed page of
> a letter, the rest of which is lost.—*Ed.*]

There's nothing unusual in the air now. Paris is being overrun with tourists who crowd the sight-seeing buses and look generally ridiculous. I met a rather nice person with Claude McKay named Donald Duff. He is a journalist who knows everyone in Harlem and has more interest in them than anyone I've seen in ages; he absolutely gets into fights about the Problem with every American who'll take his challenge. "Très, très formidable!" Still he is most sensible, says he agrees that there is no hope of the jigs every doing more than grabbing monkey-fashion all that the others are leaving to them. He says I should pass all together and not be identified with any unpopular minority unless I can be entirely independent. He is, by the way, a distant relative of the chap Hilton whom I've described before. Very, very funny combination of New England and cosmopolitan sense. The Hindu came over from London, stayed about two weeks, but I found him like the rest of his tribe sort of lost, weak, affected, not knowing whether to be Eastern or Western. I think they too are a hopeless people, as such. This Nordic and Latin myth that binds the globe has about everyone (but the Chinese, perhaps) bamfussiled, and the only thing to be done about it is to make the most of it, that is Imperialism and the rest, individually: Causes are senseless! But I need not argue that with you: you've known it all along. No?

Last week-end I went to Vaux-sur-Seine with a bunch of students from the Quarter, it's a lovely old village, there was a cozy little inn with a garden entirely unter den linden, the wild flowers in the fields (daisies, red poppies, mustard, violets near the river, corn flowers and some whose names I don't know) like California, the river visible for miles across the huge level green valley, other picturesque villages within walking distance, good food and wine, an old mechanical piano that ground out fast waltzes and the Java, songs and poetry in the open, all good friends, and all speaking French. Is there more I can say to give you the picture? I shall attend the Quatres-Arts Bal with my companion de la champagne, a really handsome architect, intelligent and refined as these people have their own way of being. This is a very "exclusive" artists ball of which you've no doubt heard. Ha! Otherwise, life here is charming in the same old way: the

great shine to me—Ha! There've been hundreds of others it seems at the 24 hour parties Louise has been staging—but these were always closest me. None of them means anything substantial to me but they're all very clever and indeed stimulating. They talk of Max Eastman, Frank Harris, Carl Sandburg, Shaw, Musolini (however it's spelled) really a friend of Louise like we might speak of [Owen] Chandler or Du Bois or Wallace Thurman.

Today I must get back on the job for a few hours at least long enough to tell de Roode about the wonderful stuff <u>he</u> must go to see and order. (I've gotten some good addresses of exclusive stuff from one of the good dressers at Louise's.)

When you [*illegible three words*] gift———don't blame me if it's a bit risqué———that seems to be a special feature of much that's bought for American houses. I hope to get it off to you as soon as I can catch de Roode in the office where I discovered it.

I say has Fay been publishing the stuff I sent?★ Love to Mama and to Grandma and you!

Anita

> [★Probably a reference to columns Anita published in the gossip sheet *Flash* at about this time.—*Ed.*]

1 rue Jacques Mawas 1
Paris 15me
29 Juin 1930

My dearest Mother and Tada—

I've just received the swell photos of you and the commencement booklet. You all sure look good—you feel good, too, I know, after so long a fooling with schools. How happy I'd be to celebrate at closer range!

But here am I—and other than longing to see you—content.

In the fall, you'll be just a step away in Washington and New York. . . . I'll run over every weekend when the Lindburgh [*sic*] Transatlantic starts business. Then, too, there's no reason why you can't come to Europe for the vacations, at least.

Lots of poor folks make the trip once a year.

Paris is sunny to-day—the blue sky reminds me of California. There aren't many days like this one but the air is always gay and full of spirit. This old town is damp, dirty, disgusting—it forces one to live above it in the clouds—we might say. This has been a lifelong habit of mine, you know, so I find here the pleasantest atmosphere because I'm not alone in the air . . . everybody is flightly.

Yesterday was clear, too, fortunately, because I gave a Cocktail Party at the home of a swell gentleman who lives alone in luxury. Tonny has just finished his portrait, and we became friends during the posing painting and gab-fest hours. He paid for the party, too (that goes without saying) and I invited the Americans who've invited me, a dozen of the most prominent artists, etc. etc. etc.

You were there too—your portraits exposed regally. I'm such a gypsy—folks are beginning to think I just growed.

It's chic to have so beautiful a family to show. The French think you two are grand, and the Americans who can't figure the possibility of a civilized shine—are the more puzzled to find a family of them————Ha!

But, in Paris, they must [illegible] an intelligent air, so of course they're always open to attack.

One of my guests was Bernard Faÿ, whose "Benjamin Franklin" you've no doubt seen. He's the classiest thing in cultured

Frenchmen and when he goes to America next fall, I'll send letters to Walter White and company, as he's anxious to "know more."

And for you, too, naturally.

There was, also, Markiovitch the young Russian (19 years) musician whose first symphony created great excitement this season.

Then, there was my old friend and buddy—Man Ray. Mr. and Mrs. Whitney, American millionaires, George Huguet critic and editor, Baring Imles [sp??] (young American who collaborated with Faÿ) and his wife, etc. etc. etc.

Hotel Bellevue
Quai de la Consigne
Toulon, France

My dear folks——

I shall be in southern France for the rest of the summer, where my address will remain the same (above) but if you wish to be sure—even until September or October—you can continue writing to 1 rue Jacques Mawas Paris 15me. The vacation will last as long as my money lasts but my trunk (tho' I expect to visit Cannes, Nice, Monte Carlo, etc.) will stay here where I've a swell room with view of the port.

I sent Tada a card from Marseilles. Mother one from Aix-en-Provence.

This is a sailors' town being the headquarters of the French Navy. But sailors and fishermen here are not the idiots they must be at Annapolis; they only make the port more picturesque. There are lots of English and French friends here from Paris—especially artists. The climate, trees, etc.——are just like San Diego: the houses all like Ramona's home; the bay all complicated with battleships, airplanes, yachts; the Mediterranean beautiful!

[*Remainder of letter is missing.*]

Toulon (Var)

2 Août 1930

My dearest Tada——

I've just finished a book called "Life of Illusions" by an Englishman: the collection of private letters written by him to his best friend—Hohun Legude—who edited the book, and if you want a picture of the inside of a vacuum covered with brutish British, take his self-confessions. The civilized people to-day (to say nothing of the savages) are getting dumber and dumber.

My honest conclusion is that the only hope of salvation lays with the half-castes. In a hundred years America will be all half-caste. I'm sure there's no stopping it. This may sound as impersonal as a Second Street Jew expounding the virtues of a second-hand pair of trousers he's trying to sell you, but as impersonally as I can see (being not excessively mixed-blood-conscious here) the world's getting smaller and smaller, all people are being mixed up—whether they want to be or not—and we half-breeds have everything in our favor. Despite the inferiority complex which holds them in subjection to-day, the 'gens de couleur' are stronger morally and physically than the "sangs purs." We haven't a hell of a lot to do with what happens a hundred years hence——we're just shining examples of superiority.

That's all I wanted to say: Aren't we just the cream!

Living just to-day, I'm finding the Côte Azur [*sic*] quite lovely. The climate is that of So. Calif. But the coast line is cut into tiny bays, all rocky and with hardly a decent plage (bathing beach) the whole length. There are excellent harbours, however, which quite naturally are "protected" by French war boats, barriers, forts, etc. Then I haven't seen an acre that doesn't seem to belong to someone—one realizes that the French are tolerant and individualistic because they've been pushed so close together they were forced to push back and fight out—each his own destiny.

Everything in France seems little to me, save the spirit of the people which is strong enough to transcend its filth (not everywhere) and crowd.

The English—on the other hand—have pushed out but never out-grown their bad God-damned pig-headedness.

In spite of their mal treatment of natives of African colonies, it's a shame that the French are not the only colonists on earth because the evil they do is never against the individual but in commercial [*illegible*], and they are sold to the idea that one drop of French blood makes a Frenchman! However—I do not hope that all the American Negroes will follow my example and force themselves in too great numbers into France itself. But they love their "ham [?] and——" too much—there's no danger.

I went for "tea" [at] the Seabrook's "atelier" (he's finishing a book on the Congo), the other day and there met some Vikings (Swedes), an American woman, two Frenchmen etc., etc. We had a jolly discussion of race which followed a remark of mine: one of the Nordics said he was "dying"—always felt the sensation of death; my answer was (in French): "I find the people of the North are always dying" . . . He repeated it to the [*illegible*] as a gem and Seabrook (who by the way is a Georgian) said that I was thinking, as he was, that the North of the world is decaying and that the next civilization will be African. This I denied but the argument became too lively on petty issues for me to explain that I meant only that the Normans live in metaphysics—This I find true but don't feel energetic enough, at the moment, to expound——take Maeterlinck as an example and prove it yourself—or Ibsen or Grieg. (My personal experiences I'll relate another time—with poets, drug-takers, etc. etc.)

I had absolutely no idea of race in my mind as I've almost forgotten it exists, being always with real artists—no Seabrooks. Howsomever my theories on the next civilization are based purely upon a very modest knowledge of English in India—Hindous in England—Negroes in America and Europe—Africans in Europe—whites in Africa, in the South Seas, everywhere——its always the same story: MIXED BLOOD! (No matter who forces it—nobody resists it.) And why not?

After the Egyptians come mixed Greeks who finally made a race; after them, Romans—a race sprung from many; then the barbarous Nordics, Gauls, Germanics, etc. Now the field is larger and if anything remains of this civilization within 2 or 200 yrs. it will have been preserved, recreated and "flowered" by a race of— what today is called half-breeds . . . There may still rest the Chinese and many Africans untouched by airplanes, gunboats, trade, railways and missionaries but the Nordic ain't got much chance to litter the earth for long—and he's wiping himself out. That's what the Americans don't want and fear. That's why they <u>hate.</u> I was thinking to-day on a boat between Toulon and a beach—way out at sea on an island, sort a Catalina—that the only people I hate are those I fear—I think it's generally true) Well, let him hate it and fight it and try to keep his race pure—I wish him luck, but I don't believe any race can go backward and forward at the same time. The only Americans who are going forward are taking inter-marriage with them—in ideal—to-day—etc. etc.

I'm all packed tonight for Nice. I've a suitcase and a small toilette case, and I'm wearing my new ensemble mode like this: [*drawing*] Cannot you see the little cape? And the way everything's longer in the back? The skirt underneath is like this: [*drawing*] isn't it just like one mother used to wear in 1906? It's grey summer open-weave wool—Rodier—and the little hat is red English felt. I don't think I've changed a d——d bit in 6 yrs but I walk a little straighter now.

By the way—I hope very sincerely that you are not really as fatigued as you looked in one of the commencement portraits.

Take care of yourself, buddy, and don't worry about little things. Remember your real life is yet to be lived and youth has to be got thru' with as calmly as possible. I'm staking all my love and luck on you, and praying you're growing stronger and stronger.

Be good to Mama until she comes to me which I even dream will be soon. Love to her, now, and kisses. Also best to Grandma—bless her heart.

I'll write you more often, I think, because I've need to clear my brain. Don't mind, do you?

> Lovingly—
> As ever.
> Anita

My address until September is Hotel Bellevue—Quaie de la Consigne—Toulon. But Jacques Mawas Paris (15me) is always good.

Agosto 8, '30

My dear Mother and Tada——

I was so near Italy at Toulon, Nice, Monte Carlo, etc. that for a thousand francs I could visit Venice, Milan, Verona, Genoa, see the Alps and Lombardi (Northern Italy) comfortably.

So here am I.

So we are here.

At Venice I found everything much as I expected just like the photos and reproductions of paintings—save that the town is naturally smaller and the people a little less romantic. These Italians are certainly a cheeky race! tho, the Mussolini-ites are not as bad as I thot they'd be. Folks had said "you'll be followed and spied upon everywhere." This isn't true. They're only kids who get a big kick out of their uniforms which are certainly chic. The country is comparatively prosperous, too. Milan, for example, has the best trams I've seen in Europe—just like Hollywood and a jolly green. One lives very well in a small hotel, with good service, sees a town and buys cigarettes for about two dollars a day.

Of course, the scenery of Lombardi is classic—lovely fields and farms—sycamore trees, palms, etc. with the tall cypress and the many campaniles breaking into the sky above hill and simple tile-roofed houses or "mission-style" church.

Our host and friend is a friend of d'Annunzio—a poet and musical critic. Also something of a diplomat. He was so delighted because of the great collection of genius in his salon—he has promised to give house and servants any time we want to entertain. But enough of cocktails in this letter to my poor dry beloveds. It was my first Parisian blowout but, I hope, at 70 or 80 to have a brilliant salon chez moi.

Well, the summer is wearing on, and I still am awaitin' my birth record. Did you send it to Chicago? If not I'd just as leave you'd file it in Los Angeles or Buenos Aires—as I'm not particular to the village in the Middle West. . . . I'll send for it there again to-day.

As I've written, I'm in no hurry to be tied but I would like to get it over with once and for all.

I have a small ensemble for the occasion—bought in advance by Tonny—made to measure (my first) beize Rodier wool, a long circular coat with cape, and a long circular skirt. The blouses will come after. I'll send you snapshots as soon as I've the hat to go with it which may also be made to order.

Sounds expensive but it's not the whole outfit suit, hat, shoes, blouse, etc. etc. May reach mille francs, or $40.00.

Claude McKay passed through Paris a few days ago on his way to Berlin where he's correcting proofs of his latest book. I didn't see him but he wrote from Germany he'll be coming back soon. I may rent my apartment to him for the rest of the summer. Can't tell yet when or where we'll go but it's sure we'll leave before August.

Countee Cullen is returning to America for good next month after having remained long enough to let drift the smoke of his marriage and divorce. He tells me he is contemplating marrying the daughter of Miller, next. (Miller and Lyles) I told him he is a d—d fool. He moved recently without giving me an address so he didn't get invited to my party. But all the better. He had some blow-outs, when Yolande was here, to which I wasn't asked.

It's a long worm that has no bumps and a dead [Nito?] who stays down for ten counts.

It's Sunday—I must make tea for a band that'll fall in here about five.

About six came home with me after cocktails yesterday. They brought eggs, etc. We had dinner here at 10:30. But it's fun!

My life's quite joyous now and I hope yours is too—And that you'll be content if you go to D.C.

Love and kisses,

Sincerely

Anita

Le 1 Janvier 1931

My dear Mother—

I was having coffee after luncheon with a friend yesterday, when she asked if I had nothing on for the afternoon would I like to go see a mystic with her. Her husband—who writes plays—wanted some dope on the business. Out of curiosity I went along and after climbing a thousand steps we found ourselves in a modest apartment apparently governed by a child of nine or ten who let us in. Her mother—the mystic—was busy with some clients and did not let us into her secret chamber for about a quarter of an hour. There we saw a very tanned, dark Jewess of about thirty, I imagine, rather pretty and much like Dora. My friend suggested cards and the dame gave her all sorts of information about herself and her family that lives in Madagascar. We took notes.

Then—being rather entranced by this freak of nature—I allowed myself to become the subject of her speculations.

Now what I'm getting at is this—she told me that you "who lived as a widow" with your son would receive a shock—as from a pickpocket—that she saw you upset—holding your hand over your heart—but that it would be not serious and that you would not be ill.

Also—and always unaided by me—who was skeptic—she gave a very good description of Tada, of his great intelligence, and of the certain success he'd have despite his "conceit." She saw him managing big prosperous things and traveling about but not very far from home. She said he was "harsh in his home" but that this year, and from now on, he'd be less harsh and that you'd be very much happier. These ideas she did not get from reading my mind because I've never thot Tada harsh nor conceited. And I've imagined you were happier there than you would be away from him.

This may be all piffle but I couldn't help letting you in on its strangeness.

And do let me know immediately about the shock.

I hope very very sincerely that if Tada has been harsh, he'll be himself "this year and hereafter."

She told me for myself that the biggest thing to happen to me this year is marriage and with a man with whom I correspond who lives in my country—"perhaps a colony because I see him in white uniform." If I marry Charlie this year—as he threatens in each letter to be coming—it'll no doubt be the uniform of his internship. That'd be a great surprise. She said that individually, I will succeed with the pen in criticisms and reviews and impressions but that I must change my environment because I'm surrounded by people who do not encourage me to write. How true! how true!

That I'd not succeed in making money like my brother who has more force. That I have no passions whatever neither for love, nor work, nor place. Not bad discovery for a mystic, eh! Well, we'll see, we'll see.

She said that it's certain I'll not marry Tonny tho' he loves me, etc, etc., but that he's young and profoundly fatalistic and will not be hurt as much as I'm afraid he will. Also that <u>his</u> mother will be probably the happiest in the lot when I marry this other gentleman because she hopes for her son a rich marriage. And that secretly she has always held poverty against me. (It isn't rich and poor in French—it's a fiancée with a dowry or one without.) For the first time—I thought of that, so later I asked Tonny if it was true about his Mother and he said—Yes, rather vaguely—but that his Mother is greedy and he'll marry whom he pleases and make enough for his family, etc. etc.

He is really about to sign up in a very good New York combination Harriman Gallery and will be independent in no time—no doubt. But it is true—I'm sick unto death of doing nothing and I'm sure I was never cut out to be "the wife of a great man"—in the doll-baby, or obedient, or shadow sense of the world. Even if I never do very much I'm afraid I just must do <u>something</u>.

This fortune teller person said I'd make some money this year in the production of films—not in acting but in giving directions for the technical perfection. That's faintly possible as I have written a scenario for Man Ray which we'll likely film this summer.

Enough of speculations and dizziness. I have a new outfit that is just charming—shall send you a snap soon.

. . . [part of page missing]

New Years Eve was the gaiest of my holiday festivities—tho' I'd been the guest of several of our friends giving little shindigs that night. I played hostess for the Count André de la Rivière whose mother was at the chateau in Brittany. He came to my place for dinner and complained that tho' there were oceans of champagne and everything was in order he detested the idea of receiving folks alone—wouldn't I come early, stay late, and experience the works. His apartment is a <u>dream!</u> You know I was enchanted! We have had, for a few months, a little left-handed crush and he is always trying to show me the point "you were born for luxury." Too bad! I draped myself in beige lace to the heels, greeted the hand-kissing and the long-robed guests, supervised the bar, danced with the youngest and shyest, etc, etc. snubbing in high tones most of the Americans . . . . Sure it was great fun! Tonny was jealous but delighted with my success in a world so society. . . . . I mean I was at home. How I wish you could have seen it. The count is only thirty but I'm the only woman he's been so attentive to since the death of his baby sweetheart, it seems. Don't worry my head's not turned—a count here is, after all, only a count etc, etc.

The first person to kiss me, at midnight, was the high and mighty American writer Lawrence Vail—I hope it's a good omen for my individual success.

Tonny gave me a modern clock for Christmas—a <u>beauty</u> of mirror and simple glass.

I told you I had had my lungs X-rayed at the American Hospital about a month ago. This week I went out again to see the result and to be thoroly examined. I am perfectly free of T. B. Well, that's that! I was getting so lazy, and so often was subject to La Grippe that I was I suppose wishing myself frail. No chance!

But I would like to have more sunshine. This damned rain rain rain is like San Francisco and <u>dull</u>! It's no wonder everybody drinks.

O yes, a friend of mine came to town the other day—a Wall Street broker named Arthur Wheeler (I met him with Man Ray) and he asked his lawyer about marriage of Americans here and how to force the city of Chicago to send me my birth certificate. The lawyer said I don't have to have the certificate at all, and that if I want to I can get married tomorrow. We all had dinner and went dancing together the other night and Tonny was relieved with the news . . . . . But I'm glad I didn't know it before because now I'd be tied up and I'm not sure I'd be as happy (happy? Contented??? I don't know what I want to say)—if I wouldn't find life just too dull to bear if I had to keep on being the shadow of another person—one whose personality is as strong as my own. One whose ego is often as great as his big young heart.

No, I don't want to marry Tonny.

[part of page missing]

Times better now than before, but he will always be the artist—self-confident and not subject to the little laws that make for peace in a home. Just imagine, for example, being all day long with your husband who, when he isn't painting—which is most of the time—is dragging at you to go out, or to cook something, or to dance, who is jealous of even the books you read that may draw your attention from him . . . . No, you can't imagine it—it has to be lived—and it's *not* funny. But we'll see, we'll see!

I've been writing a long time, haven't I? And it all doesn't mean much—like my conversation would be, but it's good to imagine you as sympathetic and patient even with my follies. At bottom, I don't think I'm much good, really; I'll be thirty this year and I'm getting more no count every day. But that's no way to talk to those who love me! Forgive me. Do give my love to Dorothy. Tell her

I've been knitting and would like to make a little [illegible] for Puffey and Brother—to send the measures. I'll write her too one day. Best wishes for the New Year to all her family. Thank her for the gifts—tho' the package hasn't arrived yet. The next time I'm not broke I'll send you all something decent.

Love and kisses to Tada (I think he's <u>perfect</u> and didn't believe a word about his being severe—ha!) Maybe he'll write me if he ain't mad. That your 1931 will be happy, Mama.

Your brat—Anita

⸻⸻

7 rue de Bourgogne 7

Paris 7e

Le 10 Fevrier 1931

My chère Maman,

Surely I have told you that I started a book last fall. It is called MOCKING-BIRD and is in the hands of an editor Wm Aspenwall Bradley, a friend, who will tell me before long whether or not I can hope to have it published one day. He received the first ten chapters yesterday, and I work every day like a trooper on the rest, in a little room high up over the palaces and river and the great Place de la Concorde, grâce à un Americain, Arthur Wheeler who pays my rent, the typewriter, etc., etc. He and his wife are from New York, know all the people we do, and are something like the Spingarns (who, by the way, live in this hotel when they're in Paris) . . . the Wheelers have an apartment not very far from here. Needless to add that they are rich and patrons of art. They give me 3,000 francs a month until the book is finished without any strings, that is if it is never published . . tant pis . . if it is, I owe them nothing.

This is the first time I ever got something for nothing and if you'd like to write someone in Paris, their address is 14 rue des Saints-Pères, Paris 7e. 'Mr and Mrs Arthur Wheeler' or just to him, n'import. Just don't be too sweet, because they must be held to think that brains is rarer than cash . . . what bull!

And please send me the dope about Grandma; she is the heroine of the story and I don't want to go on making up stuff she may think ridiculous. Love to her.

Did you get the bag and stuff I sent? That is Arthur sent it or said he did. . . . I mean he mailed it, he didn't know what was in it, so don't thank him for it. Did it get by the customs all right? I tried to make it look old. Hope I didn't ruin the bag, it's a Lanvin model.

I haven't heard from you in a long time. I see Tonny nearly every day, so if you send anything to Jacques Mawas he will get it for me. Did I tell you not to bother about that certificate? Wheeler says it isn't necessary here if you have a lawyer; he has offered his. Thanks for the magazines, I have read them and sent them to Claude McKay in Morocco. I may go down to visit him this Spring. Don't think that is scandalous; he is a fairy. And he aint got no use for nothing my color no how . . even if I were a boy. HA!

Thanks for all the news you sent last time.

Sure anybody would fall for a good looking Scotchman, why not? I tell you if you can stand shines, you can stand almost anybody.

I must get back to work now.

I'll let you know how everything is working out.

Better write to Jacques Mawas, because I may move again.

Or I may go to the Midi (Toulon) before long.

Write to Paris anyhow.

Love and kisses,

and everything.

And to the Eastons too.

Dorothy's in my book.

Yours,

Anita

P.S.

For God's sake please don't give any chance of publicity to my work here. Or to any of my ambitions. If it falls thru' there'll be no niggers to shut up. You know how it is.

Love.

Forgive typewritten—am working like a dog.

Notes

Introduction

1. Nella Larsen, *Quicksand,* in *Quicksand and Passing,* ed. Deborah E. McDowell (New Brunswick: Rutgers University Press, 1986), pp. 60–61.

2. Ibid., pp. 61–62.

3. "Draft No. 1," dated August 24, 1975 (first version of autobiography), p. 19. Anita Thompson Dickinson Reynolds Papers, Moorland-Spingarn Research Center, Howard University.

4. Thirteenth Census of the United States, 1910, Los Angeles County, Enumeration District 218, Sheet 8B; and Fourteenth Census of the United States, 1920, Los Angeles County, Enumeration District 320, Sheet 10B. Oddly, the 1920 Census also says that Anita's mother's mother was born in France with French as her "mother tongue." This suggests the possibility that whoever answered the Census deliberately misled the Census officer for some reason. Nonetheless, the family was certainly known to be black and was quite active in the black civil rights struggle in Los Angeles. As genealogists know, census records of the time are often unreliable.

5. "Draft No. 1," p. 18.

6. "The Tan Experience," draft re-titled "American Cocktail," p. 62.

7. Ibid., p. 62.

8. "Draft No. 1," p. 1.

9. "The Tan Experience," Chapter 1, p. 1.

10. "The Tan Experience," Chapter 1, p. 2

11. "Draft No. 1," p. 2.

12. Chicago City Directory of 1900 and 1901, listing for Samuel W. Thompson. The Thompsons moved by 1902 to 5401 South Wabash for two years and then to 6552 Champlain Avenue, where they shared a double with Noah Thompson in 1904 and 1905. From 1906 to 1909, Samuel Thompson and Noah shared a double at 6618 Vernon. They both left Chicago for Los Angeles after this. Both the 1910 and the 1920 census list the Thompson family at 1883 West 23rd Street, Los Angeles.

13. "Noah D. Thompson," *The Messenger* (August 1922): 466–467.

14. David Levering Lewis strongly implies that Anita Thompson and W. E. B. Du Bois had an affair at exactly this time in *W. E. B. Du Bois: The*

Fight for Equality and the American Century, 1919–1963 (New York: Henry Holt, 2000), p. 104. There are no other candidates for Anita's "intellectual giant" encountered at age twenty-two. Du Bois visited Los Angeles in the spring of 1923, when Anita was twenty-two, and toured the Hollywood studios with her. A photograph of him with her, her mother, and a child actor known as Sunshine Sammy (Ernest Morrison) appeared in the June 1923 issue of *The Crisis*. He had also featured a sultry photograph of her on the cover of *The Crisis* in January 1923, before meeting her. After his return to New York, a series of passionate letters went back and forth between them—particularly passionate on her part, as Du Bois was guarded in correspondence.

15. Ireland Thomas, "Motion Picture News," *Chicago Defender,* August 2, 1924, p. 6.

16. "Jazz Baby," words by M. K. Jerome and music by Blanche Merrill. Copyright 1919 EMI Mills Music, Inc.

17. "Draft No. 1," p. 84. She was registered initially for a course in art history given as an NYU extension course in English.

18. Tyler Stovall, *Paris Noir: African Americans in the City of Light* (Boston: Houghton Mifflin, 1996), pp. 79–80.

19. Anita Thompson to "Tada" (Sumner Matelle Thompson), 24 June 1929. Reynolds Papers.

20. Anita Reynolds to Beatrice Sumner Thompson, 10 February 1931.

21. Jacques Baron, *L'An 1 du surréalisme suivi de l'an dernier* (Paris: Éditions de Noël, 1969), p. 150. My translation. "Le music-hall, alors dans toute sa joie, rendit, dans une mesure non négligeable, sa place au merveilleux. Tout l'art des noirs Américains fut révélé à la vieille Europe. Ce n'était pas seulement la peine des hommes. C'était une conjuration contre la terre au nom du ciel. Il y avait peut-être un dieu au ciel qui n'était pas un simple entrepreneur de spectacles vulgaires."

22. Baron, p. 85. My translation. "Le Far West traversait nos murs, dans une chevauchée éperdue avec Douglas Fairbanks sous le signe de Zorro. Quant au Charlot des premiers âges, il n'était pas Charlie Chaplin mais l'éternel émigrant que nous sommes tous. Il y avait aussi le jazz."

23. Baron, p. 85. My translation. "Comme une femme qu'on aime et qu'on appelle 'mon oiseau des îles' ou 'mon orchidée du Brésil' pour la situer hors de l'espace et du temps, ou plutôt dans quelque coin du monde jamais visité où il y a beaucoup de chaleur."

24. Anita Thompson to "Tada" (Sumner Matelle Thompson), 2 August 1930. Reynolds Papers.

25. Anita Thompson to Beatrice Sumner Thompson, Paris 1929. Reynolds Papers.

26. Ibid.

27. Anita Thompson to Beatrice Sumner Thompson, 10 February 1931. Reynolds Papers.

28. "Draft No. 1," p. 97.

29. Anita Reynolds to Howard Miller, 6 October 1978, Reynolds Papers.

30. "Draft No. 1," p. 31.

31. Paul Bowles, *Without Stopping* (New York: G. P. Putnam's, 1972), p. 129.

32. Ibid., p. 137.

33. Ibid., p. 137.

34. Ibid., p. 147.

35. Paul Bowles to Bruce Morissette, January 1932, *In Touch: The Letters of Paul Bowles,* ed. Jeffrey Miller (New York: Farrar, Straus and Giroux, 1994), p. 96.

36. Florence de Mèredieu, *C'était Antonin Artaud* (Paris: Fayard, 2006), pp. 605–606.

37. "Draft No. 1," p. 203.

38. Ibid., p. 331. See also note 5 in Chapter 16.

39. Ibid., p. 267.

40. Ibid., p. 280. Anita actually had three reservations on the *Manhattan,* and she gave one to Dickinson, who had none. Ibid., p. 284.

41. Ibid., pp. 297–298.

42. Ibid., p. 298.

43. Ibid., p. 299.

44. Ibid., p. 301.

A Note on the Text

1. A letter from Frederic Wertham, M.D., to "Anita M. Dickinson" of August 2, 1947, suggests that she "work provisionally at the Lafargue Clinic beginning right off. . . . We have a lot of work there to do." Biographical notes for her papers at the Moorland Spingarn Center also state that she worked at the clinic. Reynolds Papers.

2. Richard Wright, "Phychiatry [*sic*] Comes to Harlem." *Freeworld,* Sept. 1946, pp. 45–51, quotation from 49–50.

3. Ralph Ellison, "Harlem Is Nowhere," *Shadow and Act* (New York: Signet, 1953), p. 282.

4. "The Tan Experience," MS, p. 321. Reynolds Papers.

5. Langston Hughes postcards to Reynolds dated 26 June 1960, 22 March 1964, and 4 July 1961. Reynolds Papers.

6. Juliet Man Ray to Reynolds, 16 March 1972. Reynolds Papers.

7. Anita Reynolds to Howard Miller, 6 October 1978. Reynolds Papers.

8. At one point in her tape recordings, Reynolds notes that she is "going to have to telescope some of these years, because between 1932–1935 I didn't keep a diary, or if I did I have no trace of it, and I can't remember exact dates." Draft No. 1, p. 173. This implies that she was working off of diaries for much of the memoir.

9. Anita Reynolds to Howard Miller, 6 October 1978.

10. Anita Reynolds to Howard Miller, 6 October 1978.

11. Anita Reynolds to Jean Loesch, 28 March 1980. Reynolds Papers.

Chapter 1

1. The Bonaparte referred to is either Jerome Napoleon Bonaparte or his son Jerome Napoleon Bonaparte II (1830–1893). The former, a nephew of Emperor Napoleon Bonaparte, was raised in the United States by his mother, a wealthy American whose marriage to Jerome Bonaparte (the emperor's brother and King of Westphalia) had been annulled. Jerome Napoleon Bonaparte II was a graduate of West Point (class of 1852) and an officer in the U.S. Army. He was stationed in Texas for two years until he resigned to join the French army, in which he served until 1870, when he returned to the United States and married.

Chapter 2

1. *Prélude à l'après-midi d'une faune,* Claude Debussy's famous "prelude" to Stéphane Mallarmé's poem "L'après-midi d'une faune," was first performed in 1894 and is considered by many a major turning-point in Western concert music.

Chapter 3

1. Elinor Glyn's most notorious novel, *Three Weeks* (1907), concerned a queen in the Balkans who seduced a younger British nobleman. It was a path-breaking example of erotic fiction for women. Although British, Glyn moved to California in 1920 and wrote scripts for Hollywood studios.

2. Hiram Johnson (1866–1945) was a liberal Republican and a founder of the Progressive Party who served as governor of California from 1911 to 1917 and U.S. Senator from 1917 to 1945. He supported women's suffrage and many other liberal causes. Charles M. Schwab (1862–1939) was a steel magnate, serving as the first president of U.S. Steel and then of Bethlehem Steel.

3. Jack Johnson and Jim Jeffries fought for the world heavyweight boxing championship in Reno on July 4, 1910, in what has often been called "the fight of the century." Johnson, black, was the reigning heavyweight champion, while Jeffries, white, was the former undefeated heavyweight champion, called by sportswriters the "Great White Hope" in the racially charged lead-up to the fight. Johnson dominated and won by technical knockout in the fifteenth round.

Chapter 4

1. Robert Sengstacke Abbott (1870–1940) was founder of the Chicago *Defender,* an important African American newspaper with national circulation, and was one of the first black self-made millionaires.

Chapter 5

1. David Levering Lewis strongly implies that Anita Thompson and W. E. B. Du Bois had an affair at exactly this time in *W. E. B. Du Bois: The Fight for Equality and the American Century, 1919–1963* (New York: Henry Holt, 2000), p. 104. There are no other candidates for Anita's "intellectual giant" encountered at age twenty-two. Du Bois visited Los Angeles in the spring of 1923, when Anita was twenty-two, and toured the Hollywood studios with her. A photograph of him with her, her mother, and a child actor known as Sunshine Sammy (Ernest Morrison) appeared in the June 1923 issue of *The Crisis.* Du Bois had also featured a sultry photograph of her on the cover of *The Crisis* in January 1923. After his return to New York, a series of passionate letters went back and forth between them—particularly passionate on her part, as Du Bois was guarded in correspondence.

2. Ruth St. Denis and her husband, Ted Shawn, led a famous dance "colony" in Los Angeles in the 1910s and 1920s, known as the Denishawn Dancers. They specialized particularly in "exotic" dance styles derived from India, Egypt, and Japan. Nautch dancers were female secular dancers in northern India. Their style of dance became popular in the West as a result of orientalism in the late nineteenth and early twentieth century, and "nautch dancing" was one of Ruth St. Denis's specialties. Her orientation departed from Isadora Duncan's "Greek" style and helped in the formation of modern dance in the United States. Martha Graham was one of her most noted pupils.

3. Norma Gould, a well-known dance educator, held summer classes in the Sierra Madre beginning in 1919. "Norma Gould Holds Outdoor Classes," *Los Angeles Times,* 5 September 1920, p. III 18.

4. Anna May Wong (1905–1961) was another maid-in-waiting to the princess (and a villain) in *The Thief of Bagdad* (1924). She was the first Chinese American film star.

5. The Lincoln Motion Picture Company, founded by Noble Johnson in 1916 in Los Angeles. He brought his brother George Johnson into the company to handle distribution, and George became largely responsible for the business side of the operation. Anita Thompson starred in two of their most successful films, *Man's Duty* (1919), which no longer exists, and *By Right of Birth* (1921), of which only fragments remain. The company folded in 1923. Anita Reynolds's remarks are chiefly about her role in *By Right of Birth,* the company's last film. She plays a Native American girl adopted by a white couple who move to California from Colorado. In college she discovers that she is actually a Negro, leaving her free to marry the African American college man (played by Clarence Major) who loves her. They meet before she knows that she is "black" when she falls off her horse in the woods near a stream in which he is fishing and he rescues her. Oscar Micheaux, incidentally, got his start in filmmaking by way of the Lincoln Motion Picture Company, which wanted to film his novel *The Homesteader.* Micheaux broke with them over who should direct the film and started his own company.

Chapter 6

1. The Chicago Race Riot of 1919 is often considered the most violent racial conflict in the history of Illinois as well as the worst of the Red Summer of 1919, when riots broke out in a number of cities across the United States. It was considered notable for the fact that blacks fought back en masse against their white tormentors. The riot started when a black boy swimming in Lake Michigan supposedly crossed over to the "white" section of a South Side beach area and drowned after a rock thrown by a white man hit him.

2. Edward Weston (1886–1958), who grew up in Chicago and moved to California in 1907, is one of the most influential of all American photographers. Tina Modotti (1896–1942) was an Italian photographer, stage and film actress, and, eventually, revolutionary political activist (in Mexico) who became one of Weston's favorite models (and lovers) in the 1920s. "Robo" was the nickname of Roubaix de l'Abrie Richey (born Ruby Richey in Denver), an artist who was married to Modotti but tolerated her affair with Weston. He wrote poetry, worked as an illustrator, designed fabrics, drew political cartoons, and painted. He was especially known for his work in *batik,* and his fabric designs were used for Hollywood costumes and set designs as well as stage productions. He and Modotti were thought to have the ideal bohemian marriage in the late teens and early twenties.

Carl Sadakichi Hartmann (1867–1944) was a critic and poet of German and Japanese descent, born in Japan and raised in Germany. He was an important early modernist poet and critic (and a friend of Walt Whitman's in the latter's final years). He wrote the first haiku in English and was one of the first photography critics. In the 1910s he was crowned "King of Bohemia" in Greenwich Village. In his later years he lived in Hollywood. He played the court magician in Douglas Fairbanks's *The Thief of Bagdad,* in which Anita Thompson played a lady-in-waiting to the princess.

3. Mae Walker was the adopted daughter of A'Lelia Walker (1885–1931), who was one of the well-known personalities of Jazz-Age Harlem. A'Lelia hosted much-talked-about parties and for a while owned "The Dark Tower," a townhouse in Harlem intended at first to be a hangout for writers and artists. A'Lelia's mother, Madame C. J. Walker (1867–1919, born Sarah Breedlove), had come from humble beginnings in Indianapolis but founded a hair-straightening and cosmetics business through which she became enormously wealthy. A'Lelia inherited the business when her mother died in 1919, and reputedly sought with only partial success entry into the exclusive ranks of African American "high society." Mae Walker's "Million Dollar Wedding" was one of the most extravagant African American social productions in the 1920s.

4. *La Maja desnuda* (The Nude Maja) is a famous painting by Francisco Goya (1746–1828) depicting a voluptuous nude woman reclining on large pillows on a couch and facing the viewer.

5. A well-known white author and journalist for liberal and left-leaning magazines and newspapers, Herbert J. Seligmann at the time was also an NAACP officer. Among his books was *The Negro Faces America* (1920). He was also closely associated with the modernist photographer Alfred Stieglitz and his "291" studio.

Chapter 7

1. Charles Fremont "Pruner" West was a well-known track star and football player, and later a respected medical doctor with an M.D. from Howard University, where he also coached football. He was the first African American to play quarterback in the Rose Bowl. On at least two occasions fans of opponents to his Washington and Jefferson College football team planned to attack him and / or the team because of his race but found themselves stymied by the fact that they could not pick him out due to his light skin color.

2. Noah Thompson (1878–?) was a journalist, political activist, and ultimately real estate investor in Los Angeles who encouraged black migration to that city from the South and Midwest. He and Anita's father lived

together in Chicago for several years in the late nineteenth century after moving there from the Baltimore area, and they moved at about the same time to Los Angeles as Chicago's racism grew acute in the early twentieth century. Noah, as Reynolds points out early in her memoir, was a secretary to Booker T. Washington for a while and later did work for Marcus Garvey's United Negro Improvement Association. By this time, in the late 1910s and early 1920s, he was a well-known political figure in the Los Angeles black community. He became disillusioned with Garvey over the ill-fated Black Star Line venture (the "Back to Africa" shipping project) when he felt that Garvey was misleading his followers, and ultimately spoke out against Garvey in public, a fact noted by W. E. B. Du Bois in one of his most noteworthy editorials attacking Garvey in *The Crisis*. The NAACP was strongly opposed to Garvey and supported his deportation.

3. Founded in 1921, the Lucy Stone League argued that women should keep their "maiden" names after marriage, both informally and legally. The group took its name from Lucy Stone (1818–1893), the first woman in the United States to carry her birth name through life, even after marrying. People who followed the League's ideas were called "Lucy Stoners."

4. Cleon Throckmorton (1897–1965) was a famous avant-garde set designer associated with the Provincetown Playhouse and a white contributor to the "Harlem Renaissance" as someone who lent his expertise to black theater companies, notably the Howard Players of Washington, D.C. He designed sets for white-produced Broadway sensations such as *Porgy* (1927) and *In Abraham's Bosom* (1926) after having done so, to great acclaim, for Eugene O'Neill's *The Emperor Jones* (1920) and *All God's Chillun Got Wings* (1924), which were historic in African American performance history because of the way they featured black men as lead actors in interracial casts.

Chapter 8

1. *Runnin' Wild* (1923) was one of the most successful black shows of the 1920s and the direct successor to *Shuffle Along* (1921), which Langston Hughes credited with kicking off what would become known as the Harlem Renaissance. It was created and directed by the comedians Flournoy Miller and Aubrey Lyles (who also played lead characters). After out-of-town tryouts in Washington, D.C., and Boston, it opened at the Colonial Theater at Broadway and 62nd Street on October 29, 1923, and ran for twenty-seven weeks and 213 performances before going on the road, where it was also successful. (Anita chose not to go on the road and told black journalists at the time that she preferred to turn her talents to more "artistic" work.) It was an entirely black production; not only was the cast all black, but the libretto and music

were by black composers (James P. Johnson and Cecil Mack), with contributions by Will Marion Cook and William Grant Still as well as choreography by Elida Webb. The Charleston was not a new dance, contrary to what Reynolds says, but *Runnin' Wild* was the show that turned it into a popular sensation that helped define the Jazz Age and the image of the flapper. It was therefore a historic show in the evolution of American popular culture.

2. Bill "Bojangles" Robinson (1878–1949) was one of the most famous African American entertainers of the 1920s, celebrated for his tap dancing, in particular. He later went on to star in extremely popular films with Shirley Temple, but his subservient roles tarnished his reputation. In the 1920s, he was considered a refined virtuoso of dance and a representative of African American aspirations. Jack Carter (c. 1902–1967) became an actor, best known for his starring role in a spectacular version of *Macbeth* directed by Orson Welles, known as the "Voodoo *Macbeth*."

3. H. L. Mencken, most famous as editor of *The Smart Set* and then *American Mercury,* was one of the most influential American journalists or men of letters in the 1920s and helped set the era's satirical tone. He lived in Baltimore. He was much admired by writers of the Harlem Renaissance and featured their work in *American Mercury.*

4. A normal school was a school for training teachers, usually with a shorter curriculum than a regular four-year college. Reynolds attended Coppin Normal School, which had a two-year program of study. It had been founded as part of Baltimore's Colored High School in 1900. Today it is Coppin State University.

5. Ralph Bunche (1903–1971) graduated as valedictorian of his class at UCLA in 1927 and went on to be the first African American to earn a doctorate in political science from an American university (Harvard). He taught at Howard University and became an influential political scientist and diplomat. He played a significant role in the formation and administration of the United Nations, and with Eleanor Roosevelt was instrumental in the drafting and adoption of the U.N. Declaration of Human Rights. He was the first person of African descent to receive the Nobel Peace Prize, in 1950, in honor of his mediation work in Palestine in the late 1940s. He was awarded the Presidential Medal of Freedom by John F. Kennedy in 1963.

Chapter 9

1. Ada "Bricktop" Smith (1894–1984) was an entertainer and nightclub hostess whose club, Chez Bricktop (Bricktop's), was a popular hangout in Montmartre featuring jazz. Many celebrities went there. The

Blackbirds were a group of black entertainers, chiefly singers, dancers, and blackface humorists, in the cast of the revue *Blackbirds of 1926,* which started out on Broadway and travelled to London and Paris. Produced by the white Lew Leslie and playing to mainly white audiences, it starred Florence Mills. Leslie put on more "Blackbirds" shows in 1928 and through the 1930s.

2. The Jockey Club was a well-known artists' hangout in Montparnasse, owned by the American Hilaire Hiler and decorated with cowboy motifs outside.

3. Man Ray (1890–1976) was born Emmanuel Radnitzky in South Philadelphia. He was an important modernist artist in a number of media, best known for his avant-garde photography. He had close connections with Dada and surrealism. After moving to Paris in 1921, he became a central figure in the Left Bank artistic community, and was the romantic partner of "Kiki" (Alice Prin, 1901–1953) the "Queen of Montparnasse." In 1929 he began a love affair with the surrealist photographer Lee Miller, an American woman, and broke up with Kiki.

Louise Bryant (1885–1936) was a journalist and the widow of the famous communist journalist John Reed, with whom she had travelled to Moscow in 1917–1918 to witness and report on the Communist Revolution. Reed died of typhus in Moscow and was buried under the wall of the Kremlin, a revered figure to the Russian revolutionaries. When Anita Thompson met Bryant in Paris, she was still married to her second husband, William Bullitt (a diplomat who divorced her in 1930) but living with her lesbian partner Gwen Le Gallienne, an English sculptor and sister of the famous actress Eva Le Gallienne. Bryant was also a close friend of the left-wing black poet Claude McKay, who dedicated his novel *Home to Harlem* (1928) to her. She was diagnosed in 1928 with Adiposis Dolorosa (Dercum's disease), which causes extreme weight gain, constant fatigue, and mental confusion. She became increasingly alcoholic in response to the stress and died in 1936.

4. Carl Van Vechten was then a famous music critic, novelist, and "high bohemian" based in New York who had become intimate with many African American writers and artists associated with the Harlem Renaissance and was Gertrude Stein's main champion in the United States. His interracial parties were legendary. He was very close friends with a number of Anita Thompson's black (and white) American friends. Nora Holt, a good friend of Van Vechten's by the mid-1920s, was an African American singer and nightclub hostess and at the time a hit in Paris, where she was known as "la Créole blonde." She was also the model for the character Lasca Sartoris in Van Vechten's controversial novel *Nigger Heaven* (1926).

5. Virgil Thomson (1896–1989) was an avant-garde composer from the United States who became a Paris fixture in the 1920s. Maurice Grosser (1903–1986) was an American painter and art critic. Kristians Tonny was a Dutch surrealist artist best known for his drawings using the "transfer technique," which Reynolds describes later.

6. Pavel Tchelitchew (1998–1957) was a Russian surrealist painter who moved to Paris in 1923, and then to New York in 1934. Allen Tanner (1898–1987) was an American musician; he and Tchelitchew were lovers and lived together for over a decade. They were part of Gertrude Stein's circle, as was Virgil Thomson. Eugene / Yevgeny Berman (1899–1972) was a Russian painter and set designer for opera and theater.

7. Robert Desnos (1900–1945) was a French surrealist poet particularly noted for his experiments in "automatic writing." He fought in the French Resistance in World War II, was captured by the Gestapo, and died in a concentration camp.

8. André Derain (1880–1954) was a French fauvist painter and sculptor.

Chapter 10

1. William Seabrook (1884–1945) was an American journalist from Georgia best known for his supposedly nonfictional accounts of his adventurous journeys through exotic places (Haiti, the Arab Middle East, West Africa). His book on Haiti, *Magic Island,* made him rich and, he claimed, is responsible for the term "zombie" entering the American vocabulary. It undoubtedly did help shape the popular and largely inaccurate American notions of Voodoo. In reality many of the sensational aspects of his books were fabricated, such as the "cannibal" episode in the book about his journey to Timbuktu, *Jungle Ways* (1930). He was known to, and liked by, a number of Harlem Renaissance figures and was much admired by Man Ray, who considered him superior to Hemingway because his books were supposedly based on his own experiences. Seabrook was also unabashed about what he considered his addiction to sado-masochism. His wife at the time Anita Thompson met him was Katie Seabrook, a bohemian socialite from a prominent Atlanta family.

2. Tonny at the time was very much a part of the Stein circle; she adored his portrait of her, and wrote a "portrait" of him that was included in her book *Dix Portraits* (Paris, 1930), for which he also drew a self-portrait, as did the other artists she featured in the book. These included Picasso, Tchelitchew, Berman, and Bérard.

3. In reality, Stein disapproved of the relationship between Kristians Tonny and Anita Thompson because she thought it was distracting him

from his work. According to Paul Bowles, who was also part of her circle, she conspired to get Anita to move to Tangier to work on a book in order to get her away from Tonny for a while. When he found out about this, Tonny was furious and took off for Morocco to be with Anita, ending his friendship with Stein at about the same time.

4. Caresse Crosby (1892–1970) was a well-known American patron of the arts and letters who founded with her second husband, Harry Crosby, the legendary Black Sun Press, which published a number of works by the emerging modernists based in Paris. Until Harry died with a lover in a double suicide in 1929, their decadent parties were legendary. They were fixtures of the expatriate bohemian social scene.

5. Thompson's friend most likely had loaned his gun to Michael McKendrick, a young man from Chicago who fell in with a bad crowd and started a gunfight with the jazz great Sidney Bechet in Montmartre one night in 1928. In the course of the fight, Bechet's bullets wounded three people, including McKendrick and a passing Frenchwoman on her way to work. Both men were sent to prison and then forced to leave the country. Bechet discusses the incident at length in Chapter 11 of his autobiography, *Treat It Gentle* (New York: Hill & Wang, 1960), pp. 150–156.

Chapter 11

1. *The Well of Loneliness* (1928) was a novel by the British writer Radclyffe Hall focusing on lesbian characters. It was challenged immediately in American and British courts on the grounds of obscenity and became the most well-known "lesbian novel" in the English language for decades thereafter.

2. Paul Bowles and Aaron Copland were American musicians and composers at the time. Bowles became a novelist in the 1940s; he lived most of his adult life in Tangier and set his rather surrealistic fiction in North Africa. Charles Henri Ford (1913–2002) was an American surrealist writer, photographer, collage artist, and film maker and the partner of Pavel Tchelitchew. Born and raised in Mississippi, he was part of the Stein circle in Paris and also well-known to New Yorkers like Carl Van Vechten. He was very much "out" about his sexuality from age sixteen on and was writing a novel at the time he met Anita Thompson that would be entitled *The Young and Evil* (1933), which was rejected by American and British publishers because of its openness about homosexuality but finally published in Paris. He also typed Djuna Barnes's *Nightwood* (1936) while in Morocco. He is sometimes regarded, with Paul Bowles, as a precursor to the Beats. He went to Morocco on Bowles's suggestion.

3. Abd el-Krim (1882–3 to 1963) led a large-scale rebellion in the Rif, a Berber area of northeastern Morocco, against French and Spanish rule. His guerilla tactics influenced those of later anticolonial leaders including Ho Chi Minh, Mao Zedong, and Che Guevara. His defeat of the Spanish in the Rif was an important factor in destabilizing the Spanish government, the establishment of Primo de Rivera's dictatorship, and finally the collapse of the Spanish monarchy in April 1931. However, fearful of how the Arabs' success in defeating a European colonial power might affect their own colonial rule in North Africa, the French joined with the Spanish in 1925 to defeat Abd el-Krim and his forces, who had attacked French Morocco (in the southern Rif). He surrendered in 1926 and was exiled to the island of Réunion (a French possession in the Indian Ocean), not Madagascar as Reynolds says. He was released in 1947 and took asylum in Egypt, where he once again became deeply involved in the movement for the liberation of the Maghreb, which resulted in Algerian independence just before he died.

4. The LZ 127 Graf Zeppelin, nicknamed "The Giant of the Air," was the largest passenger airship of the late 1920s and early 1930s and made numerous intercontinental and transatlantic flights until 1937, usually between Europe and South America, which would have been its destination when flying over Tangier. It could carry up to twenty passengers but made most of its money transporting mail and commercial items. Its flights were reported worldwide, and numerous countries issued postage stamps with its image, including the United States in 1930.

5. "Sandhurst" refers to the Royal Military College at Sandhurst, the British equivalent of West Point, where all British Army officers were trained.

6. The Thirty-Seventh Dogras were a battalion of Bengali Hindu soldiers based since the 1890s on the Northwest frontier of India, where they were charged with controlling the Afghan border. During World War I the regiment was in the 14th Indian Division. During the Mesopotamia Campaign, in which the British fought the Ottoman Empire for control of the region of present-day Iraq and southern Iran (the area of the Tigris-Euphrates river system), they took part in the Second Battle of Kut and the Capture of Baghdad.

Chapter 12

1. Georges Carpentier was a famous French boxer in the 1920s.

Chapter 13

1. Eslande Robeson, wife of the famous singer, actor, and political activist.

2. George Hoyningen-Huene (1900–1968), the son of a Russian aristocrat and an American woman, was a fashion photographer for the French *Vogue* (1926–1935) and then *Harper's Bazaar* (1935–1945). His photography epitomized 1930s glamour and elegance. He was a friend and collaborator of Man Ray and frequented avant-garde circles in Paris. According to a French blue guide to Tunisia of the 1950s (which I came upon at a bookstall on the Seine in 2008), the Sebastians started the whole tourist business to Hammamet when they built a large modern villa there in the 1920s. Others (including Hoyningen-Huene, in 1932) built villas nearby and a small "colony" developed. Many famous people went to visit before General Rommel took over their homes during World War II. After the war, the tourist trade established itself there, and Hammamet is one of the top tourist destinations in North Africa today. The Sebastian home, Dar Sebastian, is now a cultural center owned by the Tunisian government.

3. Ilka Chase was an American actress and daughter of the editor-in-chief of *Vogue*. Hoyningen-Huene was gay and was by now romantically attached to his frequent model Horst Horst.

Chapter 14

1. The defense of Abyssinia (Ethiopia today) against Mussolini's invasion in 1935 was a *cause célèbre* among leftists, anticolonialists, and African Americans generally. Abyssinia, ruled by Emperor Haile Selassie, was the only African nation never conquered by Europeans and had fought off the Italians in the late nineteenth century. Most of Selassie's soldiers had only primitive weapons such as bows and spears, and his air force had only three serviceable airplanes. Italy's forces not only had modern weaponry but used chemical agents that had been outlawed by the League of Nations, to which both countries belonged. Italy's conquest of Abyssinia proved the ineffectiveness of the League of Nations, contributing to its demise.

2. By "old North West frontier" Reynolds probably means the Northwest frontier of India, where Charles had been stationed in the British Indian Army and trained Bengali troops to fight the Ottoman Empire.

3. Leonor Fini (1907–1996) was an Argentine-born surrealist painter and theater and costume designer who grew up in Italy before moving to Paris and becoming part of the surrealist circle there. Much of her work has a strong feminist orientation, with powerful female figures. She was infatuated with cats.

4. At about this time Djuna Barnes (1892–1982), the American writer, would have been completing her novel *Nightwood* (1936), the work that would make her famous. Speaking openly of the gay and lesbian commu-

nities of Left Bank Paris, with which Anita Thompson was of course very familiar, it is considered a milestone in the history of gay and lesbian literature. Kay Boyle (1902–1992) was an American writer who at this time was working on *Death of a Man* (1936), a warning about the rise of Nazism.

5. The physical description of Louise Bryant reveals the fact that she was in the late stages of Adiposis Dolorosa, from which she would die in 1936.

6. Le Boeuf sur le Toit (The Ox on the Roof) is a famous Right-Bank brasserie / restaurant started by Louis Moysés in 1922 and originally located on Rue Boissy d'Anglas near the Champs-Elysées. It often featured jazz and was frequented by many famous artists, including Picasso. It has moved since but is still in existence on the Rue du Colisee.

7. *L'Humanité* was a daily newspaper published by the French Communist Party for which many important French intellectuals wrote in the mid- to late '30s. It was banned during World War II but subsequently revived. The surrealist Louis Aragon edited the weekly literary supplement in the late 1930s. *Cahiers d'art* was a prestigious magazine focusing on contemporary art, while *Figaro* and *Le Monde* were the major daily newspapers of Paris.

8. In England and the British Empire at the time, the term "nigger" was often applied to Indians as well as to people of African descent. Charles's ex-wife may well have thought that Anita was Indian.

Chapter 15

1. Jacques Baron (1905–1986) was a French surrealist poet, in fact one of the founding members of the Surrealist movement proper in 1921. A dispute with André Breton in 1929 got him "expelled" from the movement, although he stayed active in avant-garde art circles; his memoir *L'an 1 du surréalisme, suivi de l'an dernier* (1969) remains an important resource on the movement.

2. Mercer Cook (1903–1987) was the son of Abbie Mitchell Cook, a well-known African American singer and actress, and Will Marion Cook, a famous black composer and musician. Mercer Cook, who had been partly raised in Paris and held a teaching degree from the Sorbonne, at the time was an assistant professor of Romance languages at Howard University. He later became a diplomat and served as U.S. ambassador to Niger, Senegal, and Gambia.

3. Dora Maar (1907–1997) was a famous French photographer who had an intense and well-known eight-year love affair with Pablo Picasso beginning in 1936. She was the inspiration and model for many of his works during this period. Man Ray took portraits of her and taught both her and Picasso printmaking in the 1930s, and Maar was very much a part of the circle with which Anita Thompson associated in the late 1930s, photographing many of them.

4. Reynolds refers to Eric de Haulleville's surrealist novel *Le voyage aux Iles Galapagos* (Marseilles: Les Cahiers du Sud, 1934). In it a shipwrecked sailor falls in love with an exotic South Pacific island girl who reminds him, uncannily, of his wife "Anita." Kristians Tonny, incidentally, did illustrations for another of de Haulleville's books, *Le genre épique* (1929). A poem by Baron that Anita may be referring to is "Rêver de Hauteurs," which included the lines: "Donne-moi la brisure de tes paroles / Toi qui restes suspendu entre ciel et terre / Je veux revenir et creuser le sol / Avec mes frères." Jacques Baron, *L'allure poétique, 1924–1973* (Paris: Gallimard, 1974), p. 93. Originally published in Baron, *Peines Perdus* (1933).

5. Antoine de St. Exupéry was a French pilot and writer at the time most famous for books based on his aviation experience, particularly *Vol de Nuit* (*Night Flight,* 1931). He is better known today for the children's classic *Le petit prince* (*The Little Prince,* 1943). In 1935 he and a co-pilot famously crashed in the Sahara desert on a flight to Saigon and nearly died of dehydration before being rescued by a Bedouin shepherd.

6. A star boat is a class of keeled racing boat approximately twenty-two feet long and with much sail, raced with a skipper and one crew member. Rather than using a spinnaker when running with the wind, it has a special rig for the jib sail.

7. Antonin Artaud (1896–1948) was an avant-garde writer, actor, and theater director best known for his plays and essays in drama theory, which became immensely influential in modern drama worldwide. He often suffered from clinical depression and other psychological problems (what would be called today schizophrenia) in addition to being addicted to opiates. Reynolds's friend Cecile was Cecile Schramm, to whom he was briefly engaged in the mid- to late 1930s. They met in 1935 when she was eighteen or nineteen years old, the daughter of an engineer who worked for the Belgian tramways and a wealthy Flemish woman. Artaud was a major influence on such later American writers as Charles Bukowski, Allen Ginsberg, and Leroi Jones / Amiri Baraka, as well as such influential dramatists as Samuel Beckett and Sam Shepard.

8. *The Cenci* was actually a flop both commercially and critically, closing after just fourteen performances in 1935. A very disturbing play, it was an example of what Artaud called the "Theater of Cruelty." Rejecting psychological realism, Artaud sought to shock his audiences out of their "common sense" state of mind and release primitive impulses and feelings. Artaud himself played the main character Count Cenci, who is murdered by his two servants.

9. The provenance of Artaud's "magic cane" has always been a mystery to his biographers, who similarly have not been able to identify an "Anita"

who was a good friend of his fiancée Cecile Schramm (mentioned in a letter he wrote Cecile). Biographers have reported that he got the cane from Kristians Tonny, who showed it off in the Pierre Loeb gallery in 1927 and 1934. Artaud became obsessed with the cane in 1936–1937, ultimately claiming it had belonged to St. Patrick, Lucifer, and Jesus Christ. Trying to "return" the cane to Ireland led to a psychotic collapse, after which he was committed to asylums for the remainder of his life. Curiously, before this, in 1936, he had traveled to Mexico and taken up with the Tarahumara Indians, experimenting with peyote and had what he considered supernatural experiences. One wonders if the cane inspired his journey. He returned to Paris, took up again with Cecile Schramm, and then took his trip to Ireland to "return" the cane. Florence Mèredieu, *C'était Antonin Artaud* (Paris: Fayard, 2006), pp. 584–605.

10. Boris Souvarine (1895–1984, born Boris Konstantinovich Lifschitz) was a Ukrainian-born communist activist, essayist, and journalist and a leader of the French Communist Party in the 1920s. His support for Trotsky after Trotsky's ouster by Stalin in 1924 got Souvarine expelled from the Comintern, and he became a leader of the anti-Stalinist communist circle in France. By 1936, however, he and Trotsky had broken with each other.

11. The Stavisky Affair was a financial scandal in 1933–1934 that emboldened right-wing political groups to try to bring down the French socialist government. Popular demonstrations led by anti-republican groups culminated in a bloody riot outside the Chamber of Deputies in February 1934 during which fifteen people were killed. The divisions in the country between socialists and fascist sympathizers remained unhealed until World War II, and Reynolds felt that the fascist sympathizers were largely responsible for France's feeble response to German invasion.

12. André Masson (1896–1987) was a French artist closely associated with the surrealists and particularly interested in automatism (drawing with as little conscious control as possible). The Spanish Civil War proved an important influence on him, drawing him away from automatism. He was the stepbrother of the famous psychoanalytic theorist Jacques Lacan and eventually (after moving to the United States) a major influence on Jackson Pollock.

Chapter 16

1. Gaston Doumergue was President of France from 1924 to 1931. After the Stavisky Affair, which led to widespread instability, bloody riots, and the resignations of two left-wing Prime Minsters, he was called back into service as Prime Minister from February 6 to November 8, 1934, with the aim of producing a centrist government of national unity. Contrary to

Reynolds's memory, he was not assassinated but retired completely from political life after resigning as Prime Minister.

2. The Camelots du Roi were the youth organization of the Royalist "Action Française," a right-wing nationalist group. Based in the Latin Quarter, they often got into fights with left-wing youth groups.

3. Antonio Canovas del Castillo del Rey (1908–1984) was a Spanish designer who moved to Paris in 1936 at the beginning of the Spanish Civil War, in part to begin a diplomatic career. He designed accessories for Chanel. Following World War II, he was considered, with Christian Dior, one of Paris's most promising emergent fashion designers. Gabrielle Bonheur "Coco" Chanel (1883–1971) was the great Parisian fashion designer who created the "little black dress," sought elegant simplicity, and translated concepts from men's fashion to women's fashion.

4. Lyrics of "September in the Rain" (1937), written by Harry Warren and Al Dubin. First performed by Guy Lombardo, it hit number one on the charts in the United States in 1937 and later became a standard performed by numerous artists from Bing Crosby to the Beatles.

5. Fernan de Brinon, the Marquis de Brinon (1885–1947), was a lawyer and journalist who met with Hitler between 1933 and 1937 and was one of the architects of collaboration with the Nazis during World War II. He became a high official of the Vichy regime and was executed in 1947 for war crimes. Guy de Châteaubriant's father was Alphonse de Châteaubriant, who won the Prix Goncourt for his first novel, *Monsieur des Lourdines* (1911), and the Prix de l'Academie francaise for his second, *La Briere* (1923). A right-wing Catholic with strong religious priorities, in the 1930's he came to believe that Hitler's brand of National Socialism, which he accorded spiritual characteristics, held the key to human regeneration. His panegyric *La Gerbe des forces (Nouvelle Allemagne)* (1937) characterized Hitler as a prophet sent by God, and influenced important French Catholic leaders. A collaborationist during World War II, Alphonse de Châteaubriant fled to Austria after the war and was sentenced to death in absentia by the French Haute Court de justice. He died in exile under an assumed name in 1951. Born in 1904, Guy de Châteaubriant did not apparently share his father's politics but did support, during the Vichy regime, a program encouraging French workers to volunteer for work in Germany in exchange for the release of French prisoners of war.

6. Topsy and Eva are the major child characters in Harriet Beecher Stowe's *Uncle Tom's Cabin,* in which they are presented as polar opposites, Topsy being black, mischievous, and uncontrollable, and Eva blonde, sweet, and saintly.

7. Marian Anderson (1897–1993) was a famous African American contralto. In 1939, the manager of Constitution Hall, the top concert hall in Washington, D.C., owned by the Daughters of the American Revolution, refused her permission to perform there, prompting Eleanor Roosevelt to resign from the DAR and, with others including the president of the NAACP, Walter White, to arrange for her to sing on the steps of the Lincoln Memorial in a celebrated performance to an audience of over 75,000. The performance was broadcast live by radio across the United States and was widely regarded as an important symbolic victory over segregation.

8. The Gold Star Mothers were mothers of American soldiers who died in World War I. In 1930, Congress voted for funding to send them on pilgrimages to France to honor their sons by visiting their graves. However, organizers of the pilgrimage ensured that black mothers would be segregated from the white mothers and sent on a separate ship, prompting outrage on the part of the NAACP, African Americans in general, and others interested in racial equality.

Chapter 17

1. Jean Patou (1880–1936) was a French fashion designer who introduced sportswear for women, including knitted swimwear and the tennis skirt. In general, he moved fashion toward the natural and comfortable. Associated with his design tendencies was a preference for American models because they were slender, active, and engaged in sports. This gave them, he believed, longer, more elegant lines than the more curvy French models.

2. Louis Moysés was the founder and manager of the Boeuf sur le Toit, one of the famous Parisian nightclubs of the twenties and after.

3. Les Six refers to a group of French composers based in Montparnasse in the 1920s who reacted against the influence of Wagner and impressionist music. Jean Cocteau helped create the notion that they comprised a movement with him as their leader (much as Breton was the leader of the surrealists). They gathered at a bar called Le Gaya, which became the Boeuf sur le Toit, taking its name from a ballet by one of Les Six, Darius Milhaud.

4. *La dame aux camélias* (1846) was a popular novel by Alexandre Dumas, fils, that was adapted many times to stage and screen (notably *Camille,* 1936, starring Greta Garbo) and opera (*La Traviata*). Set in eighteenth-century Paris, it popularized the image of the lovely prostitute with a pure heart.

5. Le Montmarin is a beautiful 18th-century château, in Louis XV style, on the river Rance, surrounded by formal French and English gardens that date back to the eighteenth and nineteenth centuries. Located near the

Breton tourist cities of St. Malo and Dinard, it is now an official historic monument and a tourist destination open to visitors.

6. Villeroy & Boch, still a large and highly esteemed label for tableware and bathroom ceramics, dates back to the 1826 merger of the Jean François Boch Company and that of his competitor Nicholas Villeroy. Both families were French, but the Boch headquarters had moved to Germany in 1801, and the company is located in Germany to this day.

7. Solange Bazin de Jessey's life and activities in New Guinea have recently been the subject of a book, *Au pays des Papous: Solange Bazin de Jessey*, by Catherine Descrive (Paris: Tequi, 2006).

8. *Le Canard Enchaîné* is a satirical weekly newspaper founded in 1915. It features investigative journalism as well as cartoons, jokes, and leaks from the French government presented at times with a satirical tone.

Chapter 18

1. Concerning the *Canard Enchaîné*, see note 8, Chapter 17.

2. "Deep Purple" was a sentimental jazz song, originally instrumental, but for which lyrics were added in 1938 by Mitchell Parish. The 1939 recording by Larry Clinton and His Orchestra hit number one on the American charts for nine weeks that year. The lyrics begin:

> *When the deep purple falls over sleepy garden walls*
> *And the stars begin to twinkle in the sky—*
> *In the mist of a memory you wander back to me*
> *Breathing my name with a sigh . . .*

It ends "Lovers will always meet / Here in my deep purple dreams," to which Reynolds alludes.

3. Marshal Philippe Pétain (1856–1951), a hero of World War I, was the French general who was voted in as head of state to make peace with Germany after the defeat of June 1940. He became head of the authoritarian Vichy government under German occupation and cooperated with the Nazis. After the war he was convicted of treason.

4. Mme. Pétain was the wife of Marshal Pétain.

5. "Ann Morgan girls" refers to American nurses. Ann Morgan, daughter of John Pierpont Morgan, had begun an American-staffed visiting-nurses organization before World War I that became active in caring for the wounded during that war. When Germany invaded Belgium in 1940, she converted her estate at Blérancourt into a center for refugees and a regional medical center.

Index